The National Curriculum and Early Learning

THE NATIONAL CURRICULUM AND EARLY LEARNING

An evaluation

Edited by

GEVA M. BLENKIN and A. V. KELLY

P·C·P

Paul Chapman
Publishing Ltd

Paul Chapman Publishing Ltd
144 Liverpool Road
London
N1 1LA

British Library Cataloguing in Publication Data

National Curriculum and Early Learning
  I. Blenkin, Geva M. II. Kelly, A. V.
  372.19

  ISBN 1-85396-241-4

Typeset by Dorwyn Ltd., Rowlands Castle, Hants.
Printed and bound by Athenaeum Press Ltd, Newcastle upon Tyne, Great Britain

A B C D E F G H   9 8 7 6 5 4

CONTENTS

NOTES ON THE CONTRIBUTORS

All but two of the contributors to this book are members of the staff of the Faculty of Education at Goldsmiths' College, University of London. And the two exceptions have long been associated with its work.

Most of them also contributed to the two earlier books in this series, *Early Childhood Education* and *Assessment in Early Childhood Education* which, along with this book, have sought to set out an approach to early education which has long been practised and developed in courses offered by the college for both the initial and in-service education of teachers.

Geva Blenkin's work and interests lie in the field of curriculum studies in general and the early years curriculum in particular. Her main work as a senior lecturer at Goldsmith's College is focused on the higher degree programmes in early childhood education and curriculum studies. She is currently Director of a funded research project, 'Principles into Practice: Improving the Quality of Children's Early Learning'. She has published extensively on early childhood education, and her publications include the editorship of the two earlier books in this trilogy.

Eve Gregory's major area of interest is bilingualism and she has published a number of articles in this field. Her current research is into the effects of early bilingualism on beginning reading. She has responsibility for co-ordinating language courses for initial teacher education at Goldsmiths' College, and has provided a particular focus on bilingualism within these.

Pat Gura is currently Research Associate, Early Childhood Education, at Froebel Institute College, Roehampton Institute. Her main interest is in the continuing professional development of early childhood educators through collaborative action research. She edited *Exploring Learning: Young Children and Blockplay*, published by Paul Chapman (London, 1992).

Victoria Hurst is a nursery teacher whose interests lie in developing observation-based approaches to the education of the under-5s, through assessment, curriculum planning and evaluation. Her work focuses in particular on provision for play, working with parents and the outdoor learning environment. She is the author of *Planning for Early Learning*, published by Paul Chapman (London, 1991), and has contributed chapters on parents, assessment and observing play to recent publications. She chairs the Early Years Curriculum Group. She has collaborated with Geva Blenkin on the Goldsmiths' Pilot Research Project (1990–3), 'Monitoring and Evaluation in Workplace Nurseries', and is currently one of a Goldsmiths' team researching provision for children's early learning from birth to 8 years of age in England and Wales.

Vic Kelly is Professor of Curriculum Studies at Goldsmiths' College. As a student of curriculum, he is aware of the vast range of knowledge and understanding of curriculum which has been developed in recent years through the inter-relation of research and practice. He is thus committed to the view that school curricula should be planned in the light of that knowledge and understanding rather than according to political whim and ideology. That is the underlying theme of most of the publications with which he has been associated, including this book.

Chris Lloyd is a senior lecturer with responsibility for special educational needs in the Primary and the Secondary School of Education at the University of Greenwich. Her main research interests focus on issues related to integration for pupils with special educational needs in the UK and Europe. Her publications include books and articles about classroom management, partnership teaching and providing access to genuine educational opportunities to people with disabilities. A major ambition is to raise awareness of, and promote, disability as an equal opportunities issue.

Gillian Thumpston joined the staff of Goldsmiths' College after having had extensive experience of teaching in London primary schools and working as a mathematics consultant and local authority adviser. Her main responsibility at Goldsmiths' is as Primary Programme Director for the school-based element of the BA (Ed.) course. Within the broad field of mathematics education, her chief research interest is in attitudes towards mathematics, information technology and assessment and testing, and the implications these have for the teaching and learning of mathematics.

Marian Whitehead is a senior lecturer in education at Goldsmiths' College. She has published and researched extensively on language development and early childhood education and is the author of *Language and Literacy in the Early Years*, published by Paul Chapman (London, 1990). Her main teaching responsibilities are for MA work in both language and literature in education and early childhood education. Her current research is part of a project investigating notions of 'quality' in the training of early years practitioners in England and Wales.

INTRODUCTION

This book is the third in a trilogy of books on early childhood education which have been produced by early years staff at Goldsmiths' College with the support of a few colleagues from elsewhere.

The first book, *Early Childhood Education*, set out in detail a view of education as developmental and sought to explain why that kind of approach to education is especially appropriate, indeed necessary, in the early years of schooling. *Assessment in Early Childhood Education* followed that up by examining the role of assessment in early learning, outlining the appropriate forms of assessment for pupils at this stage of their education and contrasting those with the forms of assessment being advocated, planned and subsequently implemented at Key Stage 1 of the National Curriculum.

This third book aims to complete the trilogy by seeking to gauge the wider impact of the National Curriculum on learning in the early years. And it does this not merely by reasserting a developmental approach, although all of the intended contributors are committed to such a view, but rather by attempting to identify and analyse the forms of learning which current policies are leading to and are likely to promote, and to evaluate these against what research has revealed about the ways in which children's understandings develop in the early stages of their education.

It is now five years since the Education Act 1988 instituted the National Curriculum and its programme of testing for all pupils from 5 to 16 years of age in maintained schools. That National Curriculum was implemented first in schools catering for the early years of learning and the testing programme began with the testing of all pupils at Key Stage 1 (6–7-year-olds).

At the time of its institution, many criticisms were levelled at the National Curriculum and especially at its expected impact on early learning. It is now time to evaluate that impact. This is particularly important in the light of claims currently being made in documentation emerging from the National Curriculum Council and other official sources concerning its effectiveness – claims which lack the backing of supportive evidence and which, further, run counter to the experience of most of the people who are directly involved with the responsibilities of promoting early learning while endeavouring to meet the demands of the National Curriculum, whose worst fears seem to be being realized. The conflict between these two perceptions of the impact of the National Curriculum on early learning is so marked that it becomes necessary to attempt a resolution of them through as objective an evaluation as is possible of the realities of current policies and practices. This book will attempt precisely that kind of evaluation.

Its point of focus will be twofold. First, although it is too early – for anyone – to claim conclusive evidence of the actual impact of the National Curriculum on children's learning, it will seek to outline the findings of the research which has been undertaken (much of it by the intended contributors) in this field since the National Curriculum was first implemented in the early years of schooling. For this kind of research can already give indications of the direction in which things seem to be moving.

Second, it will consider what research of a wider and longer-established kind has told us about early learning, in order to assess the impact on such learning of the concepts of learning, teaching, education and curriculum which are emerging as fundamental to the National Curriculum and its associated policies.

The first two chapters seek to set the scene for those that follow. Chapter 1 outlines the skilful use of rhetoric and the manipulation of discourse which has been a feature of the strategies employed in the implementation of the National Curriculum. It poses two questions. First, how does the reality compare with the rhetoric? This is a question which all subsequent chapters will address. Second, why has this subtle power-coercive strategy been adopted? This second question provides the main focus for Chapter 2, which seeks to identify the major points of conflict between the underpinning values of the National Curriculum and those educational values which have emerged from half a century of research and practice in early childhood education and which have, as a consequence, come to be enshrined in the professional activities of those working in this field.

The main core of this book then consists of a series of explorations of those issues which seem to be emerging as the crucial features of the new curriculum policies in the early years – the lash-back effects on nursery education, the impact of testing at 7 plus, the implications for early learning in the core areas of language, mathematical development and scientific and technological understanding, and the effects on equal opportunities provision, especially in relation to those pupils who are non-native speakers of English and those deemed to have special educational needs.

A concluding chapter by the editors will then seek to draw these threads together and to point up the general features of the analysis and the conclusions of the evaluation.

There can be few people, professional or lay, who are not aware of the tensions which have resulted from the imposition of the National Curriculum on teachers, without reference to their professional expertise which common sense would suggest should have been tapped. Nor can many be in doubt that it is because of the failure to profit from that expertise that the current Secretary of State for Education has recently found it necessary to admit in public that the government has got its 'reforms' badly wrong. It is perhaps less evident, at least to those outside the profession, or even outside the early years sector of it, that these mistakes have had the greatest impact on education in the early years. Yet, as was suggested earlier, there are those who knew, and warned, that this would be the case. This book seeks to explain why this is so, why it was inevitable and what the most serious effects of the errors which have been made are.

Geva Blenkin
Vic Kelly
January 1993

1
BEYOND THE RHETORIC AND THE DISCOURSE

Vic Kelly

It is plain to anyone who has any direct experience of early years education in the UK that the advent of the National Curriculum has had the effect of turning it on its head. The direction of its development has been reversed; the advances it had made towards establishing a new and sophisticated form of curriculum have been discounted and arrested; and those teachers in the sector who continue to adhere to the values and ideals implicit in the approaches which have been displaced are struggling against all odds to maintain those values and ideals in a context which is not only incompatible but also hostile to them.

It seems no longer fashionable these days to give evidence in support of claims such as this made about education, as we shall see later in this chapter. To do so is to appear to be adopting an academic stance, to be approaching educational planning from an intellectual perspective; and it has been made quite clear that in official circles education is seen as neither an academic nor an intellectual matter. It is a matter for the amateurs rather than the professionals, for the practitioners rather than the theorists, for the untrained rather than the trained, for the inexperienced rather than the experienced.

Anecdotal evidence, however, seems quite acceptable, if one is to judge by its prevalence in official policies. And so one cannot but draw attention to the fact that educationists from other countries do not now visit the UK to study its approaches to early education, or to primary education generally, because these have reverted to being no different from, and certainly no longer superior to, their own. And, in explaining why they do not now do so, they express incredulity and amazement at the disappearance, indeed the destruction, of a system which was once their envy. And,

1

further, they evince great concern that current policies in the UK reflect not only a rejection of what they see as significant advances which had been occurring there but also movement in a direction which is the complete reverse of the directions of development to be seen in their own countries. There is a groundswell of contrary movement throughout Europe and a concomitant horror and disbelief there at the direction early education is being taken along in the UK.

For, while most other countries are increasing nursery provision, in the UK it is being reduced; while most countries are extending and intensifying courses of training for all professionals who are preparing to work with young children, in the UK these are being reduced in length and in quality. While most other countries are attempting to take full account of what recent research has revealed about appropriate forms of education for young children, policies in the UK are dismissive of such research.

The major changes which are currently being imposed on early years education in the UK, then, run contrary to trends in most other countries, are not responsive to important recent research findings and are totally uncongenial to most practitioners in the field (except possibly those recently trained teachers who have been carefully protected from exposure to all such 'woolly-mindedness' and 'idealism').

Two questions naturally arise when one appreciates this. First, in these circumstances, how have these changes been brought about? And, second, what is the impact they are having on the system? The latter question is one which is the concern of this book as a whole. The former is the first issue which this opening chapter will address.

For it is important, before we consider the impact of the changes, to consider whether those who have introduced them have good reasons for doing so. After all, it is theoretically possible that the UK *could* be the only country in the world which is getting things right in this area. That was certainly once the case. And, if it is the case now, that must change our perspective on the impact of the changes.

One has to begin by saying, however, that if there are good reasons for these changes, little attempt has been made to present these reasons to us. For most of the official documentation which has accompanied them, as has just been suggested, has consisted of unsubstantiated assertions rather than reasoned argument or the presentation of evidence. The language has been that of the politician rather than that of the professional. And the thrust has been towards *dirigisme* rather than persuasion.

STRATEGIES FOR CHANGE

It was pointed out a long time ago (Bennis, Benne and Chin, 1969) that there are three major strategies for effecting change: empirical-rational, normative-re-educative and power-coercive strategies. The empirical-rational strategy, as the term suggests, requires that those wishing to bring about change demonstrate the desirability of that change by offering either empirical evidence or rational argument (or both) to support it. The strategy assumes that human beings are rational or, at least, that they are more likely to accept proposed change if they are provided with good reasons for doing so. The absence of this kind of justification for the introduction of the National Curriculum, especially in the early years of education, must be seen as significant. For not only does it indicate that the strategy for change adopted is not of an empirical-rational kind; it also suggests either that early years specialists are not regarded in official circles as rational or that the policies are recognized as not having a basis in either empirical evidence or rational argument.

The normative-re-educative strategy seeks to bring about a commitment on the part of those who are expected to accept and implement change to the values and norms implicit in that change, and of course at the same time to persuade them to discard the norms and values which have informed their previous practice. There are clearly several ways of setting about this.

The most satisfactory of these is that which involves a link with the empirical-rational strategy, namely to lead people to a change of values by offering them evidence and/or reasons for such a change. And again it is significant and worthy of note that this has not been the means adopted to secure the implementation of the National Curriculum and its associated policies. For, again, it suggests a recognition of the impossibility of persuading teachers, especially those working in the early years, that their soundly based educational values should be changed in these ways or, indeed, surrendered altogether.

The second way of changing people's values and norms, however, is by a subtle form of power-coercion and, since this has been a major feature of current practices, it is this strategy for change we need to look at most closely here.

Power-coercive strategies seek, again as the term suggests, to effect change through the application of power or force. Those who wish to bring about change use political and/or economic power to impose those changes on others who have less power, and thus seek to take control and responsibility into their own hands.

An unwillingness to adopt more open means to bring about change is in itself a matter of some significance. There is no doubt, however, that this has been the central strategy for the implementation of the National Curriculum and its associated policies in the UK, and its significance is there for all to see. For those policies have been established by a major Education Act (1988), preceded by a number of minor Acts (1980, 1981, 1986) and followed by further legislation, on what we might call the 'Polyfilla' principle of government, by which you build, or rather jerrybuild, a framework of social policy and then fill in the gaps and stop up the loop-holes as they emerge. Furthermore, in many cases the practice has been to impose financial sanctions, both overtly, through penalties, and covertly, through funding mechanisms, for example, and an extensive programme of testing as a basis for the issuing of 'league tables', which must be seen as a device for control rather than as a means towards genuine improvements.

Thus curriculum change in the UK over the last thirty years or so has been characterized (Blenkin, Edwards and Kelly, 1992, p. 38) as displaying all three of these strategies in turn:

> During the 1960s and early 1970s empirical-rational strategies predominated through the work of the Schools Council. In the mid-1970s this gave way to normative-reeducative strategies as the emphasis shifted to school-centred innovation. Throughout both of these periods teachers enjoyed a considerable amount of autonomy in curriculum decision-making, particularly in the latter . . . The 1980s were characterized by an unprecedented shift to power-coercive strategies, and a subsequent erosion of teacher autonomy, as central government intervened increasingly in curriculum matters; this shift culminated with a vengeance in the 1988 Education Reform Act and the subsequent implementation of the National Curriculum.

There are limits, however, to how far even a government with strong autocratic tendencies can take the more overt forms of power-coercion in a democratic society. And it may well be felt that those limits have already been surpassed in the UK. Certainly, a point has been reached where actual revolt is occurring – of teachers, of parents and of governors, for example, against the testing programme and practices and the concept of 'league tables'.

And it is also the case that people's views, values and norms cannot easily or effectively be changed by these overt devices of control. Legislation can force us into doing certain things, or into doing them in certain ways; it can never make us accept or approve of them.

However, there are more covert forms of power-coercion, such as those referred to earlier, which do seek, sometimes successfully to change attitudes, to be normative-re-educative, not by offering reasoned argument or evidence but by attempting to change our views, values and norms by more subtle and hidden means. This is a more dangerous, because less readily recognizable, form of power-coercion. Yet there is little doubt that it has been a major feature of the strategies adopted in the attempt to secure the implementation of current policies in the UK. For nothing has characterized the procedures of implementation adopted so much as the use of rhetoric and the control of discourse.

And it is these features of the current scene that this chapter will consider in some detail, not only to set a context for what follows but also because the use of rhetoric and the control of discourse in this way are themselves having a serious impact on the system. For they are creating an ethos and a context for educational practice in which reasoned argument and the appeal to evidence no longer have a role. Their effect is thus, as it must be, to deintellectualize educational planning, to deprofessionalize the teacher and to turn the practice of education into an exercise for the implementation of government policies which are founded on nothing more secure than the prejudices of whatever government happens to hold power.

THE USE OF RHETORIC

The most obvious example of the use of rhetoric in the implementation of the National Curriculum and its associated policies is to be found in the Education Act 1988 itself, in fact in its very title. For the 1988 Act is not merely an education Act as, for example, the Butler Act of 1944 was; it is the Education *Reform* Act. We are, however, offered no supporting evidence for what constitutes in essence a claim to its unquestionable effectiveness; indeed it is clear that there could be no such evidence – not at least unless prophetic powers were being claimed. Some people in fact used their own prophetic powers at the time to predict that the opposite of reform would result from the policies encapsulated in the Act (Lawton and Chitty, 1988; Kelly, 1990). And subsequent events have tended to support those prophecies rather than any claims to successful reform.

The term 'reform', then, must be seen as part of the rhetoric, as part of the power-coercive strategy. And, inappropriate as it may be in what is after all a piece of legislation, we have here a significant piece of evidence that rhetoric rather than honest persuasion was to be the major device for seeking to ensure the acceptance of that legislation. And one might even interpret this as an acknowledgement from the outset both that it would be a difficult task to ensure such acceptance and that to attempt to do so by offering reasoned argument or evidence was not a workable strategy.

Nor does the rhetoric of the Act end with its title. Why should it? For the Act itself, again in spite of being an act of legislation, goes on to assert, again without evidence, what the new policies, and especially the National Curriculum, *will* achieve. Unlike the Butler Act of 1944, which set out a number of ideals which were to be the baseline for educational planning, ideals such as 'education for all according to age, aptitude and ability', the 1988 Act tells us, without fear of contradiction (or, at least, without acceptance of contradiction), not only that it is the responsibility of the Secretary of State, every local education authority and every governing body or head teacher of a maintained school to secure a curriculum which 'is a balanced and broadly based curriculum' (Education Reform Bill, p. 1, l. 21); nor only that a curriculum satisfies that criterion (or those criteria) if it 'promotes the spiritual, moral, cultural, mental and physical development of pupils at the school and of society' and 'prepares such pupils for the opportunities, responsibilities and experiences of adult life' (*ibid.*, ll. 22–5); but also – by inference – that the only kind of curriculum which can achieve these goals is one which consists of the three core subjects of mathematics, English and science, the other foundation subjects, history, geography, technology, music, art and physical education, along with religious education (with of course Welsh for the Welsh and a modern language at Key Stages 3 and 4), i.e. the National Curriculum which the Act established.

An earlier document (DES, 1987) had assured us, again without evidence, that such a curriculum *will* raise standards in four major ways:

> ensuring that all pupils study a broad and balanced range of subjects throughout their compulsory schooling.
>
> (*Ibid.*, p. 3)

> setting clear objectives for what children over the full range of ability should be able to achieve.
>
> (*Ibid.*)

> ensuring that all pupils, regardless of sex, ethnic origin and geographical location, have access to broadly the same good and relevant curriculum [i.e. the National Curriculum].
>
> (*Ibid.*)

> checking on progress towards those objectives and performances achieved at various stages, so that pupils can be stretched further when they are doing well and given more help when they are not.
>
> (*Ibid.*, p. 4)

And a follow-up document (DES, 1989a, para. 2.2) further tells us that this curriculum is 'an entitlement for all pupils'. It also informs us (*ibid.*) that the principle has been established that 'each pupil should have a broad and balanced curriculum which is relevant to his or her particular needs; [i.e. again the National Curriculum] and, further, that this principle 'is now established in law' (*ibid.*). Ergo, it must happen! It is well worth pausing here to note that this closely argued curriculum plan is to replace the 'woolly', 'child-centred', 'progressive' approach to curriculum which would be favoured and adopted by most early years teachers if they did not have the benefit of this clearly delineated alternative!

Apart from the rhetoric of terms such as 'breadth', 'balance', 'good', 'relevant', etc., to which we will return, we must also note the tactics of assertion without evidence, of unquestioned assumption and of conceptual obfuscation.

It is not the intention here, however, to go through the Act and/or the attendant and subsequent documentation which has emerged in support of it from CCW, NCC, SEAC, HMI, DFE, etc., and expose the rhetoric which is a major feature of that documentation. That interesting exercise we shall leave to the reader.

To assist him or her in that exercise, however, what we will do here is to identify the major rhetorical devices employed, so that he or she may be the more readily able to identify the many examples to be found in this documentation.

THE MAJOR RHETORICAL DEVICES

There are three main devices which need to be identified – the use of 'buzz' words, the misuse of metaphor and the manipulation, control and legitimation of discourse – and we must look briefly at all of these.

The use of 'buzz' words

The most obvious rhetorical device to be discerned in the official literature, and in the 1988 Act itself, is the use of words which carry with them warm, friendly connotations of approval. We can see this in the quotations we have already noted. Who, for example, will quarrel with the idea of an 'entitlement' curriculum? Or with that of a 'broad and balanced' curriculum? Or a 'good and relevant' curriculum? Who will argue that a curriculum should not seek to meet the 'particular needs' of every pupil or to provide 'continuity' and 'progression'? Who will disagree with the aim of 'raising standards'?

One looks in vain, however, for a definition of the meanings being given to these terms, although we know from experience (and even simply from common sense) that all of them are capable of a wide range of definitions and interpretations. And one looks in vain also for the evidence that what is proposed will actually, or even is likely to, bring about a 'raising of standards', 'entitlement', 'breadth', 'balance', 'relevance', 'progression', 'continuity' or anything else which might come within any definition of 'reform'. And one notes, as a consequence, that if neither definition nor evidence is offered, and if all proposals are couched in rhetorical terms, then the reality – of the intentions as well as of the effects – of these policies must be very different from that which the rhetoric suggests. For why should anyone have recourse to rhetoric if what is being offered is the genuine article? Rhetoric is the stock-in-trade of the politician, the advertiser and the salesperson, not of the advocate of genuine social reform. For rhetoric deliberately seeks to obfuscate truth and to usurp the place of open rational debate.

One further point should be noted here. Most of the 'buzz' words which are used have been hijacked from the language and discourse of those who, it is expected, will be most difficult to persuade and whose views of education it is intended to supplant and abolish (Blenkin and Kelly, 1993). It is easy to see that the National Curriculum, with its subject-content base and its simplistic testing procedures, is likely to be least palatable to primary teachers, and especially those working in the early years field. Hence it has been offered in a form all dressed up in the language which early years practitioners have long used in discussing and planning their work. There is no acknowledgement of the fact that the meaning given to terms such as 'process' and 'development', for example, in current policies is very different from that they have traditionally borne; the words have been hijacked but not the concepts they have previously enshrined; and it is presumably hoped that most people will not notice this.

Apart from the insult this represents to a major section of the teaching profession, it also has the effect of reducing the value of these terms to their previous 'owners' and in their earlier contexts. And, further, by deliberately promoting a lack of conceptual clarity, it obfuscates important issues and seriously limits the scope of the educational debate, thus contributing to that process of the legitimation of discourse to which we will come shortly. For to employ rhetoric is to declare oneself inimical to both conceptual clarity and open debate.

The misuse of a metaphor

The second rhetorical device which, it was suggested earlier, is a feature of current educational policies and their presentation is the use, or misuse, of metaphor.

The metaphor is a very important literary device. Without it, language of every kind would be much the poorer – our spoken language as well as our written language, the most humble piece of information in a newspaper as well as the greatest literature. As a figure of speech, therefore, the metaphor performs an important function in adding richness to language.

It also has the power to add clarity to what we are seeking to express, primarily by enabling us to offer an analogy or an illustration of what we are trying to get across. In this respect, the simile is equally helpful. It is also safer. For a simile makes it quite obvious that an analogy is being offered, a comparison made. A metaphor can insinuate itself into our thinking until we no longer recognize it as a metaphor. And so, as Eisner (1982, p. 6) has said, metaphors 'also have a cost. That cost resides in the ways in which they shape our conception of the problems we study'.

It will be worth while dwelling for a moment on some of the ways in which this can happen. A helpful distinction has been offered between 'microscopic' and 'macroscopic' metaphors (Ortony, 1979a), between metaphors at the level of individual words or sentences, which usefully perform those enriching and/or elucidating functions we noted just now, and 'systems of metaphors, or metaphoric models' (*op. cit.*, p. 4) which, as we shall see later, can become new forms of discursive practice.

For the danger of the macroscopic metaphor or the metaphoric system is that it invites us to develop arguments from analogy; it encourages us to make deductions to which the metaphor gives the appearance of legitimacy, but which, without the concealment that the metaphor provides, can be seen to be manifestly invalid. Thus, for example, if, at the macroscopic level, we get into the habit of discussing, say, 'political correctness' as a form of mental health, the metaphor/analogy can quickly lead us to conclusions about the appropriate forms of 'treatment' (including perhaps isolation through incarceration) for those who are not politically 'correct' or 'healthy'.

It is from this perspective that we need to be very circumspect about the use of metaphor in the currently accepted discourse of education. The metaphoric system which has been foisted on the world of education in recent years is the metaphor of commerce and industry. We have heard increasingly of 'providers', 'products', 'users', 'consumers', 'machinery', 'competition', 'managers', 'quality control', 'curriculum delivery' and so on. We have thus been presented with a factory, even a factory farming, picture of schools and schooling.

And it is by that device that, as Eliot Eisner has warned, our conceptions of the problems we face have been changed. For the language of industry has become the language of education, as is clear from the way in which most teachers themselves now discuss it.

If we regard the school as a factory or a factory farm, of course, there is nothing reprehensible about this. For in that case, we will see this not as metaphor but as reality. However, as long ago as 1898, the Report of the Committee on Education (1897–8), in discussing 'payment by results', declared that 'a school is a living thing, and should be judged as a living thing, not merely as a factory producing a modicum of examinable knowledge' (quoted in Goldstream, 1972, p. 162). And, more recently, the same view has been expressed by the Plowden Committee, which told us that 'a school is not merely a teaching shop' (CACE, 1967, p. 187). If we accept that view, then we are dealing here with a metaphoric system, and the effects of accepting it uncritically are that we begin to accept the conclusions we are encouraged to draw by argument from the analogy.

And so, for example, we are led and encouraged to adopt an instrumental view of the educational process; to evaluate it in terms of its endproducts; to assess educational merit in terms of cost-effectiveness and the efficiency of the 'delivery' of the content of the curriculum; to frame quality control mechanisms which do not seek to go beyond this narrow, instrumental frame of reference; to cease to ask questions about the value of what is on offer; to view the role of the headteacher as not one of academic or professional or educational leadership but as essentially technical, as Eliot Eisner (1982, p. 19) also points out; and so on.

All of this, of course, is what we are expected to do. That is the point of the misuse of the metaphor. That it is a misuse, however, becomes clear if we develop the argument from analogy to a *reductio ad absurdum*. For the factory farming analogy not only leads us to accept the necessity of testing and grading our pupils as they pass along the production line but it also encourages us to consider what we are to do with the rejects, the 'seconds', whether we are to institute some kind of 'recycling' process, or develop a scrapheap in the playground, or try to pass them off as the genuine article. As has been said elsewhere (Blenkin, Edwards and Kelly, 1992, p. 144):

> Such questions may seem absurd; if so, they demonstrate the absurdity of the analogy and the fallacy of arguments derived from it. They may seem fanciful; if so, again this reflects on the limitations of the metaphor. If, however, they

seem to us to be totally unrelated to the realities of current policies, then we should probably inspect those policies more closely.

This last point we must take up later when we consider, finally, the reality which lies behind the rhetoric.

The legitimation of discourse

We turn now to the third rhetorical device which we identified earlier as a major feature of the current educational scene in the UK – the legitimation of discourse.

We have already seen one important aspect of this in our discussion of the commercial/industrial metaphoric system which has been foisted on us in recent years. For we have seen how this has changed both the language in which we talk about education and, as a consequence, the ways in which we conceive it and the issues we regard as important within it. We must now develop this notion a little further.

Much has been said and written over the last decade or so about the status and role of discourse within societies. The importance of discourse in setting the rules and the parameters for our thinking and thus our actions has been strongly emphasized. Indeed, some have expressed the view that, in a fundamental sense, we are all the products of the discourses within which we operate. If this is the case, it must follow that we can be manipulated through the control of discourse, so that this becomes yet another useful device to the purveyor of rhetoric or the power-coercive manager of change.

It is not necessary here to delve deeply into the sociological and philosophical debate about the role of discourse and of discursive practices within society. What we must note, however, is the claim made, for example, by Michael Foucault (1980) that discursive practices are not idealist constructions but are 'materially produced by specific social, political and economic arrangements' (Cherryholmes, 1987, p. 300). Further, 'Discursive practices are not purely and simply ways of producing discourse. They are embodied in technical processes, in institutions, in patterns for general behaviour, in forms for transmission and diffusion, and *in pedagogical forms which, at once, impose and maintain them*' (Foucault, 1980, p. 200, emphasis added, quoted by Cherryholmes, 1987, p. 300).

The rules of discursive practices, as Cherryholmes goes on to claim (*ibid.*, p. 301), 'govern what can be said and what must remain unsaid . . . [and] identify who can speak with authority and who must listen'. And so, 'dominant discourses determine what counts as true, important, relevant and what gets spoken' (*ibid.*).

With this in mind, let us look again at the educational scene in recent years in the UK, and especially the field of early childhood education. One of the first features of that scene to notice is the way in which what was the dominant discourse of early years education, what we might in shorthand call the 'Plowden discourse', has been discredited and thus effectively (but not entirely) destroyed. This has been done not by reasoned argument, as we saw earlier, but by those processes of 'rubbishing' which Stephen Ball (1990) has called 'discourses of derision'. Approaches to education and curriculum predicated on the 'Plowden discourse' have been described as outmoded, as 'old hat', as unfitted to the twenty-first century. In reality, all that has happened is that they have been supplanted by approaches based on another form of discourse – 'National Curriculum speak'.

The significance of this, of course, is not merely that one ideology has been replaced by another, although in reality that is what has happened. Further than that, the new ideology through its dominant discourse has achieved a position where, rather than having to press and justify its educational values, it is able to control the degree to which they will be discussed, to 'determine what counts as true, important, relevant and what gets spoken' (Cherryholmes, 1987, p. 301) and, in short, to decide what will count as 'truth'.

Thus, for example, not only is there now no recognition of the validity of educational values other than those enshrined in the National Curriculum but also the new discourse sets the parameters within which all else in education must be conducted. Furthermore, those parameters exclude the insights acquired from earlier debates conducted within earlier forms of discourse, and attempts have been made – with some success – to invest the authority to speak with authority on educational matters in different groups of people – the politicians and the 'educrats' rather than the teachers or educationists, people with legitimate claims to understand the educational process.

And so, for example, evaluation of schools and teachers must now be done in terms of the effectiveness of their 'delivery' of the curriculum. The only data necessary for this are the results of pupil assessment and the 'performance indicator' templates applied by the agents of Ofsted. All that we have learnt from experience and research about the complexities of evaluation has been abandoned – as belonging to a different discursive system. Evaluation focuses only on the 'delivery' of the National Curriculum and not on its value or worth. Those attempting to make such an evaluation with public funding for their research are sworn to secrecy under the Official Secrets Act (it is interesting to note that the government regards the state of the education system as a potential threat to national security). Official reports informing the world about the great success of the new policies are issued before authentic research data are to hand, since it is known that those data will tell a different story. Or, as in the case of the SEAC research on testing for 7-year-olds in 1991, the evidence is suppressed (in that case because of the impending election) (Graham and Tytler 1993). To a large extent, therefore, these reports consist of assertions which lack supporting evidence or even fly in the face of contrary evidence. And it is those reports and their unsupported assertions (a euphemism for 'lies') rather than the suppressed data that constitute the new accepted discourse – a discourse of dishonesty – and thus determine, or seek to determine, the way in which we view and do things. It all gives a whole new meaning to the practice of 'story-telling' in the early years.

Another aspect of this, or another way of expressing it, is to say that there has been a significant change in the intellectual categories within which we debate and plan our educational provision. The moral category has been replaced by the mechanistic; the social by the political; the ideal by the expedient; the co-operative by the competitive. The focus of concern has shifted, or rather has been shifted, from the child to the economy. And, in the terminology of the Crowther Report (CACE, 1959), the notion of education as 'the right of every boy and girl to be educated' (p. 54) and as 'one of the social services of the welfare state' (*ibid.*) has been completely ousted by that of education as a 'national investment', as reflecting 'the need of the community to provide an adequate supply of brains and skill to sustain its economic productivity' (*ibid.*). The changes we are experiencing, therefore, are moral as well as social; our value systems are being changed as well as our practices; and our attitudes are being manipulated as well as our conditions of work. And all of this is being brought about by processes which are far more subtle than George Orwell ever envisaged.

Thus allied to, and in harness with, the use of rhetoric and metaphor, the legitimation of a new form of discourse has become a significant tool or device for effecting massive and unpopular changes by subtle, but nevertheless essentially power-coercive, means.

Some of the sociological accounts of the legitimation of discourse seem to suggest that this is an inevitable sociological process, and even that there is little we can do about it. Other contributors to the debate, however, have taken the view that to have understood it is to have achieved the possibility of controlling and resisting it. To recognize those features of discursive practices which we are identifying here and, indeed, the features of rhetoric and metaphor generally, is to be in a position to protect oneself from the attempted manipulation of one's thinking which they represent, to have gained 'greater freedom from ideological and linguistic traps, breadth of vision, the ability to "speak one's own words", direct access to fundamental negotiations of meaning' (Slaughter, 1989, p. 264), instead of 'passively decoding finished structures of meaning' (*op. cit.*, p. 265) or, in short, allowing others to do our thinking for us.

It also enables us to 'feel deeply involved in the process of cultural reconstruction and renewal' (*ibid.*). For the education system of a genuinely democratic society belongs not to the politicians and their henchpersons but to everyone in that society. And it is fundamentally antidemocratic for any group to attempt to seize control of that system by underhand methods of this kind. For an underhand method is certainly what the use of rhetorical devices of all kinds is, since it is by definition an attempt to change and control the lives of others without offering reasoned justification for decisions taken, without so much as a 'by your leave'. As such it has no place in a democratic society and none especially in the education system of such a society. In a truly democratic society everyone should have the opportunity to contribute to social planning and to 'feel deeply involved in the process of cultural reconstruction and renewal'. There is no place in such a society for those who wish, and actively seek, to deny others those rights.

Those who propound the rhetoric, however, if challenged, *might* be inclined to respond by asserting that their claims are not rhetorical but have a firm basis in reason and evidence (although one might then speculate on why they do not present the reasons and the evidence to us). It is not enough, therefore, merely to recognize their rhetorical techniques. In order to demonstrate that they are rhetorical, we need to be able to show them to be untrue or invalid. We must, finally, in this chapter, therefore, attempt some evaluation of the reality behind and beyond the rhetoric – in case it is not rhetoric at all.

THE REALITY BEYOND THE RHETORIC

Subsequent chapters will be seeking to identify what is actually happening to early childhood education as a result of the changes imposed by the 1988 Act and the related policy decisions which have followed. The final section of this chapter, therefore, will seek to do no more than to highlight some of the broad issues which must be addressed, and to look at some of the more extravagant claims which have been made, and continue to be made, for these policies. Three large claims in particular need to be given close consideration:

- That the new policies *will* raise standards.
- That they *will* offer a broad and balanced curriculum for all pupils.
- That such a curriculum is an entitlement for all pupils, i.e. that all pupils *will* experience such a curriculum.

The raising of standards

We noted earlier the assertion made in the consultative document which preceded the passing of the Education Act 1988 that 'a national curriculum backed by clear assessment arrangements will help to raise standards of attainment' (DES, 1987, p. 3). And we also noted there the four ways in which it was claimed that this would be achieved.

It was also clear that there was no intention to offer any evidence in support of this claim. It is quite reasonable, therefore, after four or five years of the new policies, to ask whether this assertion has been verified by the results of the implementation of those policies.

It is, of course, easy for politicians and their aides to make assertions without evidence. That after all is their stock-in-trade. To respond, however, is not so easy for those of us whose respect for intellectual standards is such as to create in us a need for some justification for any pronouncements we may wish to make. It is, therefore, difficult to offer a view on the effects of these policies on standards in the early years in the absence of any really solid evidence.

One can begin, however, by noting that there is no convincing evidence in support of the claim for improved standards, although the assertions continue to be made. One can also comment on the fact that few, if any, teachers of early years pupils can be heard to agree with the claim. In fact, if the anecdotal evidence is to be given any weight, the view of most teachers in this sector can be seen to be quite the opposite, and their reasons for that view well grounded, as subsequent chapters will reveal.

There is also some more objective evidence, however, which is worthy of note. The most obvious source of impact on the work of teachers in the early years has been the testing of pupils at Key Stage 1. And, as we shall see in later chapters, attempts have been made to assess this impact and its effects. In particular, one of the few pieces of politically independent research in this area, that undertaken jointly by the National Union of Teachers (NUT) and the School of Education of the University of Leeds (NUT, 1993), has presented a number of findings which would seem to have some significance for the question of standards in the early years.

The focus of this research has been on the effects of the testing process itself. And its findings are interesting in that they demonstrate quite convincingly that the impact on classroom activities during the actual period of the testing is, on any definition of 'standards', detrimental to those standards. That there should be, on the evidence of a very large majority of teachers, less collaborative working by pupils, for example, less catering for their individual needs, less allowing them to approach teachers for support, less hearing children read, and less talking to children about their work, can be interpreted in no other way than as a lowering of the quality of provision during the periods of testing and thus, it must be assumed, of standards of pupil attainment.

Further than this, however, that same survey also found that 'four out of every five teachers felt that pupils were less well prepared for Y3 than had been the case in previous years' (*op. cit.*, p. viii). This, they suggested, is 'due to the loss of teaching time caused by the SATs' (*op. cit.*, p. 15). In other words, the general view of teachers, who are the only people in a position to offer such judgements, since, unlike the testers, they have a basis for comparision, is that standards have effectively fallen as a result of the new policies, and especially the testing at Key Stage 1. In relation to the testing programme and its impact on standards, someone recently remarked that no one ever grew taller by constantly measuring him or herself, or heavier by constant weighing (a relief, no doubt, to weight watchers!). It seems, however, that it is possible to become smaller through this process.

We may finally note that the declared intention now to reduce the length of all courses of teacher training and to plan them as periods of apprenticeship rather than professional education is difficult to reconcile with the stated intention of raising standards. For it can hardly be argued that one of the routes towards improved standards is by lowering the quality of teachers.

Such evidence as we have access to, therefore, far from supporting the rhetoric of a raising of standards, points very clearly in the other direction. And subsequent chapters will reinforce that view.

A broad and balanced curriculum

We noted earlier that one of the ways in which, we were assured, standards would be raised was by 'ensuring that all pupils study a broad and balanced range of subjects throughout their compulsory schooling' (DES, 1987, p. 3). The question of whether the National Curriculum represents such a broad and balanced curriculum for all pupils or, to express it differently, whether its effect has been to provide them all with such a curriculum especially in the early years, is an even more difficult question to address than that about standards. For a moment's thought will reveal the complexities of concepts such as 'breadth' and 'balance' when applied to the school curriculum (Kelly, 1986), and will demonstrate that whether we regard the National Curriculum as offering breadth and balance will depend entirely on our definition of these terms.

We can, however, comment on the apparent meaning given to them within current policies – or rather the confusion of meanings within such policies. The quotation from the consultative document which we have just noted firmly defines breadth and balance in terms of the *subjects* included in the National Curriculum. And this is confirmed by the National Curriculum Council (NCC) in the third document in its *Curriculum Guidance* series. For there we are told, in no uncertain terms, that 'the National Curriculum [i.e. the core and foundation subjects] will offer a broad and balanced education for all pupils providing progression and continuity from 5 to 16 and beyond' (NCC, 1990, p. 1). However, earlier on the same page, we have also been told that 'the National Curriculum alone will not provide the necessary breadth' (*ibid.*), and we have only reached page 2 of that document when we learn that 'a balanced whole curriculum must furnish opportunities for additional subjects'. So, is the National Curriculum balanced or not? NCC, it seems, is not sure. Or does the National Curriculum require to be augmented in some way? NCC, it seems, believes that it does.

It will be enlightening to explore this a little further. This particular NCC document is entitled *The Whole Curriculum*, and is concerned to argue that the whole curriculum has to be seen as more than a collection of subjects. In particular, it is concerned with what is happening to personal and social education as a result of the new policies. And it has a right to be so concerned. For, as some people said at the time when the National Curriculum, and especially its testing programme, were being introduced, that curriculum is assessment led and will lead teachers into 'teaching to the tests', concentrating their efforts on the subjects of the National Curriculum and especially on the core subjects which the Standard Assessment Tasks (SATs) seek to test, to the detriment of other important aspects of their role as educators (Kelly, 1990). And, as we have noted, the research is already indicating that we were right to offer that warning. For if teachers are having less time to give to such things as collaborative working by pupils, catering for individual needs, allowing children to approach teachers for support and talking to children about their work (NUT, 1993), then an important dimension of a broad and balanced curriculum is being lost.

By any definition, a crucial element in the curriculum of children in the early years is the opportunity to 'become a pupil' and, as part of that process, to learn to work with others in a properly structured social environment. To create such an environment and to support this kind of development are tasks which early years teachers traditionally have seen as central to their role, and further as vital to the provision of a properly balanced early years curriculum. To put that vital element at risk by the imposition of a subject-based curriculum and, worse, to seek then to reinvent it through the metaphysics of 'cross-curricular' 'dimensions', 'skills' and 'themes', is at best perverse, and at worst pernicious.

At all events, in our present context, it seems to cast some doubt on the validity of the claim that we now have a broad and balanced curriculum in the early years of a kind we did not have before. The only thing which has changed – and it is a mighty change – is that large helpings of subject content have been added, especially scientific and technological content. And, while it may be claimed that this has added a balancing factor on one definition of curriculum balance, we also need to ask what has been jettisoned to make way for it. And the answer to that question begins to look very disturbing indeed. It seems it is the 'whole' curriculum rather than the National Curriculum which is broad and balanced, and that the National Curriculum excludes some important balancing elements. Yet it is only the National Curriculum which schools are required by law to teach, and those other important elements remain optional and thus, as we have seen, and shall see again in subsequent chapters, at risk.

Entitlement

Let us now turn to the last piece of rhetoric we said we would explore further, the claim that the National Curriculum is an entitlement curriculum, that 'a curriculum which meets these general criteria [i.e. those of the National Curriculum] is an entitlement for all pupils' (DES, 1987, para. 2.2), and that 'the ERA . . . entitles every pupil in maintained schools . . . to a curriculum which is balanced and broadly based' (DES, 1989a, para. 2.1.).

The wording of these statements is at best ambiguous, and it is noteworthy, if not sinister, that the word 'entitlement' does not appear in the 1988 Act itself. Yet the term does bring with it connotations of equality, and some of the supporting documentation confirms this. We hear, for example, that, again as we saw above, one of the ways in which this new curriculum will raise standards is by 'ensuring that all pupils, regardless of sex, ethnic origin and geographical location, have access to the same good and relevant curriculum' (DES, 1987, p. 4).

We might perhaps note the naivety, or the duplicity, of the claim that what, since 1944, several generations of well meaning, committed and hard-working professionals have failed to achieve a few, possibly not well meaning, committed or hard-working amateurs will bring about by a single act of legislation. However, some kind of equality of provision seems to be the goal. Or, again, is it merely the rhetoric? Let us consider the reality.

Again, when these policies were being framed and developed, there were those who warned of the inequalities which all the research evidence indicated were built into this new curriculum (Kelly, 1990). In particular, two kinds of research evidence were cited, that relating to the inequalities of streaming and selection and that concerned with the alienating effect of forcing children into a curriculum which reflects values at odds with those of their own cultural – social as well as ethnic – background.

The evidence for the inequalities of streaming and selection processes is massive and totally convincing. For it makes it absolutely plain, first, that in the days of selection by way of 11-plus testing for selective forms of secondary education, most primary schools placed their pupils into streamed classes at 7 plus; second, that the children who found themselves in the 'A' stream at 7 plus were mostly winter-born children (who had had the benefit of as much as two whole terms more schooling – 33.3 per cent – than their summer-born counterparts); and thus, third, that the best chance any child had of passing the 11 plus was to be born in the winter. Nor does the early admission to reception classes of summer-born children, to enable them to have the same amount of full-time schooling as the others, solve the problem, although it is a policy which is currently being adopted in many places in the attempt to do so. For it is not merely a matter of the length of time spent at school; it is also a matter of the level of maturity reached by children at the point of testing.

There was further evidence too of the significant part played by social class in educational success, not only at 11 plus but later too, such as that produced by the researches of the Early Leaving Report (CACE, 1954) and the Crowther Report (CACE, 1959). And there also began to emerge similar evidence in relation to pupils from ethnic minority groups (Coard, 1971).

In an attempt to combat these problems, the 11 plus was abolished in most places, comprehensive secondary education was introduced and streaming gave way to mixed-ability groupings in most primary schools and in many secondary schools too. The conditions created by current policies now put all of those developments at risk and presage a return to the worst forms of educational inequality. For testing at Key Stages 1 and 2 is already leading some primary schools to the reintroduction of streaming. And the evidence is beginning to emerge, notably through that survey undertaken by the NUT and the Leeds School of Education, to which we referred earlier, that the same groups of children are now at risk.

For example, the report of that survey offers convincing evidence to support its claims that 'at both subject and Profile Component levels, significant differences were found in favour of *winter-born* children, in English, Mathematics and Science (NUT, 1993, p. x); that 'at subject level, there were significant differences in performance between the ethnic groupings in all four subjects' (*op. cit.*, p. 51); that 'at PC level, significant differences were found in favour of English-speaking children on English PC2, Mathematics PC1 and Science PC1' (*op. cit.*, p. 52); and that 'in both Teacher Assessments and Standard Assessments there were significant differences in favour of pupils from *higher neighbourhood status groups'* [the new term for 'social class'] (*op. cit.*, p. x).

We have seen it all before. And, in the light of the evidence both from this contemporary study and from the many earlier studies of inegalitarian procedures, we are more than justified in asking in what sense of 'entitlement', other than the rhetorical, are current policies offering entitlement. For most children, again primarily those who are already socially disadvantaged, the entitlement is to failure. And, in support of this, we may cite the comment made by HMI in their annual report for 1990–1, that 'progress on equal opportunities is best described as patchy . . . too often the gap between policy and practice is unacceptably wide' (DES, 1992, para. 28).

This problem, of course, has particular implications for the education of non-native speakers of English and for those deemed to have special educational needs. The situation of pupils in both of those categories will be fully discussed in Chapters 8 and 9. We must note here, however, the hollowness of the claims that the National Curriculum offers such pupils an entitlement on a par with that of other pupils, and we must recognize this as further evidence of the rhetorical nature of these claims. We perhaps should also note the implications of this for that promised 'raising of standards' we discussed earlier. For, in terms of language development, the bilingualism of non-native speakers of English has hitherto been regarded as an enormous advantage; it has now become a handicap. And, in relation to pupils deemed to have special educational needs, we may also note that the policy adumbrated in the Warnock Report (DES, 1978b) of integrating them, wherever possible, into ordinary schools, in order to ensure that there would be little or no reduction in the educational standards they were encouraged and assisted to aim for, has been replaced by a system of increased segregation and exclusion. We have thus identified two major categories of pupil for whom standards of educational provision can be seen to have been reduced by the advent of the National Curriculum.

Let us, finally, remember what we once knew about alienation. Alienation is that state of disaffection which results from a feeling of powerlessness in the face of the apparent rejection of one's own culture and values. It is the concept which was once used to explain the disaffection from the school system of those many pupils whose culture and values were at odds with the culture and values implicit in that system and especially in the school curriculum. Thus children from working-class homes were seen to be put off schooling by being offered a predominantly middle-class curriculum. And black children were driven from formal education by a curriculum designed for pupils from a white, Anglo-Saxon, even Christian culture. In both cases, the problem was compounded by that rejection of their own culture and values which were implicit in the offering of a curriculum which seemed prepared to pay scant attention to them.

Again, therefore, a good deal of effort had been put into attempting to correct this situation, in order to eliminate the inequalities which it clearly engendered. To do this, however, it is clearly necessary to permit some variation of curriculum content, to allow, for example, some pupils to develop their historical understanding by studying the history of Mogul India rather than merely that of Tudor England or to study black jazz rather than white European classical music.

The National Curriculum permits none of this flexibility. And one has only to look at the history orders to see the truth of this. It is a nationalistic rather than a national curriculum. For this reason, some people have been warning for some time that the alienation of large groups of pupils must result from the introduction of a curriculum as rigidly focused on one section of society as the National Curriculum clearly is. And perhaps the worst feature of this is not the refusal to take proper note of the evidence, but the fact that, as a result of current policies, that alienation and disaffection which was once a feature of secondary education is now to be seen also in the early years (Barrett, 1989).

We have thus identified yet another significant group of pupils for whom the National Curriculum will not only fail to offer any genuine form of entitlement but for whom it will also mean a reduction rather than a raising of standards.

Finally we must note another dimension of this, and one which affects all children in the early years. That is the inevitable alienation from schooling of all young children if they are presented with a formalized, subject-based curriculum at an age and stage when intellectually and cognitively they are unable to respond to it (Katz and Chard, 1989). 'For a curriculum divided into subjects is, potentially, the most alienating form of curriculum for young children because it formalizes experience too soon and, in doing so, makes it distant from the everyday, commonsense knowledge and learning that the young child is familiar with and responsive to' (Blenkin and Kelly, 1993, p. 58).

And so we see that there is more reason to expect that the impact of the National Curriculum on all pupils in the early years will be to lower standards of attainment than to accept the claims of the documentation that it will raise them.

Again, therefore, we have to recognize the claims that what is being offered is an entitlement curriculum to be mere rhetoric. Indeed, we must also recognize the internal incoherence of a set of policies which purport to be based on the principle that 'each pupil should have a broad and balanced curriculum which is also relevant to his or her needs' (DES, 1989a, para. 2.2.), and which seek at the same time to meet the needs of every individual pupil with one rigid and inflexible curricular offering.

Entitlement is to that which the government, through its Secretary of State for Education, prescribes, i.e. to what is relevant to what *it* perceives as *its* needs, not to what might count as 'good and relevant' or 'broad and balanced' in the eyes of the individual pupil.

To promote a genuine form of entitlement, a curriculum must not only be common to all but it must also be 'genuinely suitable for all, not suitable only for the middle-class or most academic' (Warnock, 1977, p. 84). 'A system must be devised so flexible that it can be made to accommodate everyone, whatever his ability, whatever his cultural background' (*ibid.*). And 'it is possible to devise a curriculum which is both common and non-middle class, adaptable for all, and within which no-one is doomed to failure or frustration' (*ibid.*). The present National Curriculum is clearly very far from being this kind of curriculum. Indeed, it is its polar opposite.

As Mary Warnock also points out (*op. cit.*, p. 26), 'there is a difference between claiming that everyone has an equal right to education and saying that everyone has a right to equal education'. In a democratic society, 'entitlement' should mean more than entitlement to access; it should mean entitlement to full and appropriate provision (Kelly, 1990). And the younger the citizens in that democratic society, the greater their entitlement to this kind of consideration. On this kind of definition, then, the National Curriculum is not only not an entitlement curriculum but it also falls a good deal short of being a suitable curriculum for a democratic society.

Rhetoric it all is, then, since far from finding evidence to support these claims, we have unearthed some quite compelling evidence to refute them. That evidence will be expanded and developed in the chapters which follow.

SUMMARY AND CONCLUSIONS

This chapter has sought to set the scene for what follows by clearing away some of the conceptual lumber created by the massive use of rhetoric by the government and its aides in its attempt to impose its current educational policies.

It began by looking at some of the strategies available to those who wish to bring about curriculum change, and suggested that the power-coercive technique is the only one which could be adopted by those who are aware that their proposed changes are not acceptable to the community on which they plan to impose them.

It then considered some aspects of the subtle use of rhetorical devices as a major component in the power-coercive methods used to implement the National Curriculum, and its associated policies, in the UK.

And, finally, it explored the reality behind some of the more extravagant claims which have formed a large part of the rhetoric with which society has been bombarded in recent years.

It is that exploration which the chapters which follow will seek to extend and deepen.

2

EARLY LEARNING AND A DEVELOPMENTALLY APPROPRIATE CURRICULUM: SOME LESSONS FROM RESEARCH

Geva Blenkin

Habits, in general, may be very early formed in children. An association of ideas is, as it were, the parent of habit. If, then, you can accustom your children to perceive that your will must always prevail over theirs, when they are opposed, the thing is done, and they will submit to it without difficulty or regret. To bring this about, as soon as they begin to show their inclination by desire or aversion, let single instances be chosen now and then (not too frequently) to contradict them. For example, if a child shews a desire to have any thing in his hand that he sees, or has any thing in his hand with which he is delighted, let the parent take it from him, and when he does so, let no consideration whatever make him restore it at that time.
(Witherspoon, quoted in Greven, 1973, p. 91, and also in Swann and Gamage, 1993, p. 36)

I think it is possible to claim that during the last century or more we have moved away from the repressive Victorian attitudes to early education and training which are expressed with such apparent enthusiasm in this extract from Witherspoon's advice to parents and teachers. Although echoes of this view can be detected in some of the arguments mounted, for example, by politicians as they attempt to justify current policies and their effect on young children learning in group settings (the 'against sparing the rod' brigade), or as they try to rally support at party conferences (with policies which should apply to everyone else's grandchildren but not to their own), most interested and thoughtful adults – parents and professionals alike – would find such brutalizing approaches to the rearing of their own or other people's children abhorrent.

Our present-day disinclination to attempt to break the will of our children in order to educate them in obedience is not attributable, as these same politicians would have us believe, to simple-minded, child-centred practitioners. Nor is it traceable to the insane advice of kindly but 'woolly-minded theorists' and 'post-Plowden progressives' who are said still to reside in and control the teaching profession, especially that part of it that functions in State nursery and primary schools (all imaginary characters, by the way, who appear in several myths to be exploded in Chapter 5). On the contrary! This disinclination on the part of parents and practitioners to apply simplistic methods of a mildly sadistic kind to the training of children is one of the results of their acting intelligently upon the findings and recommendations of the extensive research studies into early learning and early childhood education.

And this international research has not only been extensive in scale but also remarkable for the consistency of its recommendations and findings. It is also, on the one hand, leading us to develop a clearer picture worldwide of what a developmentally appropriate curriculum for young children would look like. And, on the other hand, it is identifying the demands that such a curriculum makes on early years professionals and, as a result, it is clarifying their training needs.

Further than this, it is being accepted on a remarkably extensive scale worldwide that the education of our youngest children is an important, demanding and complex undertaking. Indeed, it is being widely conceded that more investment into high-quality provision for young children, and into the upgrading of training and status for early years practitioners, will yield an important economic bonus in the long term (Beruetta-Clement *et al.*, 1984; Jowett and Sylva, 1986; Andersson, 1992).

One would be a dolt if one were to ignore such powerful evidence and the worldwide trends that it is leading to. To fly in the face of this evidence and these trends, and to advocate provision for early education of a kind which contradicts them on nearly every count, would appear to be the action and consequence of lunacy. Yet this is precisely what has been done by current policies, and especially the National Curriculum which has been implemented in infant schools in England and Wales to form the first stage of the four-stage curriculum required by the Education Reform Act 1988.

In Chapter 1 we explored the use of rhetoric as a power-coercive device employed to establish the National Curriculum. In this chapter we will begin by considering why power-coercion seemed to the architects of the National Curriculum the only mechanism by which they could hope to ensure its implementation. It is not surprising, in the light of the evidence to which we have just referred, that they rejected the possibility of persuading the teaching profession of its value or the chance of encouraging teachers to accept and implement it on its merits.

The only general reason for this can be that they realized that the National Curriculum, and the values it encapsulates, would be unacceptable to the profession, or at least to large sections of it, and that its merits would not be recognized or even identified, so that its implementation must be brought about by imposition rather than by persuasion. This suggests in turn that they were fully aware that the values implicit in the National Curriculum are fundamentally at odds with the values on which most teachers, especially those working in the early years, have hitherto based their practice and, indeed, with the values and the commitments that attracted them to take up their profession in the first place. In addition, it must have been apparent that there was very little in the field of empirical research that supported the National Curriculum, and that, especially in early childhood education, the empirical evidence about early learning was loaded against the acceptability of this particular form of curriculum. They must have been particularly aware, therefore, that it would be in the early years of schooling that the impact of the National Curriculum would be greatest and where the conflict with existing values and practices would be most significant.

This chapter will begin, therefore, by attempting to identify the main features of the approach to education which has been taken and favoured by almost all early years specialists as it has developed over more than half a century, and to introduce the research evidence that supports this acceptance. Questions may be asked about the effectiveness with which this approach has been translated into practice in some places, but there can be little doubt about the level of consensus among practitioners in this field over their educational values. It is those underlying values which this chapter will first seek to identify in order to compare and contrast them with the basic principles of the National Curriculum. It will then go on to consider some of the effects on the quality of educational provision in this sector of the attempt to implant a new and alien set of educational values in a soil quite unfitted and unprepared to receive and nurture them. In this way it is hoped to identify the many points of conflict and rejection which constitute the general causation of those problems which subsequent chapters will explore and develop.

THE TRADITIONAL VALUES OF EARLY CHILDHOOD EDUCATION

'It is nothing short of a miracle that the modern methods of instruction have not entirely strangled the holy curiosity of enquiry' (Einstein, from an autobiographical essay quoted in Bernstein, 1973, p. 69). Early educationists are traditionally committed to nurturing curiosity and not to killing it. It must be emphasized at the start of this section, therefore, that there is a long tradition in Western cultures of viewing the earliest stages of schooling differently and with more care and sensitivity from those that come later. This tradition can be traced back to the early period of our civilization. We are advised, for example, by Plato in his *Republic* to take particular care when educating 'the young and tender', since 'in all things the beginning is the most important part'. And this recognition of the sensitivity of children at the early stages in their learning is carried through the Judaio-Christian tradition. It is even defined for us, by the Jesuits, as the period from birth to 7, and it is claimed by them that it is during this crucial period that future attributes and abilities will be settled and future life chances effected.

One of the main reasons why this tradition has been so persistent is the recognition that young children, certainly to the age of 8, are not only dependent and vulnerable but are also highly impressionable and learn more rapidly during this early stage than at any other period of their lives. We need to pay especial attention, therefore, to how they are educated at this stage, and we need to be aware that they must be protected from approaches to schooling of a kind which are commonly adopted and accepted at later stages, if their capacity to learn and develop is to be nurtured in positive ways. For, as Einstein complains, in the essay from which our earlier quotation is taken, much that is offered in the name of education can actually delay mental development, and this can be particularly harmful during the earliest stages of learning.

Although this tradition of taking special care over the education of our youngest children is a long one, however, it is during the present century that attention has been paid to the clarification of the values that must underpin our attempts to educate the young. And it is also during this period, and particularly during the latter half of the century, that the essential features of a developmentally appropriate curriculum for young children have begun to emerge.

The characteristics of this approach, and the values that underpin it, have been documented elsewhere (DeVries, 1987; Spodek and Saracho, 1991;

Blenkin and Kelly, 1988; 1992). To set the context for this discussion, however, some of its salient features need to be highlighted briefly, since, however imperfect they may have been in implementing this form of curriculum, or indeed in giving expression to its underpinning values, most early years practitioners would be committed to several inter-related theoretical positions.

First, they would see education as development rather than as the mere acquisition of knowledge, and some would argue that in early childhood education this has always been a distinctive concern. For example, Spodek and Saracho (1991, p. x) note that 'making curriculum decisions for young children requires the educator to be more concerned with the individual's level of development'. They go on to claim that, although there are common elements to educational provision throughout the stages of schooling, 'the structure, process, and content of the programs that are developed in early childhood education are unique' (*ibid.*), and they have developed in a more sophisticated form because of the need to focus on developmental processes in the early stages of learning.

This leads to the concern to establish a developmentally appropriate curriculum which provides for and nurtures the child's development through a range of symbolizing activities. Here a useful distinction is made between an intellectually stimulating curriculum and an academic curriculum. And it is argued that, at this early stage, the curriculum must not be 'formalized' or structured in an 'academic' manner, since this is likely to alienate young learners by overestimating their academic ability while ignoring, or underestimating, their intellectual ability (Katz and Chard, 1989).

Education is defined, therefore, in terms of its processes rather than its content or its extrinsic 'aims and objectives'. And provision and experiences are planned in relation to, and in harmony with, the developmental level of the individual child.

Cognitive development is seen as dependent on, or interlinked with, psychomotor and affective development. This leads to a holistic approach to curriculum planning. In addition, the social context of learning is identified as the most crucial element in human learning. Informal and interactive styles of instruction are, therefore, advocated. Finally, the importance of play in learning and development is emphasized.

These principles, which inform what can be seen as a consensus of opinon on what is an appropriate approach to early education, can of course be seen as applying equally well to education at later stages. There are, however, four broad themes which recur in the discussions of appropriate forms of curriculum for early childhood education, and which are peculiar to that stage of education.

First, the young child is dependent on adults and is new to institutional life. The process of learning to be a pupil is thus of great importance.

Second, rates of development and learning are at their most rapid during this stage of education, and they are highly susceptible to environmental constraints or advantages. The young child, therefore, needs to be stimulated by a wide range of experiences rather than confined to a narrow and restrictive programme.

Third, although social interaction is important at every stage of learning, it is of particular importance at this early stage, since young learners are not able to make sense of experiences which are presented in a more formal or abstract way. This means that young children are particularly dependent on real experiences and on talking through these experiences with an interested adult. Their capacity to learn from the more formal demands of schooling depends on their being helped to make mental bridges or links between their common-sense world and this more abstract world (Hughes, 1986). Because of this need, sharing experiences and helping children to make sense of these experiences is the key role of the early educator.

Fourth, early education must not only provide a rich array of practical experiences but it must also nurture the playfulness of children. For secure mastery of skills or knowledge depends on play, because it is through play that the child is able to test out, informally and personally, what is newly learnt.

It is these aspects of early learning that have provided a focus for empirical research into early childhood education. And this research, in turn, has yielded supporting evidence for the provision of a developmentally appropriate curriculum.

EVIDENCE TO SUPPORT A DEVELOPMENTAL APPROACH TO EDUCATION

> We shall not cease from exploration
> And the end of all our exploring
> Will be to arrive where we started
> And know the place for the first time.
> (T. S. Eliot, *Little Gidding*, v, ll. 26–9)

It has taken a long time, much exploration and experience, research and careful thought to enable us to begin to understand what might be a developmentally appropriate curriculum for young children. And it is this recognition of the complexity of the task of educating the young human child that has led to modesty and diffidence on the part of reflective practitioners, and has rendered them particularly vulnerable to those with simplistic remedies.

For obvious reasons, young children are not good candidates for the examination halls. Traditional tests of performance also yield results that are less and less reliable the younger the performer is. It is notoriously difficult to employ standardized tests to deduce very young children's ability and potential ability, as rates of development vary so much in the early years, and the child's levels of concentration and interest fluctuate considerably (Powell and Sigel, 1991). Before the introduction of the National Curriculum, there were ethical reasons too that made it difficult to collect data that would show the differential impact of different approaches to early education. For it would have been unthinkable to provide children with less than the best that we could manage.

With improvements in technology, which have enhanced the reliability of observational studies of performance, however, and with the more open attitudes of teachers and other practitioners to classroom-based research, a considerable amount of evidence is being built up to support a developmental view of education in the early years. This body of research is enhancing our understanding of how children learn and, therefore, enabling us to appreciate also how they can best be taught.

A brief glimpse of some of this research, and of some of the children who feature in it, will illustrate this point. It will also show that the principles outlined above, which form the traditional theoretical position of most early childhood educators, are not simply ideological, as it is often claimed (O'Hear, 1991). For they are, as was argued in the introduction to this chapter, firmly grounded in research evidence of an overwhelmingly convincing kind.

The first set of evidence supports the view that adults must mediate between young children's experience of the common-sense, everyday world of their homes and communities and the more formal and abstract world of school learning. Supporting this sense-making process, as was noted above, has been shown to be essential if the child is to become a successful learner in school (Donaldson, Grieve and Pratt, 1983). And if the adult is paying attention to lesson content or assessment of performance rather than to the sense that the child is making of procedures, then genuine learning is put at risk (Donaldson, 1978).

It is the process of becoming a pupil that features strongly in research studies of adult and child interactions in classrooms, and these studies show, alarmingly, that many children can become disaffected and alienated from school at a very early age (Barrett, 1986; 1989). This is particularly likely to happen if the teacher is not sensitive to the effects of the socialization process on the individual child, because he or she is not participating in the child's sense-making activities. If learning to become a pupil is left to chance, the evidence shows that children will become passive and bored, or will be confused by their new role and seem, from the teacher's viewpoint, to be disruptive and rude.

Willes (1983), for example, shows that most children on starting school learn very quickly to conform to a stilted classroom discourse which is entirely under the teacher's control, and that, once established, this style of talk is resistant to change. She also observes, however, that the culture, routines and expectations of school are not always self-evident to all budding pupils. Her tapes show that Neil, for example, is being checked constantly by his reception class teacher for not conforming to the implicit and unexplained rules of 'classroom conversations'. And yet it is clear, from his contributions, that he is confused rather than disobedient, because the exchanges show that he is trying to converse with his teacher in the real sense of that term, while his teacher is instructing and assessing rather than instigating a genuine dialogue. Neil, at 5, has not yet understood these uncritically accepted rules of schooling (*op. cit.*, pp. 78–9).

Being a good pupil, however, should mean learning effectively in a group setting. And this social and interpersonal context for learning is especially important for the very young child who, both at home and at school, learns best in conversations with friends and, in particular, with friendly adults. But the conversations must be genuine. When teachers realize this, and challenge the stilted roles of the pupil and the teacher, children can reveal, in the classroom as well as in the more intimate and secure home environment, their abilities as powerful thinkers, as the following extract from a teacher's records of her 4-year-old pupils in discussion shows:

Frederick, upon rehearsing the tale of Jack and the Beanstalk, immediately makes an important connection for himself and the small group at the snack table. My role is somewhat akin to the ancient Greek chorus.
Frederick: Does the giant's wife like Jack?
Teacher: She seems to. I wonder what Jack would say if she asked him to stay.
Christopher: He said no. He said, 'I gots a mother already'.
Teacher: But maybe the wife is lonely. What will she do?
Petey: Buy a friendly fox.
Jonathan: No, let her get a dog or a cat.
Mollie: They can live with Jack and his mother.
Petey: And the cow.

Barney: They sold the cow and the mother would say no.
Frederick: She doesn't like bad guys.
Teacher: Unless there is a way to change the giant to a good giant. I wonder if there is.
Emily: A fairy godmother.
Teacher: Like Cinderella's?
Petey: She couldn't get in the door. Of that Jack and the Beanstalk place.

(Paley, 1988, p. ix)

But research evidence shows, as was noted above, that many practitioners who work with young children do not realize the power of the culture's stereotypes of 'teacher' and 'pupil', and do not work against these stereotypes for the benefit of a better learning role for the pupil in the manner that Katz (1977) suggests is essential. Many children, therefore, behave more like the 'good pupil' that is found in comics and playground games. They become, in short, obedient and passive, and always play safe.

It is only when teachers learn to decentre, and understand problems and experiences from the young child's point of view, that they are able to develop effective dialogues in group settings. And, as the studies above show, this is put at risk if the teacher is under pressure to cover lesson content or is preoccupied for most of the time with assessing children's behaviour and performance. If such risk is to be avoided, the teacher needs to be highly sensitive to, and possess an expert understanding of, how children develop. Indeed, it is now accepted internationally, although not in official policies for England and Wales, that child development should be the core content and the basis of sound professional practice with young children. For, as two American experts recently argued, 'Knowing how children grow, develop and learn is viewed as more critical than any particular content area . . . In essence the early childhood teacher is expected to be an expert in and an applied practitioner of child development' (Peters and Klinzing, 1990, p. 67).

Teachers who have a thorough understanding of child development, and who have learnt to translate research findings about human development into effective practice, are equipped to observe children and be guided by these observations. And, if they are secure and confident with their group, young children will be direct and honest in their appraisals of classroom experiences. Indeed, this spontaneity and honesty, although unnerving on occasions, can be the greatest attraction and source of delight for teachers working with young children. In this age of accountability, we receive our most honest accounts, and are, therefore, appraised most fairly, by our youngest pupils. That is if we permit them a voice and listen to what they say.

My favourite young appraiser of the quality of schooling in the research literature is a 5-year-old traveller child called Sonnyboy, who constantly questions the rituals and routines of the West Country reception class that is being studied. Cousins, the researcher, records that

> Over the weeks, often quite accidentally, I was able to pick up some of his pearls of wisdom. He was scathing about the absence of real money in the classroom shop; couldn't fathom out what was meant by playtime; questioned why school scissors were always blunt and didn't see why you couldn't eat snacks when you felt hungry. He put on extra clothes for PE because it was cold in the hall and decided assembly was the time to dream . . . School time caused him a lot of trouble and the only thing which made Sonnyboy very angry was when his favourite games were interrupted by either bell or clock. One playtime I could hear him grumbling, 'That don't make no sense . . . I just got to the interestin' bit . . . I don't care about the time . . . that's plain stupid . . . time's as long as it takes'.
>
> (Cousins, 1990, pp. 30–1)

Sonnyboy clearly is an exceptional child. At 5 he was able to look after other children, especially those from his own travellers' community. He was acutely sensitive to the responses of others and tried, if he could, to sort out the confusions of his friends by mediating in an expert way between their experiences at home and at school, to the great benefit of those who were less confident and more confused by school life. But Sonnyboy is also a child who is most at risk if the narrow socializing aspects of schooling are emphasized rather than the educational and developmental aspects. For it is clear that he cannot remain passive and silent in the face of things that do not make sense to him at all.

The observations of Sonnyboy also remind us of the fact that playfulness and informal activities absorb children and are essential to the secure development of their understanding. To ignore this in early education, and to demean play as trivial, can undermine the quality of children's learning and, indeed, can be quite stressful to the child. For, as Guha argues,

> To give time for play in school is not to give a 'break' or rest from learning; it is not a concession to immature minds. Rather it is a way of making teaching and learning more productive . . . We do not know what the knowledge is, and the skills are, that the children of today will most need in the future. Flexibility, confidence and the ability to think for oneself – these are the attributes one hopes will not let them down. If play is conducive to the development of these, we had better have it in the school.
>
> (Guha, 1988, pp. 78–9)

Most adults think that schooling is a serious business, because they recognize that it affects greatly children's life chances. Parents and teachers, therefore, have tended during the past few years to push play to the fringes of school life – even for many of our 4-year-olds who are now to be found in reception classes designed for children of compulsory school age.

In Elkind's view, this undervaluing of play can be seen across a range of capitalist societies. He argues that

> It is not play itself that is being opposed, but rather play in infancy and early childhood. In contemporary society, play is often seen as something you can do and enjoy only as an adult, not a child . . . In Japan, where many children are pressured academically even during the early years, the college student takes four years off to play.
>
> (Elkind, 1990, p. 16)

He explains this curious phenomenon by arguing that, on the one hand, 'earlier is better' for academic study has become an entrenched position in capitalist cultures, particularly those of the USA and Japan while, on the other hand, ability is defined in these societies 'as a matter of the individual rather than as that of a group of individuals' (*op. cit.*, p. 7). And much of the play that goes on in the early years depends on group interaction and co-operation, and is often viewed as relaxation. It is small wonder, therefore, that 3-year-old Jack, when I visited him recently, greeted me with a rather earnest 'Are you interested in toys?'!

And yet, as Fromberg (1990) points out, there is a proliferation of studies which show that play contributes to the development of language, social competence, cognitive skills and imagination. She goes on to say, however, that 'at the same time that the research literature on the value of play appears to be expanding geometrically, the presence of play in early childhood classrooms has been dwindling impetuously' (*op. cit.*, p. 237). The evidence is mounting to show that playfulness is crucial to early learning, and yet it is being ignored by parents and policy-makers alike.

The same is true of what that research, to which we referred earlier in this chapter, has told us about the long-term advantages of high-quality early education. And it is worth spelling this out in slightly more detail here. These longitudinal studies were largely undertaken through the High/Scope project in the USA, but some were conducted in Europe, most notably in Sweden and in the UK. These studies have shown that high-quality, well resourced and cognitively orientated provision for education in the early years has far-reaching effects. In reporting on this research, Sylva (1992a, p. 687) shows that

> In addition to demonstrating that pre-school attendance [up to 6 years of age in the USA and 7 years of age in Sweden] led to lasting and better functioning in the domains of school, employment and community adjustment, Beruetta-

Clement also established the costs and benefits of early education . . . It became clear in the US that high quality early education literally 'pays off'.

With such powerful evidence at hand, it is not surprising that Weikart, the Director of the High/Scope Research Study, argues that his country cannot afford not to invest in high-quality early childhood education (Beruetta-Clement *et al.*, 1984).

Sylva also shows in her own study, conducted with Jowett in British preschool settings (Jowett and Sylva, 1986), how well resourced early education, provided by qualified teachers who are mindful of what a developmentally appropriate curriculum is, gave working-class children an advantage when they started compulsory schooling over those children who had attended low-cost provision, and had thus experienced a narrow and ill-thought out curriculum. In Sylva's words, 'Children in this study demonstrated their greater readiness for school by independence in learning, resourcefulness in the face of task difficulty, and use of teachers as learning resources' (1992a, p. 687).

Again, however, we must note the unwillingness of those responsible for current policies, in relation both to the school curriculum and to the preparation of teachers to work with children in the early years, to acknowledge the strength and the significance of this research evidence. We must note further how odd this is when that evidence points up the cost benefits to society of high-quality early education, as well as the advantages it offers to individual children and the extent to which it points us in the direction of a curriculum which can offer genuine entitlement to all pupils.

It is to a consideration of this disturbing tendency to ignore, and even denigrate, what research tells us about effective learning and how we can nurture such learning in schools that we turn next. For it is clear that the recommendations made for the National Curriculum contradict at almost every turn what has been shown to be thoroughly researched, well informed and widely supported professional practice in the early years of education.

THE UNDERPINNING VALUES OF THE NATIONAL CURRICULUM

Both art and play, like imagination and fantasy, are not regarded as a part of the serious business of schooling. To be serious requires clear goals, a well thought out plan for achieving them and, perhaps most of all, hard work . . . In a society with Calvinist roots and a prevailing anxiety about school productivity, the idea that either play or art should be considered a part of the core of education is not particularly likely.

(Eisner, 1990, p. 43)

This grimly instrumental and worryingly simplistic picture of what schooling should be about is the view that is prevalent among lay people in the USA. It also has much in common with the view that is dominant in the UK at present.

Eisner goes on to argue that this view is based on deeply held cultural ideas (prejudices?) – that individuals learn through competing alone rather than by co-operating in a social group, for example, and that proper learning is a solemn business and the sooner that children get down to it the better. Indeed, it is based on all the assumptions and punitive attitudes to children which were discussed earlier in this chapter. He notes, however, that such views are not supported by the evidence about worthwhile teaching and learning. And, because those who promote such views ignore the research evidence, they marginalize some vital experiences and activities which should be central to what children are offered in school.

Even worse than the narrow instrumentalism that occurs when such simplistic ideas are espoused is the assumption that, if learning doesn't hurt, it is not worth doing. And, if anyone challenges this punitive approach, as Whitehead (1993) does when she asks 'Why not happiness?', he or she is ridiculed as being too permissive with children or is accused of having frivolous intent.

Worst of all, however, is to find this folk-view of schooling accepted and implemented by government, and to discover that it is possible for a government to step in and assert, with breathtaking confidence and certainty, but with no basis more reliable than this folk consciousness, that they will put everything to rights because they know both which skills and knowledge it is best for children to learn and also how to test this with accuracy. And yet this is precisely what has happened with the introduction of the National Curriculum into early childhood education in the UK.

There is a sense in which, therefore, it is fruitless to look for the underlying values of the National Curriculum or for reasoned explanation or justification of the form it has taken. For it has been established without recourse to informed argument or research findings. Like most educational 'reforms' that have been implemented on this kind of scale, the current policies in England and Wales reflect what Friesen (1987) refers to as the standard preoccupations with money, accountability and child performance, but they do not adhere to any coherent or defensible educational philosophy. This is why, as we saw in Chapter 1, the National Curriculum has been implemented by power-coercive rather than by either empirical-rational or normative-re-educative strategies. Laws have been made and every kind of rhetorical device employed but no attempt has been made to offer an argued rationale.

If we wish to discover the underlying values of the National Curriculum, therefore, we must pick them out for ourselves from the actual policies and the legislation. For we will nowhere find a clear statement of them. We must look beyond the rhetoric.

When we do so, perhaps the first thing which stands out is the evidence that these policies fail to evince any kind of concern for children. The central concern is with the subjects and the subject content children are to assimilate, the targets they are to attain, the levels of knowledge they are to reach, rather than with the contribution such learning or attainment is likely to make to their own learning and development as human beings. Indeed, the impression one gets is that these policies have been framed by people who not only do not understand young children but who also actually seem to dislike them. Certainly, there is no sense of caring for them at any level beyond that of regarding them as potential adults and employees. Indeed, one finds oneself wondering whether these people were ever children themselves.

The first underpinning value that can be identified, therefore, by even the most superficial perusal of these policies, is that they do not place the child first. And this is the central reason for that head-on clash with the traditions of early childhood education that we have referred to on a number of occasions.

From that first principle of the National Curriculum, several other values immediately follow. First, it is essentially instrumental, concerned more with what children are to become than with what they are here and now, focused on product rather than on process. Hence it is obsessed with planning by 'aims and objectives', to the exclusion of any allowance for spontaneity, for what we have long known as 'unintended learning outcomes'.

Second, it is not even towards the child's long-term interests that this product orientation is primarily addressed. The concern is with what are seen as the needs of society, the material demands of the economy (insofar as anyone with the present government's record for economic mismanagement is likely to be able to foresee these) and the political concern not just for law and order but, further, for conformity.

Third, when it is not these political or economic demands which are to the fore, when some attempt seems to be being made to engage in planning which might be claimed to be educational, it is still not the needs of the child which prevail but those of the subjects selected for inclusion, either as core or foundation subjects, in the National Curriculum. Thus the much vaunted 'progression' and 'continuity', which we are told the National Curriculum will bring, are defined in terms of the assumed structures of the subjects rather than what is known about the ways in which children structure their learning.

And, fourth, as we suggested at the beginning of this section, education, having been conceptualized as product orientated, is seen as a competitive rather than as a collaborative enterprise. Educational attainment is regarded as a solitary pursuit; the 'arms round work' syndrome returns; and children are encouraged not to improve their own performance but to better that of their peers, so that summative rather than ipsative forms of assessment are favoured, and pencil-and-paper tests are preferred to more sophisticated forms of assessment to enable easier comparisons between, and ranking of, children, even at ages 6–7.

There is much more one could say in developing the story of these underpinning values. Perhaps, however, enough has already been said to demonstrate their central thrust.

One last point must be made, however, before we compare this value system with that we considered earlier in this chapter, the value stance of those who embrace and advocate a developmentally appropriate curriculum for the early years of schooling. For, whereas we have been able to point to the extensive research evidence upon which their case is based, not even the strongest advocates of the National Curriculum can produce similar evidence in support of theirs. It may be argued that all value stances are ideological. It must be accepted, however, that some are more ideological than others, and that the term 'ideology', especially if it is being used as a term of abuse, as we have seen it is by at least one uninformed critic of the developmental approach to education in the early years (O'Hear, 1991), is far more appropriately used of theories for which there is little intellectual justification beyond economic and political interest, or even blind prejudice.

ESTABLISHING A DEVELOPMENTALLY APPROPRIATE CURRICULUM: THE CLASH OF VALUES

The changes in children's lives have been phenomenal. Did you know that 95 per cent of the scientists who ever lived are alive today, and current estimates of the pace of change suggest that only 2 per cent of the knowledge a child will need by the age of 40 is available today?

(Irvine, 1990, quoted in NBEET, 1992, p. 41)

The issue of how to establish a curriculum for young children that will support the development of the knowledge, skills and values that will enable them to function as effective – and productive – citizens in the next century, when our current understanding is developing and changing at the speed described above, is an international preoccupation. And the solution adopted by most policy-makers, including those in the Australian government, from whose advisory document the above quotation is taken, is to attempt to establish a developmentally appropriate curriculum.

A preoccupation with how to describe and implement this curriculum can be identified in documents from New Zealand (ECCE Working Group, 1988) and from Canada (Ministry of Education, 1990), in policies for most European Community countries (Pascal and Bertram, 1993), in the advisory papers in the USA (Elkind, 1989) and in the commitment of the US federal government over more than two decades to research into high-quality early years programmes (Hohmann, Banet and Weikart, 1979). And the irony is that it is evident that these countries are, on the one hand, moving towards a model of early education that is close to the developmental model, described above and well established as the traditional approach to early education in the UK, and, on the other hand, are up-grading the training and status of early years practitioners to graduate level, a level long established in the UK. As we have seen, however, policies in the UK are moving in exactly the opposite direction and, as the National Curriculum is being implemented, evidence is beginning to emerge which reveals that teachers are being pressed into methods which are more formal and didactic, subject teaching is on the increase and there is a growing tendency towards whole-class teaching rather than individual or group provision, even in the early years. In reporting on the influence that the National Curriculum is having at Key Stage 1, the Primary Policy Task Group warn about the damaging effects that such shifts could have and suggest that they will 'hinder children developing skills which were gained in group activities, such as problem-solving, decision-making, predicting, hypothesising and summarising' (quoted in O'Connor 1993a, p. 6). They go on to report high levels of stress among teachers in early childhood education, a finding that is even acknowledged as a problem by the government, through its chairman of the School Curriculum and Assessment Authority (NCC/SEAC, 1993).

The government's answer to teacher stress is, of course, to attribute it to overload and to call, therefore, for an even more simplified, 'back to the basics' kind of curriculum at Key Stage 1. And this is approved of by government supporters, and even offered by one as evidence that the

Secretary of State has outmanoeuvred his opponents and opened the way for a basic curriculum to be introduced, which is 'what the Government and a great many parents wanted in the first place' (Shakespeare, 1993, p. 14).

This stress is partly attributable to overload. For many early years teachers, unlike their colleagues at Key Stage 3, have tried to meet the requirements of the law, while attempting at the same time to protect the young children in their care from being too overtly aware of the more negative effects of summative assessment and also seeking to continue to offer the children a developmentally appropriate curriculum. It can be seen, too, however, as the direct result, of their trying in their practice to find a compromise solution to the clash of educational values when such a compromise is not possible.

For the National Curriculum is not just a different curriculum from the traditional early years curriculum; it is its mirror image, its exact opposite in every respect. Hence the two are quite incompatible. And this presents early years teachers with very serious problems and difficulties. For many are attempting to maintain the educational values and practices that they are professionally committed to, and are being encouraged to do so as they see a groundswell of support worldwide hailing these values and practices as the foundations of a developmentally appropriate curriculum for young children, in the context of the imposition from without of a curriculum which is alien to those values and which, as the research shows, is also alienating to a majority of their pupils. It is difficult, if not impossible, therefore, for them to maintain their own professional standards in the face of a legal obligation to do otherwise.

These professional tensions and the loss of quality in early education which is resulting from current policies will be recurring themes in subsequent chapters. In the context of this chapter, however, it is worth noting in general the effects of those policies, and in particular the National Curriculum, on what worldwide research is showing to be developmentally appropriate provision and practice in early education.

THE IMPACT OF THE NATIONAL CURRICULUM ON A DEVELOPMENTALLY APPROPRIATE CURRICULUM

Despite the fact that primary schools are responding to curricular and other 'reforms' on an unprecedented scale, the culture of primary teaching has not changed overnight . . . the National Curriculum had begun to force a reap-

praisal of such important matters as the place of subjects within the primary
curriculum . . . aspects of the National Curriculum programmes of study are
receiving differentiated treatment even at Key Stage 1 . . . the discussion
paper is also encouraging a dispassionate examination of that most sacred of
primary 'sacred cows' – the class teacher system.

(Ofsted, 1993b, p. 18)

The speed with which the National Curriculum has been required to be
implemented in the early years, and the manner in which that implementation has been brought about and monitored, are both causes of teacher
stress. The follow-up report, from which the above quotations are taken,
was published in January 1993, a mere twelve months after the original so-called 'Three Wise Men' Report (DES, 1992) had been issued, and had
concluded that 'at school level, teachers will have to abandon the dogma of
decades' (*op. cit.*, p. 54). And both the original and the follow-up reports
ignore any of the powerful challenges to their views, which show that what
they choose to dismiss as 'dogma' may be the articulation of a highly
sophisticated form of curriculum. The speed of the follow-up, which could
be seen more as checking-up, and the tone of both reports verge on harass-ment. Furthermore, both reject any notion of debate, and both ignore all of
the views, referred to above, which seek to incorporate the research evi-dence in support of a developmentally appropriate curriculum.

It must, therefore, be asserted again and again that the 'findings' of both
these official reports are open to significant criticism and challenge. For
example, a complementary report to that of the 'Three Wise Men', and
known as the 'Three Wise Women Report' (David, Curtis and Siraj-Blatchford, 1992), challenged the assertions and recommendations on nearly
every count and argued that 'poor quality of teaching . . . seems unlikely to
be associated with any particular educational "doctrine" or "dogma" . . .
and may be as relevant to didactically taught, subject-based classes' (*op. cit.*,
p. 7). The writers go on to cite research evidence that shows that 'progres-sive' teaching methods are a great rarity (DES, 1978a; Desforges and Cock-burn, 1987; Tizard *et al.*, 1988; Bennett and Kell, 1989), and they assert, very
reasonably, therefore, that these informal methods 'can hardly be blamed for
alleged low standards within the system as a whole' (David, Curtis and Siraj-Blatchford, 1992, p. 7). All such reasoned challenge and the research evi-dence that is cited to support these counterarguments are ignored which, in
itself, is also a form of harassment as it indicates that those in power can
ignore reasoned debate and assert their own will.

They thus reflect that attempt to impose the new curriculum by the
power-coercive use of rhetoric and to control the discourse of the

educational 'debate' which we explored in Chapter 1. And they reinforce the points made there, by demonstrating only too clearly why empirical/ rational and normative/re-educative strategies were not an option. To persuade teachers to accept policies which run counter both to the research evidence and, as a consequence, to their own professional judgement was clearly not possible; imposition by more subtle means was the only route. The only conclusion one can reach from this is that teachers are now to be made to do what the politicians demand and not what their own professional judgement dictates. And it is this that is at the root of the tension teachers are feeling – an attempt to deprive them of their professionalism and to force them away from the paths that their professional judgements would lead them into.

Education, however it is conceived, involves making judgements. To deprive teachers of that capability or, worse, to seek to make their judgements for them, and without providing them with a reasoned rationale for decisions made, is a certain recipe for a loss in the quality of educational provision. For it leads not only to teacher stress; it leads also to teacher alienation. It involves a reduction in the levels of skill and competence required of teachers; and this is reinforced and reflected in the currently proposed reductions in the extent, and thus the quality, of their training. To inform teachers, whether explicitly through official documents or implicitly through imposed policies, that they do not need to know as much to teach young children as they would if they wished to teach at a later stage of education; to imply that all they really need is increased knowledge of the subjects they are now required to teach; to suggest that, unlike teachers of young children in almost every other country, they do not need any understanding of child development; all of this is to deintellectualize and to deprofessionalize them, and it cannot fail to reduce the quality of their provision. It reflects a reduction in what society requires of teachers, and must be matched, especially when the profession is staffed largely by those teachers who are the products of the new, reduced forms of training, by a reduction in the ambitions teachers will have for their own professional performance and for the attainment of their pupils (except in that limited and limiting sense of attainment which is endemic to National Curriculum assessment).

SUMMARY AND CONCLUSIONS

Later chapters will offer evidence of this depressing process of deterioration. They will also pick up and elaborate on the points made earlier about the alienation of pupils and the reduction in their ambitions for themselves and their expectations of their schools and teachers. What this chapter has sought to do is to stress the extent to which current policies fly in the face of research and represent an attempt to oust a form of curriculum which is so soundly based that, while it is being destroyed in England and Wales, it is being embraced and promoted in almost every other country. The chapter has thus added to what was said in Chapter 1, and reinforced the arguments for asserting that, whatever the rhetoric of standards and quality, it is only on a very limited definition of these concepts that anything other than deterioration can be identified.

3
THE IMPLICATIONS OF THE NATIONAL CURRICULUM FOR NURSERY EDUCATION

Victoria Hurst

There is much uncertainty about what is involved in the education of Britain's under-5s. Nursery education must be defined before we can begin to discuss how the issues raised by the coming of the National Curriculum affect it.

Educational terms are prone to change their meaning, services evolve over time, and sometimes there is a blurring of boundaries of meaning for a particular purpose. It is interesting to note, for instance, that statistics on nursery education now incorporate those for under-5s into other forms of provision. As a result, it is now hard to detect what levels of nursery education provision are currently made (see, for instance, the 1992 Statistical Bulletin – HMSO, 1993). And so, in 1992, John Major was able to claim that Britain had one of the best (instead of one of the worst) records on educational provision for under-5s in Europe, as a result of adding in the figures for children in other forms of provision as well. It will be as well, therefore, to make some points about nursery education which will enable readers to identify it. Nursery education is

- publicly financed and provided in nursery schools, in nursery classes attached to infant and primary schools, and in combined nursery centres where education and social services finance and staff the centres jointly;
- staffed by trained nursery teachers and nursery nurses;
- subject to DFE regulations about space indoors and outdoors and about staffing and equipment;
- supported by the local education authority advisory service;
- free of the requirements of the National Curriculum but linked into the primary education system; and

- independent in its processes of curriculum planning, assessment and evaluation of the effectiveness of its provision.

There are places for approximately 26 per cent of British under-5s in nursery education. About 75 per cent of these places are part time, reducing the number of children who can make use of them. Many children cannot have a place at all because there is no provision in their area.

PRINCIPLES OF NURSERY EDUCATION

Practitioners of nursery education often refer to the principles of their approach although their practice may vary. Hartley (1993, p. 2, original emphasis) identifies the underlying intention of such practitioners:

> What is interesting about some nursery schools is that they are institutions which purport not to be institutions; that is, they try to allow the children to *be themselves*, free of institutional constraints. To take this view is to share the romantic view of the child held by Rousseau. Other nursery schools may take a different view, perhaps regarding the purpose of nursery education as a more formal preparation for primary school, equipping the child with the rudiments of language, number and appropriate behaviour. Thus nursery education means different things to different people. My impression, after having talked to nursery educators, is that their views incorporate the moral philosophy of Rousseau and the developmental psychology of Piaget, especially the latter.

Hartley's definition makes it clear that, although practice may vary, it is the developmental rather than the preparatory philosophy that characterizes for him the essential nature of nursery education. But it is necessary to say more about what this means in practice, in terms of the curriculum, the provision and management of the learning environment, the monitoring and assessment of children and the kind of evaluation that is chosen.

Children should be enabled to be themselves

Is this romantic nonsense? Many people think so, and justify their belief by reference to themselves as children along the following lines. 'Children are lazy little beggars, they never work unless you force them to. I was just like that myself.' 'If they're allowed to run wild they'll never get a sense of discipline – it's hard enough at later stages. We gave our teachers a terrible time, they were always sending notes home.' This constitutes a statement about human nature, a pedagogic theory of original sin.

To this, a pedagogy founded on research in children's development and learning responds by referring to the body of research which shows children constantly striving to make meaning out of their world (Wells, 1987; Trevarthen, 1992), striving in play and in pictorial representation to discern patterns, roles and relationships that they will use in growing up (Bruce 1991), exploring the world and hypothesizing about it through activity and conversation (Wood, 1988) and encountering literacy, mathematics and scientific thinking through their self-motivated talk, play and exploration (Blenkin and Kelly, 1988; Whitehead 1990). These statements form the principles of nursery education, and are shared by early years practitioners throughout the years before eight (Bruce, 1987; Early Years Curriculum Group, 1989).

Being realistic about children

Nursery teachers and nursery nurses do indeed have to be wise in the ways of human nature, and to be realistic about the children with whom they work. All children are expert at handling adults and other children in order to accomplish their own ends (Dunn, 1988), and most children need guidance on how to get on with other people (Harris, 1989). But a part of this realism is in seeing how much more effective education can be if it works with the grain of the child's motivation to learn than against it, and in using personal sensitivity to get to know the child so that this can be achieved. From this fundamental purpose all the nursery education processes take their quality – they are all designed to get to know the child, so that the child's education may be the most appropriate possible.

The curriculum in nursery education is the under-5s' version of the developmentally appropriate curriculum as outlined in Chapter 2, and in Blenkin and Kelly (1988), and assessment follows the ipsative model, in order to record how the individual child is developing. Evaluation is the process by which practitioners make judgements about the effectiveness of their provision for learning and plan how to develop their work in the future. Evaluation in nursery education is based on these ipsative assessments of the children concerned. The progress of the children provides the evidence, and the principles of nursery education, as summarized above, provide the criteria for judgement, as we shall see in detail later.

How does the pedagogy of nursery education fare when it confronts the National Curriculum? The three processes of curriculum planning, assessment and evaluation have been identified; they will be explored. First, however, we need to look at the process that underpins everything in nursery education – observation of individual children.

OBSERVATION: THE ESSENTIAL TOOL OF NURSERY EDUCATION

Important as is the understanding of how young children develop and learn which practitioners get from their studies of child development, their understanding has to be applied to individual children through the process of observation if it is to be of any benefit at all. Observation is a complex and sophisticated pedagogic process through which practitioners learn about individual children. It is the way in which teachers and nursery nurses gather evidence for use in curriculum planning. This is the challenging professional task of reconciling the established understanding and skills of children with an appropriate 'next step' in the learning we wish them to acquire. It is the source of evidence for monitoring and assessment of individual children, and the way in which practitioners evaluate their own provision, defining effectiveness in terms of the degree to which the educational opportunities provided meet the children's learning needs. Lastly, it is also the stimulus to professional development in the way that it often challenges practitioners to rethink their attitudes and established ideas about their work.

At classroom level there is a great need for the monitoring of education. Parents seek to know how their children's education is going so that problems can be identified in time; and practitioners seek to know how each child is getting on and whether different approaches or strategies should be tried. Increasingly, practitioners are required to justify their practice in the face of pressure from those who would prefer formal education to the developmental nursery curriculum. What could be more reliable for this justification than the learner's progress as recorded stage by stage?

Observation provides the only true test of the quality of the practitioner's work and offers the most reliable information about each child's progress. Using it turns the practitioner into a learner and often brings about a transformation of perspective, since the open-minded stance necessary makes practitioners question previously held assumptions and rethink their practice. The development of a greater degree of autonomy in practitioners is not, however, always seen as a good thing, as we shall see later, since – in the early years of education at least – it tends towards criticism of established views about what should be happening in classrooms.

It is relevant here also to focus on some of the new processes that this cycle of assessment, planning and evaluation through observation identifies. The issues are to do with what I have called 'analysis' and 'reflection'.

These were identified as important stages during the research in evaluation, which is discussed below.

A difficulty that practitioners and students often report is in knowing how to use observations, and sometimes this results in people saying 'I didn't find anything in my observation' or 'I can't see how to get any ideas from what I've noted' or even 'She didn't do anything while I was watching'.

Analysis is the process of thinking about the data from observation and what information it has brought. It is subtly different from checking an observation to see how well a child is doing in a particular area or at some particular task – the adult has to have an open mind, and to be willing to learn something new – frequently something completely unknown previously – from each observation. Reflection is the process of thinking about what has been learnt and accommodating oneself to this new information. Reflection is the stage at which changes in practice are likely to take place, as the practitioner develops greater understanding of how education may best be negotiated with individuals and groups. A brief example of these two processes now follows:

15.5.91: in playground. Two staff present. Watching J (girl, 3.6) and K (girl, 3.4) as they take out empty buggy, carrying handbags and wearing hats.

1.52   Standing watching other children, no talk.

1.55   Still standing watching in silence.

1.57:   J pushes buggy tentatively forward, then back again. K holds on. Both looking at busy children.

2.00:   Still standing in silence (observer called away briefly).

2.05:   Seen over by fence, still watching in silence.

2.07:   In home corner, silent, putting hats back, investigating tea-things.

(Observation ends here.)

Addendum
Next day: J's mother says she told her she went into the playground on the way to school this morning – likes the home corner better.

Analysis of this observation would involve asking questions which did not start from the assumption which might immediately spring to mind on reading the observation, but from a more objective viewpoint. The following framework to guide analysis is from Lally and Hurst (1992, p. 90):

Questions to provide a framework for analysing observations of the learning experiences of individual children.
1.   From what you know (or have been told) about this child, what would you say is the significance of this observation? (e.g. does it indicate pro-

gress, regression, the development of a new interest or skill, a change in attitude etc?)

2. What does the observation tell you about this child's interests, experience, skills, attitudes and knowledge? What information would you want to add to his/her record?

3. What additional information would you like to collect to gain a clearer picture of the child? (i.e. what questions about this child has the observation generated?)

4. How could you use the information you have gained from analysing this observation to plan to support and extend this child's learning? (this should include a consideration of the provision of equipment and experiences as well as possible adult involvement).

Reflection is the process of pondering on the answers to these questions and their implications for the learning environment and the adults. Here practitioners use all their personal sensitivity and personal experience as well as their knowledge of the children and of child development to draw from the observation and the analysis of it what they need to develop and improve their provision of opportunities for learning.

Readers will have a range of thoughts and speculations about the observation given above. Care for the children as persons will necessitate thinking about both their emotional and social states as well as how their interest in imaginative domestic play can be supported and extended. This will mean self-criticism about the structure, management and staff roles in the nursery as well as an examination of the plans and provision available. The list of questions will go on, because reflection works at many levels, and because each practitioner brings something unique to the development of the learning environment. This is where both the individuality and the quality of nursery education come from.

THE PRESSURES OF THE NATIONAL CURRICULUM

A professional development course on assessment on starting school undertaken with nursery and reception teachers in Buckinghamshire (Lally and Hurst, in preparation), has identified some of the problems teachers encounter in trying to reconcile a developmental approach with the National Curriculum's concept of early years education as basic instruction. The following dilemmas were identified by participants on the course:

Many reception teachers felt under pressure to assess immediately (i.e. as soon as the child is admitted) to provide a 'baseline' to refer back to when the children participate in SATs at 7 years of age. The idea that you can get a clear picture of 'where a child is' from a series of 'tests' during the first week or so in the reception class conflicts with an early years perspective (based on research evidence) which highlights the stressful nature of transitions and the importance of children being settled into a new situation if they are to be able to show what they know and can do. A very real challenge for nursery and infant staff is to develop approaches to assessment which are compatible with widely acknowledged principles of early years education.

It was not just what was assessed that was at stake; it was the conflict between open methods of assessment, where practitioners observe and note what is there to be noted, and closed methods where tests or even screening methods are used to find out whether children can perform a certain range of tasks, and to establish precisely what they cannot do.

This concern, placing assessment (correctly, I believe) at the heart of the problems posed by the National Curriculum, was expanded by the teachers into the areas of the curriculum most likely to be influenced. Play and the National Curriculum might be incompatible or at least separable, and there was doubt about whether we should be assessing children's play, although it is in fact the best way to get to know children's interests and established understandings of the world (Hurst, 1993). Teachers were anxious about giving children autonomy in the classroom, fearing the loss of control of their learning, although some people doubted whether we can actually control children's learning whatever we do. However, the perceived need to achieve a balance between child-initiated activity and directed activity aimed at covering parts of the curriculum which have to be taught shows the influence of the idea of 'instruction' as being a necessary part of National Curriculum practice.

This also set up conflicts between nursery and reception staff. Reception class staff said that they often feel like the filling in the sandwich facing pressure from nursery colleagues to offer children more freedom of choice, while at the same time being pressured by Key Stage 1 staff to work more formally. The requirement to show an end-product conflicted with young children's learning which often does not produce tangible results. This tension applied to teachers as well. Some teachers said they felt guilty about observing; though they recognized its value, they were not convinced that others would.

ASSESSMENT AND BASELINE ASSESSMENT

Baseline assessment, identified by the teachers as posing very serious problems, epitomizes the conflict between the nursery curriculum and the National Curriculum. If children have attended nursery school or class, to what extent can the assessment profile completed by staff in these settings have links with the first assessment in the infant school? If that assessment is seen as a baseline for the National Curriculum, the nursery staff must see their work either as preparation for basic instruction or as unconnected with the work in the infant school. Neither can be acceptable. Again, how can a whole-school policy on early years assessment link the nursery class with the rest of the school in a simplistic subject-based system without diminishing or even denigrating the value of nursery work?

The National Curriculum exerts pressure towards basic instruction in subjects through its emphasis on simplistic assessment in a way which can easily undermine established good practice in nursery schools. The Buckinghamshire teachers were worried that many practitioners in nursery and reception classes have not been trained to work with such young children and have had few opportunities to focus on their own age-phase specialism in in-service education. They felt that this would become an increasingly serious problem because of the assumption which underlies the National Curriculum that the subject curriculum is the only source of quality in teaching.

There are serious objections to baseline assessment, yet what lies behind it is the search for ways to inform ourselves – parents just as much as practitioners – about individual children and their educational progress. There can be no objection to that aim, and it is right to look for ways towards it. The objection lies in the nature of the assessment that is proposed, since it runs counter to the aims of the developmental curriculum in that it structures a predetermined and rigid set of behaviours to be demonstrated by the pupil and is not open to what the individual child brings to school.

However, there are criticisms of this positive or ipsative approach, for do not teachers need to know what it is their pupils cannot do? To this, we might reply that first it would be helpful to explore some ideas about what pupils can and cannot do. Here we uncover the lines of the division between the broad developmental aims of the nursery curriculum and the precise and behavioural ones of the National Curriculum. Any curriculum which incorporates precise specification of what pupils should be able to do into each subject at each level has already petrified its curriculum around external objectives and has committed itself to the fulfilment of those objectives as itemized in the assessment structure. The Early Years Curriculum Group (1989) explored ways in which many of the elements of the attainment targets (ATs) of the National Curriculum could be identified by observation of children as young as 3 years of age, but the achievement was neither structured nor sequenced in the way demanded by the ATs and their assessment procedures. It was structured by the nursery children's own mental pictures and maps of the world as they knew it, and sequenced according to their own development processes.

So we come back to the problem of what it is thought that young children should be able to do, should know, and what understandings we want them to have. There is a real opposition between those who would define this in terms of the child's own growing independence as a social and thinking person, and those who would see young children in subject terms and as absolute beginners. Even with the aim to reconcile the two, the sides continue to pull apart and, as was suggested in Chapter 2, may be irreconcilable.

An example of this would be the following analytical record of a child's development in which a developmental structure for the observations is applied to National Curriculum objectives. It is clear that either the child or the National Curriculum will have to be marginalized, and that the teacher of this boy of 4½ is already having difficulty accepting his very normal social, emotional and physical needs within the structure of the reception class:

CHILD'S NAME: Jamie, DATE OF BIRTH: 23/6/88, DATE OF RE-
CORD: 14/11/92
SOCIAL DEVELOPMENT: Settling in quite well with some of the other children [see with Michael H, below] but finds it hard to manage in large organised groups e.g. P.E. or assembly [see earlier record, 31/10/92].
PHYSICAL DEVELOPMENT: Very active, rushes around room. Always climbing on things or jumping on and off tables, dolls' beds etc. [but no accidents – good gross motor dvpt]. Fine motor skills not so well dvpt – paint everywhere! Can't write name on paintings and not interested in trying – says 'You do it for me'.
EMOTIONAL DEVELOPMENT: Still very adult-dependent, especially when Mum has just left and in p.m. session [see earlier record, 31/10/92]. Disaster if Michael H is not present in morning when he arrives. Frightened of playground, poor eater at dinner-time.
SPONTANEOUS INTERESTS AS SHOWN IN PLAY, ACTIVITIES AND CONVERSATION: Made a 'caravan' with Michael H with big blocks [see photo + sketches attached]; playing going on holiday, going to bed with blankets from dolls' beds, making the dinner 'with a fire', meeting 'Nannie Johnson' at her house 'down at my Birchington', driving ' a long long way' very vigorously with loud engine and tyre noises [particp. obs. 10/11/92].

AREAS OF LEARNING AND EXPERIENCE
Linguistic and literary: playing story with Michael, carrying it on for whole
   p.m. to staff, recreated and expanded it with 2 others.
Creative and aesthetic: N/A.

Mathematical: some interest in symmetry – tried to balance 'wheels' on sides of caravan [circular paper from easel] [Photograph attached].

Technological: fixing caravan to blocks ['my Daddy's car'] with coloured wool. Told me where all the beds would be at night and how they fold away.

Historical/geographical: told story of holiday and visit to Nannie, knew she was his 'Mum's Mum', 'my other Nannie's died when she got ill'. Not interested when I asked him to draw map of where the family went when they visited Nannie.

[Separate entry for projected developments in classroom.]

INFORMATION NEEDED FROM PARENTS: How is he at home? Any worries?

OTHER INFORMATION NEEDED, FURTHER PLANS FOR OBSER-VATION: Watch during organised work time. Is he able to understand what to do? Does he seem anxious or purposeless?

DEVELOPMENT OF PROVISION: According to results of observation.

ANY SPECIAL ACTION: Perhaps change of class organisation to provide more play opportunities for Jamie, Michael and others of same age, depending on observations of them.

(Observational material collected by V.H. in a reception class)

We see from this example that it is not possible to restrict the argument about baseline assessment to the procedures or the information sought, because of the influence that the underlying educational aims or objectives will have on how the assessment is targeted. As Wolfendale (1993) points out, baseline assessment in the sense of early assessment of children is not new, and we must 'safeguard effective current and time-honoured proven early years assessment practice and only introduce innovative on-entry or baseline approaches that stand up to rigorous educational standards' (p. 2).

In turn, the orientation of the assessment will determine how the curriculum is perceived, and how the practitioner plans it. It is therefore not viable to propose that nursery education should contribute to what goes on in the infant school without taking into consideration that the fundamental aims of the two may not be in accord, and that if this is so there will be a severe disjunction between the two which will affect children, parents, teachers and the whole of the transition process.

Yet there are ways in which the links can be very powerful, exercising an influence on the reception class that is much needed when so high a proportion of under-5s are admitted well before they are technically 'rising-5s'. If supporting links are to be made, it must be mainly through the assessments which nursery teachers and nursery nurses make of children, which are later passed on to their reception teachers. These records, in charting children's development over time in nursery education, show the reception teacher much more than a 'snap-shot' assessment can.

But reception teachers have large classes and a higher child:teacher ratio than nursery teachers. They seek to know about where they need to intervene to help children as well as how they can build on children's strengths. Can nursery education's assessment processes, which are ipsative (Blenkin and Kelly, 1992) or prospective (Athey, 1990), accommodate information about what children cannot do as well as what they can? Nursery assessment can and does identify areas of weakness or underdevelopment in children, since the records would show either a gap or a level of achievement that was lower than expected.

The advantage of using this approach, rather than a basic skills one, is that we have not yet clarified and agreed how basic skills relate to later achievement, nor how any skills relate to understanding, interest, knowledge, insight and creativity. There is a correlation between mastery of reading and writing skills and later literacy, but how they relate to each other needs to be discovered. Which causes which? Is it the acquisition of skills that helps a child to understand the uses of literacy, or is it the understanding of the role of literacy in our lives that spurs the child to acquire the skills as the key to this transforming process?

We have good reason to suppose (as is shown by Pat Gura (1992) in analysing the Froebel Block Play Project and in Chapter 7,) that skills are developed by the interaction of the child's purposes and growing understanding with the environment, and that it is the child's purposes which we should assess.

There is another difficulty with assessment of skills in early childhood. The skills measured in the infant school depend upon large and small body movements, yet these are well known to be particularly challenging to the immature nervous and muscular systems of young children. Assessment of performance is likely to lead to a much lower and narrower rating of ability and achievement than is assessment through what children show in other ways. Again, as so much depends upon the degree of physical maturation, it is hard to see how children can be given a fair chance to show their best since there will always be faster and slower developers at this age.

The presence or absence of particular skills, therefore, may tell us about the child's physical development but not about the individual and characteristic ways the child understands and learns about the world. Premature reliance on skills performance bears more harshly on those whose coordination and general motor development are slower. Might this perhaps be one of the causes of boys' lower levels of interest in academic-type tasks in infant school, and their higher levels of disaffection from school at later stages?

While we lack general understanding of how skill and competence relates to fundamental understanding, personal internalization and self-confidence, we should not rush ahead on the basis of assumed links, but build up our experience of using existing well tried methods. It could be hazarded that most of the difficulties caused by the National Curriculum in the early years of education arc due to the doubt cast on existing good practice, as shown in the dilemmas reported by the Buckinghamshire teachers. If we could work from an understanding of what children already know and do, we could help our 'slower learners' rather than simply note their difficulties.

The evidence for the links between quality in early education and subsequent success in learning is strong (Sylva, 1993). It seems unlikely that rigidly structured forms of baseline assessment focused on basic skills will have much contribution to make to later educational achievement.

EVALUATION AND THE NURSERY CURRICULUM

We have seen how restricted ideas of what young children are capable of cause assessment to be limited and to influence the curriculum offered to them so that emphasis is placed on the acquisition of a narrow range of knowledge and skills which are easily measurable. We cannot apply fore-ordained measures of effectiveness – such as early achievement of 'basic skills' – without over-riding the principles on which education in early childhood is based. These principles derive from children's needs for supportive relationships, for play, for exploration and for a curriculum that is developed by their practitioners to match their present levels of understanding.

Just as different kinds of assessment spring from different ideas about what children can and should learn, so do different kinds of evaluation of the effectiveness of provision for their learning. Particular values lead to particular approaches to evaluation, which influence the curriculum in their particular ways. Evaluation of practitioners' work by a checklist of basic information and skills that are required to be taught is one example – it will put pressure on practitioners to 'teach' these skills. However, if evaluation is a process that explores how well the practitioner has connected the content intended for learning with the child as active meaning-maker, the curriculum will be directed towards a developmental model. Recent research shows how such evaluation presents itself.

Researching practitioners' evaluation

A pilot research project investigated evaluation in the years before 5, focusing on the monitoring and evaluation of education in two nurseries providing for children whose parents need full-day provision for them (Hurst, forthcoming). The project studied the process of evaluation in two nurseries, one of which was a combined nursery centre employing three nursery teachers, three other teachers and nursery workers who were predominantly qualified NNEBs (nursery nurses) or equivalent in their training.

The project involved an action-research framework for the study of evaluation, in which the researchers worked with the practitioners to study the children and learn more about how best to provide for their learning needs. The researchers began by making observations of the children in order to acquire understanding of the task in each nursery. They then collaborated with practitioners in articulating aims for children as individuals or in groups, and supported staff in observing and reflecting upon children's progress.

Evaluation by the staff of the nurseries studied was found to be directed towards meeting the individual learning needs of children. Practitioners' evaluation was founded on observation and assessment of children, and was linked with principles of child development and curriculum knowledge in order to match learning needs. Practitioners felt that levels of professional support and in-service training should be adequate to allow staff to monitor and evaluate their work to the standards they saw as appropriate, which involved working to a very high standard.

This challenge to professionalism, the challenge of the nursery curriculum, comes from its focus on very young learners as individuals and on their individual perceptions of the world. Practitioners believed that they must seek to establish connections with what children already know and can do and extend these connections towards further knowledge, competence and understanding. Nursery education was seen as a personal foundation in learning, in attitudes and capabilities that are of lifelong importance. Practitioners felt that they needed to be expert in the observation and assessment of children, well informed about child development and to have the curriculum expertise to match children's individual learning needs.

THE NURSERY CURRICULUM AND THE NATIONAL CURRICULUM

It is surprising that the introduction of the National Curriculum has not led to a greater emphasis on the value of nursery education. Research shows marked differences between nursery-educated and non-nursery-educated children in their achievement at Key Stage 1, in spite of the fact that the nursery-educated children were from less favoured backgrounds (NUT/ University of Leeds, 1993). The National Curriculum claims to develop educational quality and raise standards, as we saw in Chapter 1, and it would appear prudent to have regard to the foundations of the maintained education system on which subsequent developments must build.

This is not the only reason why nursery education should be given high priority. Without nursery education or an equivalent standard in other forms of provision there cannot be equal access for all children to education, whatever the National Curriculum's intentions. The research recently reported in the UK and USA (summarized in Sylva, 1993) makes it clear that quality of early learning has lasting educational, social and economic effects which are particularly marked in children from deprived backgrounds. Is it really the case that the National Curriculum is opposed to this, or is there some other factor at work?

Practitioners in nursery education report themselves as bewildered and confused by the current turn of events, as is shown by the comments of the Buckinghamshire teachers above. The essence of their professional expertise is marginalized and their pedagogy hijacked in the interests of very different aims. The developmental curriculum is being undermined in various ways, and nursery education, as the first stage of the developmental curriculum, is affected adversely too. The factors in this process of undermining such a well established and well researched curriculum are threefold in that the National Curriculum has imposed a simplistic model of learning; caused a downwards pressure for a subject-based approach; and legitimized a 'back to basics' trend in thinking which presents itself as based on common sense but which conceals an inadequate view of human beings in general and children in particular.

The pedagogy implied by the National Curriculum

The simplistic model of education that lies at the heart of the National Curriculum is certainly one reason for the low morale of nursery practitioners. A reductionist view of the process of teaching which sees it as transmission of subject knowledge in which there is no place for children as active thinkers runs completely counter to the interactive pedagogy of the developmental curriculum, and leads to those many inadequacies explained elsewhere in this chapter and in every other chapter in this book.

Top-down pressure

The downward pressure of the National Curriculum affects both infant education and the preschool services. In the infant school, teachers are under pressure to demonstrate that they are producing results in terms of the Key Stage 1 assessment. This works against the provision of a developmentally appropriate curriculum and affects teachers' perceptions of the assessment process. The curriculum for the youngest children in the infant school is not seen as laying sure foundations for understanding of the academic disciplines through a personalized curriculum but as an introduction to a few limited basic skills. This means too often the loss of the opportunity to link children's developing understanding of their world with the power and complexity of language and literacy, and the empirical investigation and recording processes of mathematical and scientific thought. Design and technology, too, a particularly strong area in good nursery practice, which can bring a practical perspective on the curriculum throughout the infant school (Gura, 1992), is seen in terms of meeting requirements to achieve preset targets.

This malign influence extends into the preschool area, where practitioners are under pressure to formalize their curriculum, and where parents are encouraged to see as a selling-point of all forms of preschool provision their likeness to 'real school'. Play is increasingly seen as the enemy of education, and the outdoor learning environment is neglected in favour of rigid and prestructured tasks.

It seems likely that the children who suffer the most are the 4-year-olds in reception classes, or in similar provision in infant schools. This is counted as nursery provision in DFE statistics if more than 50 per cent of children are under 5, but it has none of the essential characteristics of nursery education. At an age when they need close relationships with caring and well prepared adults, these children are in classes where pupil numbers are permitted to go up to over thirty with only one teacher who may or may not be trained for their age-group. Although many reception teachers make heroic efforts to provide for these children, they themselves are concerned that adequate provision is not possible. In too many classrooms children learn to sit for long periods in silence while their peers in nursery classrooms are active in and out of doors; and infant school worksheets take the place of exploration and experimentation. Play is increasingly relegated to the margins of their school experience, in spite of all the evidence about its centrality to children under 7.

'Basics' and 'common sense'

The ever-present trend towards defining early years education along the lines of the elementary school curriculum of basic instruction in a limited range of knowledge and skills has never been stronger than it is at present. A Ms Susan Elkin, described as teaching English in Kent, writing in *The Independent* newspaper under the heading 'Three Rs and a bit of common sense' (1 September 1993), asserts that the one-year post-war emergency training should be reinstated for infant teachers. She does not specify what she would recommend for nursery teachers, but it is hardly likely to be a longer or more academic course:

> First, it is simply not as demanding intellectually to teach six-year-olds the basics as it is to teach A-level students, and it is patently ridiculous to pretend otherwise – even though the unions have always insisted it is. Of course, someone preparing pupils for Oxford or Cambridge in, say, physics, will need to have spent several years studying science at a high level as well as having been trained how to teach it.
>
> An infants' teacher working on the three Rs needs a quite different set of skills which do not, I suggest, take as long to acquire. After all, the potential infants' teacher already has the subject knowledge. She can already read, write and count. The training therefore can, and should, focus entirely on practical teaching strategies. It is a shameful waste of resources to insist that every infants' teacher spend three or four years in higher education.

This view, of course, confuses the difficulty of the subject content with the difficulty of the task of teaching it – it leaves out the learner from the educational process. This is the level of thinking that assumes a higher level of academic ability in junior or secondary teachers than in infant teachers.

Mary Archer, herself an academic chemist, welcomes the recent educational changes in her introduction to *The Sunday Times Parent Power* series (15 August 1993) under the headline 'Here is the good news: help is at hand'. After asserting that the well educated school-leaver is 'all too rare a bird' and discussing the government's other initiatives, she identifies access to information about schools as the most important factor in helping parents get the best possible education for their children:

> Above all, the information, published by the government for the first time last year about state schools' GCSE and A-level results, has put a powerful new tool into the hands of parents in reaching a decision on where to send their child . . . Admittedly, the tables that can so far be compiled are narrow in compass. The government intends to publish other information about truancy rates and career courses taken at 16. League tables can then be more broadly based, but until intellectual ability on entrance becomes the baseline, the

value added by the school itself will not be rateable, let alone adjustable for socio-economic factors or unit cost.

It seems from this that Archer sees assessment as a kind of commercial insurance policy against getting too low a return for the investment in the product. It is directly analogous to, and perhaps derived from, the 'value-added' marketing policy of stores such as Marks & Spencer which have found that the return on prepared meals is much better than that on the raw materials. It is humbling to reflect that the consumption of a Friday evening supper may have contributed to the evolution of policy on meeting the learning needs of the nation's youngest children.

Interestingly, along with her advocacy of a value-added base for evaluating schools, she confirms Hughes' findings (1993) that parents' first criterion for their choice of school is that the child should be happy there, which seems to favour a rather different pedagogy of a somewhat more developmental tendency:

> At Cheltenham Ladies College [Lady Archer's old school], we did some discreet market research a few months ago, and perhaps our parents may speak for all.
> First and foremost, parents want their children to grow up happily in a school that feels right for them. They want good academic standards, good order and discipline and good reputation. Oh, and they do not mind at all whether or not their girls turn out to be 'ladies'.

REDRESSING THE BALANCE

Rather than embarking on a lengthy analysis of the assumptions behind these two, fairly typical, comments on early education, we might note simply that each writer assumes that statements need not be justified by anything other than an appeal to established ideas of what is right in education. Might this be a clue to the hidden agenda of their messages? In the years since the writers had their formative experiences, practitioners and researchers have begun to establish different ways of justifying what is done in schools. This has shifted the weight of authority from traditional practice to reasoned choices, and it has given to practitioners a new authority. Now educational policy decisions can be taken for professional reasons, without having to have recourse either to what was good practice shortly after the Second World War or to what is deemed good practice in the social circles where government ministers are found.

If it is the case that much of what is bewildering and demoralizing in public attitudes for nursery practitioners today is actually a powerful backlash against the developing autonomy of practitioners rather than evidence that something is wrong with what teachers and nursery nurses do in school, we can determine upon a relevant course of morale-building which draws upon permanent sources of strength.

Strong home–school links in partnership with parents

There are good educational reasons why these are high up in nursery priorities, and parents and practitioners have mutually supportive interests in effective education. Often, however, the very assertions that undermine practitioners also confuse and mislead parents, so that they feel they should seek early formal education for their children. This can best be combated by demonstrating knowledge of each child and justifying educational provision through observation and assessment.

Additionally, where parents are able to participate in the education of their children on a partnership basis, each side contributing what it is best at, the long-term effects are seen to be striking and cannot help being recognized by parents. A long-term British study has shown that nursery education involving parents can be associated with measured (and maintained) IQ gains both for participating children and for their non-participating younger siblings (Athey, 1990). Giving high status to what parents do as the first educators of their children and helping them to develop their role, has been linked in English, as well as American, studies with escape from disadvantage. Parents should be helped to see the point of a curriculum which places the learner at the centre.

Strong links with other practitioners

There is much anxiety among nursery teachers, nursery nurses, playgroup and nursery workers and infant teachers that the needs of the under-7s as a whole are being overlooked. The pressure for a formal basic curriculum is at least as strong in playgroups and day nurseries as it is in nursery schools and classes. Reception teachers in particular are vulnerable to this pressure, and therefore keenly aware of it. Provision for play, and for outdoor play in particular, is minimal in reception classes and in Years 1 and 2 in the infant school. The emotional needs of under-7s cannot be met with present staffing levels, funding and school organization in many infant schools. Learning itself is being compartmentalized in ways that are foreign to and, as we saw in Chapters 1 and 2, unsuitable for young learners, and education is defined in many early years groups – including some under-5s provision –

as being the opposite of play. We must ensure that practitioners stand together and help each other to demonstrate that early learning can only take place within a developmental curriculum, and that practitioners of all kinds are sufficiently well supported and well trained to be able to maintain high standards within a developmental framework.

Classroom-based development of practice

Developing an appropriate pedagogy for the needs of the youngest children is a task that is, by its nature, never completed. All nursery practitioners have an interest in keeping their practice under review, and in taking whatever opportunities offer to research ways to meet children's needs more effectively. If the strength of the reaction to the assertion of professional autonomy is seen as significant, it may be that what it tells us is that reasoned professional judgements and decisions are a very powerful factor in the development of practitioners' independence.

Justifying these judgements and decisions, and maintaining professional independence in public, is not something that always comes easily to practitioners, but there are certain tools that we can use to help people understand what we are trying to say. We can appeal to the need to foster qualities that are usually agreed to be important for young people, for instance. Now that the pace of economic, technological and political change is so fast, industrial and commercial leaders frequently emphasize the need for the ability to adapt intelligently to new circumstances. Autonomy, creativity and lateral thinking are essential for this.

In order to show how they help children to learn how to live in society, and how to adapt themselves to the changing demands of contemporary life, those who provide high-quality education in the early years can emphasize the role of play, fantasy and the imagination. Through imaginative responses to challenges and dilemmas children extend their learning beyond the current situation and their existing solutions to difficulties, and – because they transcend their present – reach forward into new ways to move towards their goals.

Provision for play is central to high-quality education in the early years, and explanations of the curriculum for the under-5s should demonstrate how this is understood by practitioners in terms of children's developing understanding of the world and resourcefulness in dealing with it.

Leadership is another quality much valued in the world of work, and this is also developed through play. Practitioners can point out that it is hardly likely to be developed through the passive experience of basic instruction.

NURSERY EDUCATION IN THE FUTURE

What can we do to ensure that nursery education continues and grows in influence? The first thing is to decide what are the essential elements that must be promoted, and how best to articulate and communicate them.

More than anything, it is the developmental curriculum with its informed and reasoned planning and evaluating processes that embodies what is most effective in nursery education. Many people are uncertain of what this curriculum is like, because it is available to only a minority of children and non-existent or nearly so in many local education authorities. If more parents knew what it was like, and what opportunities it offered to their children now and for their later development, they would be more assertive in their support for it. Practitioners, parents, governors and councillors must publicize the value of this developmental curriculum for the youngest children and explain how it supports later learning. We must also be clear sighted about what is good nursery practice and what is not. Nursery schools and classes, and nursery centres, must continue to be professionally self-critical about their practice, and connect their evaluations of their work with the principles of the developmental curriculum.

Hartley (1993) has distinguished between institutions that aim for children to be themselves and those that have other aims, such as preparation for a later stage of education. His is a helpful formulation, since there is a bewildering variety of institutions that come under the name of nursery school or class in addition to the nursery schools, classes and centres maintained by local education authorities. There is also an array of approaches to nursery education to come to grips with. Many of these have distinctive names which give an idea of the person or programme providing the central pedagogic philosophy. The names of Froebel, Montessori and Steiner live on in this way. And there are new approaches such as High/Scope. How are practitioners and parents to evaluate the provision of such different institutions? Again, among the maintained nursery institutions as well as among the other institutions, there are vast differences in standards of educational provision offered. For both of these reasons, we need a set of criteria which enables us to judge the effectiveness of any kind of nursery education provision among the different forms of nursery education that are to be found in Britain.

We also need, just as much, criteria for judging other kinds of provision for the under-5s. The Rumbold Report (DES, 1990) emphasized the importance of reviewing the effectiveness and value of the provision that is made, but left it up to the practitioner to decide how this should be done. It would be a move towards improving and equalizing standards if the whole under-5s field could agree on the principles and criteria that all practitioners should use in their different settings. This chapter focuses strictly on 'nursery education' as defined here, but if a coherent way of making judgements about the quality of nursery education can be identified and articulated, it may be that it can be applied to other forms of provision as well with due allowance made for structural differences, since the needs of the children are the same whether they are in a day nursery, playgroup, private school or nursery school, centre or class.

SUMMARY AND CONCLUSIONS

There are many assertions and assumptions about education in the early years which run counter to the best of what nursery education has to offer. Practitioners need to remember that the only true test of any educational proposal is in the progress that individual children make.

The quality of their work, and its justification, will be based on the accuracy of the observations and the insight and understanding that they bring to the interpretation of these observations.

Educational research has a role to play in working with practitioners to investigate these processes and to make sure they are generalized. Collaborative research with practitioners can document and communicate to others the quality of nursery education. Long-term research (much needed in the UK) could show how the benign effects of maintained nursery education continue into later schooling and young adulthood in Britain as they do in America (Schweinhart and Weikart, 1993).

Practitioners have a very important role. They can communicate to parents, governors, councillors and the community what is being done right there in the nursery. These will all be powerful forces in educational decision-making when those who presently misunderstand and denigrate nursery education have passed on to other topics, and they are our natural allies.

But, and it is an important but, the influence to be fought against continually wherever it appears is the perennial pejorative view of young children, which fails to see in them all that is most creative, exciting, hopeful and vulnerable about human beings. There will always be a risk of devaluing young children, and therefore devaluing nursery education, because there will always be people who are ill at ease with that side of themselves, preferring some kind of a package of knowledge and understandings about the world to their own, personal, reasoned and experienced version. The National Curriculum has been the occasion for one outburst of this attitude; there will be others. This should only strengthen the will of nursery practitioners to meet the challenge by demonstrating, as we can through documenting children's progress, that nursery education really works at the level which matters most – the present and future development and learning of individual children.

4
THE IMPACT OF TESTING AT KEY STAGE 1: SOME EARLY RESEARCH EVIDENCE

Gillian Thumpston and Marian Whitehead

On the outskirts of every agony sits some observant fellow who points.
(Woolf, 1931, p. 213)

This epigram is a telling commentary on the false notions of objectivity which sometimes bedevil educational research and it sustained us as we undertook the work described in this chapter.

We want to emphasize the historical importance of the first full year of national testing at Key Stage 1 of the National Curriculum: the year 1990–1 was an educational watershed comparable with 1870, 1944 and 1988. Looking back from the perspective of 1993, we can claim that our early research evidence was already finding those weaknesses which have subsequently been recognized by professional bodies and central government.

SETTING THE SCENE

The project began in June 1990 when Goldsmiths' College awarded a 'starter' research grant for a small-scale pilot study of the first year of testing at the end of Key Stage 1 (KS1) in an inner-city borough. We planned to monitor and share in this first year of national testing with teacher colleagues in two Year-2 classes in the chosen borough. The borough had been selected for the size, diversity and complexity of the social and cultural worlds it encompassed, plus its maintained educational sector of 53 nursery classes, 2 nursery schools, 77 primary schools, 17 secondary schools, 8 special schools and a large further education college.

Some factual information about the two schools visited is given in Table 4.1, but a few general comments will help to set the scene for the following discussion. The two schools A and B are at the extreme north and south boundaries of the borough. School B is in an attractive modern building near the river frontage, in an area with a long history of neglect, poverty and the consequent social dislocations and deprivations. School A is in a building which is over one hundred years old but is in the southern residential part of the borough where good council housing, leafy roads, owner-occupation and some degree of affluence are the norm. The full research report also involved a third school in the borough whose Year-2 class teacher contributed a set of teacher reflections.

We observed and participated in the weekly experiences of the two Year-2 classes in schools A and B as they approached and negotiated

Table 4.1 The schools, 1990–1

	School A	School B
School		
Number on roll	251	191
Teaching staff: full time	9	9
part time	2	1
Other classroom support staff: full time	2	3 (1 for statemented child)
part time	nil	2
Number of classes	8 (including Nursery)	7
Grouping of children	Chronological	Chronological
KS1 class		
Number of children at KS1	29	26
Number at KS1 receiving free meals	3	15
Home languages spoken	English 27 Turkish 2	English 24 Turkish 1 Chinese 1
Preschool experience of nursery and/or playgroup	23	11
Time in infant school by end of KS1: 3 years	9	10
2 years (2 terms)	11	5
2 years (1 term)	9	10
2 years	nil	1

testing at the end of KS1. It is often claimed, perhaps rather smugly, that the observer sees most of the game, but there did appear to be real advantages in being observant 'outsiders'.

Our visits were frequent enough to enable us to establish good professional relationships with staff and children and appreciate the impact of National Curriculum testing on the schools, the teachers, the children, the curriculum and the organization of teaching and learning.

M.W. also had long-established professional links with both schools. However, we were distanced enough to avoid being drawn into all the minutiae of coping with running a school and the new external demands for assessment. In summary, we would claim it as a 'plus' that we saw things clearly because we were outsiders, but we were also aware of the dangers inherent in this position. The trap which it was essential to avoid was that of indulging in the facile criticism of our overworked and stressed teacher colleagues. We attempted to counter this by rejecting a detailed case-study analysis of the project and by inviting some reflections from the Year-2 teacher in a third school in the borough.

The rejection of a traditional case-study analysis took us back to the basic need in research to ask questions and investigate taken-for-granted assumptions. We were increasingly aware of the unchallenged status and origins of the National Curriculum demands which were particularly marked in the tone and implicit values of the documentation which purported to monitor the implementation of the core subjects (NCC, 1991a). Perhaps early years practitioners are especially sensitive to such hidden agendas because they derive from an approach which is not common in the British early years tradition. As we analysed and discussed our experiences of the project we found ourselves coming back again and again to the fact that our school visits had been a way of testing the rhetoric of the documentation (Webb, 1990, p. 266) as it was put into practice by our teacher colleagues, seeking for that reality behind the rhetoric which was discussed in Chapter 1. Asking questions about the National Curriculum assumptions and claims became the theme of our research.

CHOOSING ANCESTORS

The account which follows will appear to some to be a strange kind of 'research', being neither fish, fowl nor good red herring. But we believe that many primary teachers will recognize something of the flavour of classroom life as they have experienced it in recent years. We even claim for our report a respectable mongrel status and have chosen our ancestors carefully. Three identifiable sets of forebears have contributed to our account's distinctly 'qualitative' characteristics: the action-based practitioner research family, the ethnographic tribe and the narrative clan.

From our practitioner-research inheritance we derive an emphasis on professional development through systematic self-study (Stenhouse, 1975) and collaboration between teachers and researchers and practitioners in other educational institutions. This approach emphasizes the grounding of all ideas, or theories about education, in actual classroom practice and ongoing evaluation of real teaching and learning events. This is, in effect, the 'action-based' dimension of practitioner research which aims to take particular classroom outcomes and conclusions and disseminate them widely, in order to improve practice. Theories are thus created in the pursuit of improvement and are more readily accessible to teachers (Bassey, 1983).

It is a natural transition from the close study of small groups in classrooms negotiating cultural meanings and social transactions (learning and teaching) to the concerns of ethnography. Ethnographic research is a branch of anthropology and is mainly focused on group life and the ways in which deeply held and usually implicit values, meanings and beliefs are shared and transmitted, and come to shape the lives of group members. Language and literacy practices are central to these activities and can be of great interest to the educational researcher. However, 'classic' ethnography operates with long time-spans, for example, ten years in both the studies by Heath (1983) and Wells (1985), and requires an almost total immersion in the life-style of the groups being studied. Nevertheless, it should be noted that teacher practitioners are in many ways already genuine classroom ethnographers: they are involved on a long-term basis with their classroom groups; they are participants, committed to and part of the groups' daily negotiations and meaning-making; and they also have a professional obligation to monitor, record and analyse the world of the classroom. Teachers are both participants and observers.

The description and evaluation of classroom life and of teaching and learning encounters, or 'events', can only be satisfactorily conveyed by accounts which do justice to the richness, complexity and allusiveness of public and hidden agendas. Reports of ethnographic research are often narrative accounts (Heath, 1983; Wells, 1987). These stories about closely observed homes and classrooms, teachers and children (Armstrong, 1980; Paley, 1981; 1990) and the stories created by the participants themselves, support radical yet ancient ways of planning educational curricula and practice (Pollard, 1985; Egan and Nadaner, 1988; Rosen, 1988). The narrative approach to telling 'how it is' (Cortazzi, 1991) gives both a sequenced account of teaching and learning 'events' and an evaluative interpretation of them. The interpretation produces not so much a sullying of the purity of objective research, whatever that might be, but a remarkable insight into the cultures of teacher and pupil participants. In narratives of research, the keys to understanding the assumptions and values of the participants are to be found in their use of recurring metaphors (Eisner, 1985). Trivial examples of this would be the tendency of some teachers to talk of children in terms of 'brightness' or 'elasticity' . . . the art of stretching children! Or the fact that at present official government documentation avoids identifying teachers as professionals and prefers the 'operatives who deliver the goods' metaphor. Yet, by their 'stories' you shall know them, and self-knowledge begins with the stories we tell ourselves. Narrative accounts of research are an invaluable way into systematic self-study. Metaphors and stories are a reminder that the ancestors we have chosen will be useful guides to the 'hidden' as well as the 'formal' curricula of classrooms. Our antecedants are also more likely than most to sensitize us to the slippages between official documentation and classroom practice, and to the problems which arise when children, parents and teachers are drawn into an experiment whose outcome is uncertain (Campbell, 1989) and, as we saw in Chapter 1, into the acceptance of metaphors which are not their own.

BROAD AIMS

Our broad aims for the research arose partly from the processes of practitioner and action research, and partly from the questions we wished to ask in our specifically local setting. The processes of practitioner and action research have been defined as 'any systematic enquiry, large or small, conducted by professionals and focusing on some aspect of their practice in order to find out more about it, and eventually to act in ways they see as better or more effective.' (Oberg and McCutcheon, 1989, p. 117).

We wished to help ourselves and our class teacher colleagues to find out more about testing at KS1, particularly as these procedures were new and essentially untried, apart from the 1989 pilot runs. We certainly hoped to be able to find ways of being more effective as assessors and we also wished to monitor any unknown side-effects and unintended outcomes of testing 6- and 7-year-olds. From the start of the project we also had a secondary aim which was very much concerned with involving ourselves in cushioning the impact of the National Curriculum on young children and their teachers. This was not an entirely defensive reaction, but a forward-looking professional concern to help practitoners 'inhabit the system creatively in order to work towards change through action at the micro-level' (Webb, 1990, p. 30).

At the micro-level of our own inner-city context we originally proposed to ask questions about

- the impact of National Curriculum testing on the LEA's obligation to ensure equal opportunities and cater for special needs in education;
- the impact on the children as individuals;
- the impact on the infant school curriculum; and
- the impact on the teachers.

A CASE STUDY?

The approach we took, with its emphasis on field notes, diaries, participant observation and unstructured 'interviews', should have resulted in case studies of the classes and teachers involved in the project, but this presented another kind of problem. We were not really able to develop with our teacher colleagues any kind of action-research cycle in which we identified our problem, imagined a solution, moved in the direction of this solution, evaluated the outcomes and reviewed the problem again (Gregson, 1990). We were all involved in implementing the statutory requirements of the Education Reform Act 1988 in the first year of national testing at KS1. The obligation was as simple as that! There was little room for school experimentation, teacher initiatives or alternative curricula. Any detailed analysis of how each individual teacher and class coped seemed increasingly inappropriate and unprofessional. Teachers and tutors were faced with a difficult situation because an insensitively written report of the research could easily fail the schools we had worked in, as well as failing the challenge to monitor the impact of the National Curriculum.

We thus turned our attention to the official monitoring report (NCC, 1991a). The judgements in the document provided the pegs on which we could hang our own classroom-based work and observations and provided a way of 'showing how much change actually occurs in practice; identifying the unintended consequences of policy initiatives; exposing the contradictions in policy which are apparent when it is implemented' (Finch, 1988, p. 190).

We do not offer any rigorous case studies as such, but we do provide some glimpses of contradictions and unintended consequences, and perhaps the beginnings of a way of inhabiting the system creatively and even generating 'transforming' theories of practice.

TESTING THE RHETORIC

The NCC report on the implementation of the National Curriculum core subjects, 1989–90 (1991a) provided us with a useful set of claims against which we could set our own small-scale and localized findings. The NCC case-study schools revealed that changes in teachers' planning and teaching caused by the introduction of the National Curriculum included

- more observations of pupils;
- more use of investigations;
- more group work;
- more support in the classroom;
- greater awareness of the need for curriculum differentiation;
- increased time spent on science with consequent reductions in other activities; and
- increased sense that every moment in the classroom had to be used to good effect (NCC, 1991a, p. 17)

MORE OBSERVATIONS?

The first three changes are particularly interesting because claiming that they are happening is very much a matter of what is already in the eye of the beholder! Whereas the NCC data identifies more observation of pupils, more investigations and more group work, we saw more checking up on pupils, more imposed projects and more groups of four to six children sitting at tables for longer periods of time. The teachers in the two schools were increasingly obliged to keep tick-off checklists of each child's performance, and records of their own professional planning, in terms of attainment targets, statements of attainment and standard assessment tasks (SATs). We also shared something of this huge checking and recording burden by spending periods assessing children. It was quite obvious that, as we also saw in Chapter 3, this prescribed information-gathering was driving out more detailed approaches to individual observation such as target child observations (Sylva, Roy and Painter, 1980). What might be described as holistic approaches to observing and recording children's physical, social, communicative, and linguistic, mathematical and scientific, moral and aesthetic development, were no longer high priority, let alone practical. Detailed and probing investigations of children's reading development, for example, miscue analysis and teacher–child interviews, were not in evidence.

MORE USE OF INVESTIGATIONS?

The main evidence we saw for investigations in 1990–1 was an increase in science-focused classroom and whole-school projects such as 'Change', the latter demonstrated by displays of rotting fruits and leaves in the early part of the autumn term. However, while these well planned displays, which took a lot of teachers' time to organize, sometimes languished on the display tables, the children were rushing in from the playgrounds with armfuls of fallen leaves and plane-tree fruits. The problem seemed to be one of too much of a focus on the preplanning of what children *ought* to take from 'seasonal change', rather than observing the children and sharing in, and then extending, their delight in the changes brought by the autumn. As a national approach to curriculum planning it all seemed very cart before horse!

However, when teachers were relaxed and confident enough to experiment themselves, real investigations did occur and indicated the potential of a broader and richer curriculum approach. One example of this emerged in the early autumn of 1991 in school B; significantly it happened before the pressures of testing built up. The children and their teacher had been exploring ideas about 'going back in history' and each child set about investigating what he or she had been doing, wearing, eating and travelling in, 'six years ago'. The final recording of the results of the research was in the form of a vivid wall painting depicting babies, baby clothes, prams, pushchairs and representations of baby-talk! This investigation had been rich in home-and-school involvement, as well as talking, remembering, searching for evidence, painting, drawing, collage, reading, writing, calculating and measuring. Indeed, it demonstrated an approach which is the basis of the developmental early years curriculum (Blenkin and Kelly, 1988) and is reflected to some extent in the non-statutory programmes of study. But this was exceptional and it is sad to have to agree with the NCC (1991a, p. 17) findings that 'It was apparent that teachers were tending to use attainment targets and statements of attainment rather than programmes of study as the basis for their planning. In the first year teachers had still to take full advantage of non-statutory guidance in the core subjects.' Interestingly, this history example, one of our positive exceptions to the dominance of a target driven curriculum, is not in a core subject.

MORE GROUP WORK?

.oo easy to mistake the practice of grouping children for the conveniencￚ of allocating tables and chairs or organizing different classroom activities for group work. Certainly, the children in the two classes sat in groups of four or six and were usually set a 'group activity', for example, writing a book review, copying notes from the board about the weather and the air temperature, completing worksheets on clock-time, sewing hand-puppets with a parent and drawing a selection of plants. If this is all that is meant by 'more group work' one must claim that in the primary sector it predates the Education Reform Act by many years and as yet shows no signs of diminishing.

However, we would propose that another conception of group work, one in which children are expected to collaborate and extend each other's learning, language skills, thinking and social adaptability, is not just far from increasing, it is extremely rare. We found little evidence of joint co-operative work planned for groups of children and would suggest that the aims and practices of the National Curriculum are so focused on individual summative assessments and gradings that in practice they militate against planned collaboration in the curriculum. Furthermore, it might even be foolhardy of responsible teachers to go too far down the genuine group-work road when they are required to report in a highly individualized way on each child's solitary achievements of levels and targets.

INCREASED TIME SPENT ON SCIENCE?

It must be clear by now that we certainly noted the increased time spent on science, predominantly 'natural' or biological science, and the subsequent reduction in other activities. Both teachers were quite outspoken about the losses from the curriculum in their classes as they attempted to meet all the KS1 demands for assessment. The teacher in school A talked of a loss of balance in the curriculum and noted that art, play and drama and a general spontaneity in responding to and following up 'exciting events' with the children had been pushed out. In school B the class teacher regretted that art work had been greatly diminished in order to develop science and technology. Several children in the class had learning and behavioural problems and their restlessness and need for constant reassurance and a variety of ways into the curriculum, plus flexible teaching styles and a network of caring support, made it difficult to narrow the curriculum down to reading, writing, mathematics and science. Consequently, in this class some excellent work in PE, dance and drama continued to flourish well into the spring term.

Problems with science do not arise simply from the time it is taking up in the curriculum of the schools: there are problems with the nature of this science. Where infant teachers still feel strong and confident, for example with the biological sciences, lively work continues and there are enough 'nature tables' and nature walks and expeditions to gladden the heart of Susan Isaacs or Margaret McMillan! But the National Curriculum model of science as demonstrations and experiments, facts to know and phenomena to classify and label correctly, appears to be importing an unhelpful emphasis into the infant classroom. The traditional secondary school model of the tripartite sciences, 'hard' physics and chemistry and 'soft' biology, de-skills young children and leaves their teachers orchestrating the 'experiments' and 'telling' the facts. We saw prisms, magnets, lenses, ramps and slopes, and the now notorious floating and sinking exercises. Our colleagues in the schools were obliged to go through these procedures but we saw little evidence of children catching alight and really investigating their world. The current National Curriculum science assessments do not appear in practice to promote child-led hypothesizing, testing, questioning and the kind of intense involvement associated with creative thinking and play (Bruce, 1991). The danger is that knowing the name of something is already coming to be preferred to knowing something (Feynman, 1988).

CURRICULUM DIFFERENTIATION

Curriculum differentiation, or the discrete subjects approach, is a central and defining feature of the National Curriculum. Curriculum is defined in terms of core and foundation subjects and the linked requirements of testing children's knowledge of subjects reinforce the legislation. As far as the schools are concerned, there can be no choice about greater awareness of the need for curriculum differentiation, it is a legal requirement.

The only possible room for discussion focuses around the NCC's choice of the words 'greater awareness' and 'need'. Both schools visited were 'aware' of curriculum differentiation, they could not have been more so, but were also doubtful about the 'need' as it is being promoted by the official agencies. The Year-2 teachers and their colleagues were much exercised by the promotion of a traditional secondary school model of subject timetables. There was also the awareness of some pressure to reinstate an even older 'three Rs' model: 'I use class lessons a lot more to ensure that children will have experience of the targets they must reach' (school A).

'It's very compartmentalized . . . it's much more like it used to be . . . in some ways it's easier, it simplifies teaching' (school A). In a discussion of history and geography, the teacher in school B said that she had been trained to treat these as part of a general environmental approach and although this influenced her a great deal, she was aware that she would need to highlight them as subjects.

USING EVERY MOMENT TO GOOD EFFECT?

The level of support in the classroom when SATs are being administered is closely related to the claim that there was an 'increased sense that every moment in the classroom had to be used to good effect'. Apart from the deeply offensive suggestion that most professional teachers do not aim to use classroom time effectively, this claim is assuming a great deal about what constitutes 'good'. It actually begs the question of quality, effectiveness and the evidence that these have occurred. There is also a masking of the loss to other classes and groups in the schools caused by the diverting of highly skilled and experienced specialist teachers and support staff to Year-2 classes. In the particular schools visited, there was an overwhelming sense that every moment had to be spent on preparing for and meeting the teacher assessments and SATs. But there was some unease about the value, in terms of young children's education, of such priorities. During one snowy week in February, the Year-2 class teacher in school A commented, not for the first time, on the loss of spontaneity in her teaching: she could only spare the briefest of sessions to dwell on the spectacular snowfalls before getting back to the assessments.

During the period of formal standardized assessment (April/May), or testing as it was universally called, the use of classroom time changed noticeably. Priorities had to be focused on individuals and groups 'doing' a SAT and the remaining children had to be quiet and occupied and avoid interrupting the teacher with requests for help or information. This situation lasted for several weeks in all schools; a national survey suggests a minimum of four weeks of total suspension of normal teaching and learning (NUT, 1991). It is probably the case that the time-filling occupations which we noticed thoughtful teachers driven to use during the SAT period are typical. For example, copying a letter of thanks from the board, cutting pictures out of old magazines, and colouring in outline pictures or templates. But even during these less than 'good' uses of children's time the human need to make sense surfaces. When one of us questioned a child about his views on colouring in templates he assured her that 'colouring is good for you and it gives my hands exercise'!

Our teachers were positive and conscientious professionals, seeking to make the best job they could of the classroom testing of 6-year-olds, and they are not as outspoken in their criticisms as many teachers have continued to be in the media and in submissions to unions and professional organizations. However, it was clear that they were very concerned about not teaching PE and dance, or not listening to children read (apart from SAT procedures), or not developing new themes and interests. They obviously considered these 'lost opportunities' to be the crucial elements in using every moment in the classroom to good effect.

As well as the changes outlined in the NCC Report (1991a), our study also found that in school A the class teacher had to devise two timetables, one for the SATs and one for the other activities. The most difficult organization problem was that presented by children who were absent from school when their group was undertaking a SAT. These children then had to be incorporated into another group on their return, which meant that they appeared to have to be in two places at the same time: in one to do the SAT they had missed and in another to be with their group which was doing the next SAT!

A further difficulty was highlighted in school B where the teacher found that as the summer term progressed she was spending increasing amounts of time with the group undertaking the SAT, and correspondingly less with the rest of the class. This teacher had no extra support in her classroom and this was causing increased pressure on those children with behavioural and emotional difficulties. Evidence of this, the teacher believed, was most apparent at the end of sessions when she was spending less time supervising the finishing of activities and the essential 'tidying up' of the classroom. It is always important that resources and equipment are returned correctly in order that the next groups can begin their work promptly. However, it is also a time which can cause children some anxiety as it is less structured, demands a developed sense of responsibility, and, in this case, without the teacher to supervise them, the children were finding it difficult to cope.

Increased time spent on SATs in the summer term led to a reduction in the amount of time given to some curriculum areas. In school B the class teacher regretted these areas of neglect as she considered that provision for her class should not be restricted to reading, writing, mathematics and science. This group of children was particularly in need of constant reassurance, a variety of ways into the curriculum and supportive, flexible teaching styles. This was demonstrated by one incident on a sunny May morning when the teacher took the class for an outdoor PE lesson, for the first time that term. The children responded extremely well to the lesson and the teacher felt that this was also reflected in the quality of the work they undertook during the rest of the day. But this raised a further dilemma for the teacher because she was then concerned that she had previously done the children a disservice: perhaps they would have performed better in the SATs if she had included PE more often! However, this would have prevented her and the children from finishing the SATs. Both the teachers had attempted to fit the SATs into their topic, but in school B the teacher felt that this was not as satisfactory as she had hoped it would be. The constraints of the SATs were causing the integration to be contrived and the SATs could not be fitted in as unobtrusively as she had wished.

More observation of pupils and more work with individuals and small groups was difficult to substantiate. We certainly saw the class teachers working with small groups of children, observing what those children were doing, and recording and assessing the children's activities. All these procedures would be expected, indeed required, as part of the teaching activities in a primary classroom. However, as we saw earlier in this chapter and in Chapter 3, during the National Curriculum assessment and testing, we noted that the observations were focused on the child's performance at a prescribed task, not on observing what the child was doing for the sake of informing future planning and provision. It was observing for the sake of testing, not teaching. There appeared to be no time for reflection on what was observed, apart from the dilemma of which level to record. In order for teachers to teach, rather than lecture, as was stressed in Chapter 3, observations which are reflected on and then acted upon are a prerequisite. How else can a teacher gain insights into what children understand, know and, perhaps more importantly, enjoy knowing?

RECORD-KEEPING

The NCC survey evidence also noted some common problems with record-keeping:

- Its heavy demands on teachers' time.
- Uncertainty and confusion about the judgement-making process.
- Major reservations about checklist-style records (NCC, 1991a, p. 18).

These three problems recurred in the nationwide surveys (NUT, 1991; DES, 1991a), in anecdotal evidence and in the responses of the inner-city teachers we observed. It would be difficult to exaggerate the overwhelming nature of the burden which this itemized checklist style of record-keeping, and the preceding checking and judgement-making, placed on our colleagues, a burden now fully recognized by the government's own adviser (NCC/SEAC, 1993). Furthermore, our visits and observations did not reflect anything of the long hours the teachers spent in the evenings and very early mornings, writing up assessments and planning the next batch.

Sadly, the time spent appears to have been out of all proportion to the value of such 'quick-check' summative assessments. The teachers we visited were accustomed to building up detailed, long-term records on individual children, identifying patterns of developments and difficulties in the cognitive, affective, linguistic, aesthetic, physical, social, mathematical and scientific domains. The teachers were particularly bothered by the doubtful reliability of the instant judgements they were being asked to make. This concern is a recurring theme in the many conversations we had.

Early October, school A

The class teacher voiced her worries about the vagueness of some National Curriculum targets, especially 'drawing geometrical shapes'. How mathematically accurate do the shapes have to be?

Early November, school A

Once again we found ourselves discussing the issue of subjectivity and teacher judgements. Despite all the claims for national standardization it was quite clear that ticking so-called attainment levels was highly subjective. We also noted that once a task, skill or concept is achieved and demonstrated it might not show up when a teacher tests it a few months later. The class teacher and her part-time colleague referred to their general experience: children often appear to know something and seem able to do something but, a few months later, with another teacher perhaps, they do not appear to be confident in the attainment. We talked generally about the fact that learning may take considerable time to become established and can only really be said to have taken hold if the understanding and/or competence is transferable to other situations and contexts.

Mid-March, school A

The teacher points out that her children can write interesting 'sentences', but the counting of full stops and capital letters would immediately mark them down: 'What are we doing, when we assess writing by young children who are only 6 years of age, by counting full stops?'

Late April, school A

The class teacher has noted that in response to the 'Write a story SAT' some very competent and confident individuals are 'playing it safe'. They were aware that this was a testing situation and chose to write their stories about very simple 'walks to the park and back home to bed', using only those words which they knew they could spell accurately.

Early March, school A

A rather heated discussion with the staff about 'the nature of the evidence' for assessing children at particular levels. The teachers voiced a strongly held opinion which they would like to put 'on the record'. If teachers' assessments are so worth while they should be taken seriously and the professional judgements they represent trusted. In other words, with good teacher assessments there may be little need for SAT procedures at the end of KS1.

BENEFITS FOR PUPILS?

The NCC monitoring survey and case-study data suggest that many primary teachers support the National Curriculum because it confers educational benefits on pupils and staff. The benefits for pupils are listed as:

- providing a better balance of knowledge and skills;
- greater coverage of science;
- better progression and continuity; and
- target-setting and common goals (NCC, 1991a, p. 14).

The assumptions behind these kinds of claims have already been discussed, but the first listed benefit is a particuarly bold example of undiscussed and undefined assertion. Educational planning and evaluation should at least try to start from an analysis of what is 'knowledge', what are 'skills' and what might a 'better balance' of these look like? The NCC assertion fails to indicate that there are a variety of ways of defining knowledge. A taxonomy model of lists of very traditional 'subjects' which consist of fairly static, finite bodies of 'facts' to be acquired is exemplified in the National Curriculum. But there are other conceptions of knowledge which highlight the provisional, evolving, socially constructed and personally created nature of human knowing (Vygotsky, 1978; Bruner, 1986; Kelly, 1986) and lead to different forms of curriculum (DES, 1975; Blenkin and Kelly, 1988; EYCG, 1989, 1992).

Any argument by assertion also fails to probe the nature of skills: how are they related to knowledge, is acting skilfully, for example, different from acting 'thoughtfully? Can schools train children (and teachers) as skilful operators but still fail to educate them? Our own visits and observations indicated that many skills and specific operations were in evidence, for example, tracing over handwriting patterns, counting to 100 and responding to Yes/No questions on computer software programs. All are useful in short-term ways, but of limited wider application and not necessarily generating knowledge, that network of connections, symbolic representations and meanings which extends the power of our thinking and hypothesizing.

It is interesting to note that one of us caused some anxiety among the staff in one of the project schools when she departed from the class procedures for assessing 'response to stories' (E, AT 2, Level 2), by introducing a picture book (*Bye Bye Baby*, Ahlberg and Ahlberg, 1989), and supporting the children's spontaneous discussion of how a baby could get himself born without having a mother! This actually provided evidence of far greater social, literary and scientific knowledge among these 6-year-olds than could be gleaned from limited and limiting checking procedures.

It is possible to train children to remember facts and give skilled performances, and it is necessary to train teachers to deliver, assess and test the National Curriculum. But does all this training and compulsion amount to quality education?

Consider the following response from a group of Year-2 children who had been working with one of us on writing book reviews. The children had some previous experience of writing reviews, although this was the first time they had worked with the researcher. They had spent time discussing their choice of book and the reasons for writing a book review before the following exchange occurred:

> *Researcher:* What are you going to be thinking about when writing your book reviews?
> *Chorus of children:* Capital letters, full stops, commas and not lots of 'ands'.

As the teacher in school A recounted, 'I asked them to write a story and S—— was back in five minutes. I thought she couldn't possibly have finished, but there it was, good spelling, good punctuation, two sides. Boring story, but that doesn't matter for National Curriculum.'

Greater coverage of science has already been discussed and is far from being an unalloyed benefit, as we have indicated. The NCC claims for better progression and continuity would seem to be based on the assumption that working through levels 1–10 in the attainment targets (ATs) provides automatic progression and continuity. There would seem to be little recognition of the anxieties expressed by many teachers and their professional associations with regard to the hierarchical format of the ATs and the discrete subjects approach. During the three-week period when SATs were being adminstered there was often a lack of continuity for those children who did not attain Level 1 and, for all children, few links between work in the core subjects. Shortage of time meant that some activities such as MA Level 2/3, making the mathematics game, had to be curtailed and the children were not able to finish constructing the game to their own satisfaction, nor solve the problems that arose from this. The pressure of time was perhaps felt by the children, as one child in school A remarked: 'This is just like a factory, innit . . . making games?'

There was very little evidence to support the view that pupils were setting their own targets and had perceived common goals. The children and teachers were working within an imposed curriculum that had assumed widespread acceptance of common goals. For some children MA 3 Level 3 SAT seemed to demonstrate the opposite of common goals. In this SAT the child should be able to recall number facts immediately, with no obvious working out, but how does the child perceive this common goal when asked in class discussion (school A):

> *Teacher:* How many children are here today, if there are 29 in the class and 3 are away?
> *Child immediately raises hand to answer.*
> *Teacher:* I won't ask you, I can see you didn't think about it, but just put up your hand?

BENEFITS FOR STAFF?

The benefits for staff are listed as:

- greater attention to curriculum planning;
- a catalyst for extending staff co-operation;
- teaching is better organized; and
- increased awareness of content requirements for each subject (NCC, 1991a, p. 14).

The unpleasant suggestion behind all these claims is that, before ERA, staff paid little attention to curriculum planning, were divided, isolated and unco-operative, as well as being poorly organized in their teaching and ignorant of subject content. Our exaggerated summary serves to focus attention on the simplistic 'before and after' attitude to teachers which pervades the documentation. In practice, the picture in the schools is rather different. Sophisticated curriculum planning has almost disappeared and in its place there are 'timetables' which are simply ways of showing an intention to cover, or deliver, the core and foundation subjects.

Professional teachers have always seen co-operation with colleagues and extra activities with parents and children, extending well above and beyond the call of duty, as part of their remit. This quality commitment and professionalism has been undermined by personal exhaustion and public disparagement. It is no coincidence that most young children were comparatively unscathed by their first experience of testing in 1990–1, while their teachers were reporting high levels of stress and exhaustion (NUT, 1991). Clearly teachers took it on themselves to protect their very young examinees from public failure and humiliation.

The teachers we visited were acutely aware that a high price was paid for 'better organized' delivery of the National Curriculum. This price included the rejection of children's playful and unpredictable responses and the exclusion of risk-taking and 'going beyond the information given' (Bruner, 1973). Yet these elements of imaginative projection and 'leaps in the dark' are at the heart of creative scientific, mathematical, historical and literary thinking – to name but a few domains of knowledge. The issues of subjects, subject content and curriculum differentiation have occurred frequently in this account, but for most 'staff' they were, and continue to be, a matter of implementing the National Curriculum definitions of what constitute English, mathematics and science. Both teachers felt they were under pressure to increase their own awareness of what the National Curriculum stated was the content requirement for each subject, in order to be able to provide the best opportunities for the children in their classes. The arbitrary nature of this pressure was demonstrated when the content of mathematics and science changed suddenly in the middle of the testing season in 1991. It is interesting to consider how changes could be, and continue to be, made to subjects which consist of sets of 'known facts'. The Year-2 teachers in both schools were committed to making the teacher assessments and SATs work. They were also determined that the children in their classes should not be upset by the testing and that the assessment should be a true reflection of the children's abilities.

GENERATING THEORY

Positive ways of reflecting on the experiences of the past few years must be developed in order to generate some theories of hope, as befits the professional needs of those who work with the youngest members of society: 'Theory is always for someone and for some purpose' (Cox, 1986, p. 207).

In educational theory the first someone is always the child and the following notes indicate ways of generating theories which will enhance the quality of education for all our children:

- Schooling should confirm and constantly reaffirm children's ability to learn. Furthermore, the demands of the curriculum should make sense and have relevance for the learner. This theoretical perspective is clearly missing if children are required to float pieces of fruit and create games that cannot be played!
- Teaching and learning are most successful when teachers are partners with children in the process. This important relationship is undermined when teachers are forced into the role of 'unhelpful examiner': our report demonstrates that the learning situation degenerates when young children are cast adrift by this unpredictable change in teacher role.
- Teacher assessment is fundamental in education and should be recognized as such. It is based on knowledge of the learner and of the context of learning. In addition it acknowledges the human dimension of learning and the unique, multi-faceted nature of teaching and learning.
- Parental and community understanding of what teachers do and of how children learn is crucial for an effective education system which aspires to be more than schooling, or training. But there is now a need to explain publicly the potential conflict which exists between parental awareness of the singular individuality of their own child, or children, and the blanket uniformity of a system of national testing.
- Education involves feeling as well as knowing. The intuition of parents and carers that their children should be happy in school must be articulated and valued, not derided. The lessons learnt by overwhelmed, frightened and confused children are not ones which education should deliver.
- Qualitative research jointly undertaken by teachers and researchers which seeks to develop the participant observer approach is a positive strategy. One which can be adopted in order to generate theories which enable teachers to inhabit the system creatively. We have in mind those research accounts which 'tell it like it is', the stories of classrooms in all their complexity (Jackson, 1979; Armstrong, 1980; Paley, 1981). Such stories use narrative form and the language of human encounters, in

preference to numbers and charts which obscure rather than illuminate the realities of the classroom. It is an irony that the curriculum for children prescribes speaking and listening in the core areas, while the stories told by teachers have until now fallen on deaf ears. We need to create the public context in which teachers and researchers can tell true stories about classroom life, true that is to the spirit rather than the rhetoric.

SUMMARY AND CONCLUSIONS

The current situation finds us frozen on the horns of a dilemma! We originally summarized our research as a set of dilemmas and creative possibilities. The dilemmas clustered around three main issues:

• The practical need for teachers to be researchers in their own schools and classrooms, although this is proving to be increasingly difficult in the context of a legally imposed and highly centralized curriculum.
• A curriculum fit for children should do justice to the scope of their minds: wider forms of knowing are possible and evaluation must be able to capture such richness and diversity.
• Assessment is being used for social control; we are valuing children as w, 1, 2, 3, 4, etc. This is reminiscent of gentling the masses with training, short sharp exams, terminal assessments, league tables, well resourced schools for a selected few, and concerted attacks on the graduate status of the teaching profession.

It is now publicly acknowledged that the weaknesses which many researchers identified in the first years of testing at KS1 have led to a state of breakdown in the National Curriculum. The decision to 'freeze' further changes (NCC/SEAC, 1993) does not resolve the dilemmas and it is more important than ever for professional educators to explore creative and innovative ways forward. Our original suggestions for this are still relevant:

• Continued research and work on teacher assessment of pupils.
• Evolving a language which renders the subtleties of the classroom accessible to many more people.
• Involving children in forms of self-assessment which are purposeful, enhance self-esteem and put learners in control.
• Helping parents and communities to understand the issues involved in testing the 'basics' and in children's learning.

- Advocating the pleasure principle: sharing the notion that play, risk-taking and experimentation are central to human development and learning.

5
LANGUAGE DEVELOPMENT IN THE EARLY YEARS: MORE THAN NATIONAL CURRICULUM ENGLISH

Marian Whitehead

Two roads diverged in a wood, and I –
I took the one less travelled by,
And that has made all the difference.
(Robert Frost, 'The Road Not Taken', 1955)

CLEARING THE GROUND

Any attempt to review the journey which we have all, teachers and pupils, been required to make in recent years from 'language in education' to National Curriculum English is likely to be overwhelmed by confusion and misinformation. Thus a little ground-clearing and myth disposal is essential before the road behind and ahead can be mapped. This introductory section aims to dispose of two prevalent myths: one generally applied to early years and primary teaching, Key Stages 1 and 2 in National Curriculum parlance, and one specific to the study of language and literacy.

A myth almost always contains a grain of truth which has become so over-laid with metaphors and extra stories that it is increasingly obscure and even misleading. Such myths, however, are not necessarily the stories of antiquity: they are constantly created and reworked and can be as modern as motorway ghost stories or tall tales of EC regulations and bureaucratic muddles. The implementation and monitoring of the National Curriculum has generated many new myths and the two referred to above must be challenged before they acquire the status of absolute truths.

The first myth focuses on the intellectual and professional abilities of early years and primary teachers and is of very recent vintage. It makes the general claim that Key Stages 1 and 2 teachers are unable to cope with the

87

full range of the ten (inclusive of religious education) National Curriculum subjects. Obscured by this rather surprising assertion is one indisputable grain of truth: the proliferation of levels, attainment targets, assessment tables and the cumbersome procedures for recording them, have placed an intolerable burden on teachers. This was highlighted in the previous chapter on the experience of testing at Key Stage 1 (KS1) in an inner-city area in 1990–1. Even if this load is about to be lightened somewhat (NCC/ SEAC, 1993), the myth remains and grows. The myth actually shifts attention away from the Kafkaesque nightmare of paperwork and documentation out of control and suggests that professional teachers cannot teach English, mathematics, science, history, geography, art, technology, music, physical education and religious education, to children up to the age of 11.

This dangerous and misleading myth must be challenged. First, it is an insulting calumny against the professionalism of early years and later primary teachers, many of whom do have a considerable subject expertise but who pride themselves on being 'teachers first'. That is, experts on learning, child development and the pedagogic skills. This professionalism is not that of the 'Jack or Jill of all trades, master or mistress of none' generalist, but is at its best a finely tuned ability to understand and relate formally constituted bodies of knowledge and generally accepted 'facts' to the needs, interests and experiences of young learners.

A further sub-myth should be nailed down at this point: it really is no great achievement to know and disseminate the material which is so mechanically set out in the National Curriculum ring-binders. It is hardly an intellectual challenge to get to grips with the outdated notions of 'subjects' and 'facts' in this new late nineteenth-century primary curriculum.

The 'teachers can't cope' myth is also dangerous on the grounds that it diverts attention away from the real message which professional early years teachers do wish to get over to parents and central government. This is that, as we have seen, in earlier chapters, the narrowly subject-based curriculum is not appropriate for young children and fails to take account of, and build on, the powerful thinking strategies which they use in their engagements with their own worlds of people and events. The apparently deliberate ignoring of all that has been researched, modified and published over the years about young children as learners, from Piaget (1926), Vygotsky (1986) and Bruner (1986), to the Early Years Curriculum Group (1989; 1992), is inexplicable, except in terms of institutionalized ignorance and anti-intellectualism.

A third reason for challenging the myth of early years teacher incompetence is that it is now being used as a means of splitting the teaching profession into those who do the basic baby-stuff and, therefore, require minimal preparation, and those who teach real subjects at 'higher' levels. The latest proposals (DFE, 1993b) for the non-education of early years teachers encapsulate the full range of misleading mythical claims discussed here: primary teachers are generally incompetent, young children are simple and unchallenging thinkers, and early years teachers do not need degree-level education and training.

The current debate about literacy and the appropriate English curriculum for schools is also distorted by an old and deep-seated myth: that there is just one unambiguous set of literacy skills which schools must pass on. The grain of truth here is the notion that literacy is a powerful tool for national and personal survival and development in the modern world. The obfuscation is caused by oversimplification and historical and cultural ignorance. This is the 'literacy myth' (Graff, 1987) which uses the rhetoric of decline and decay to suggest that things were once so much better and modern education is to blame for falling standards of literacy, as well as all other ills afflicting the nation.

In addition to debunking the notion that a return to 'basic literacy skills', of the kind appropriate for a nineteenth-century clerk, will produce economic miracles and social stability, Graff also highlights the complexity and variability of oral and literate behaviours in communities outside the confines of schools and work places. Shirley Brice Heath, in the Foreword to Graff's work (1987), emphasizes the warning inherent in all his studies: 'Responses to questions surrounding oral and written language beliefs and behaviours lie deep in the self-definitions, sociocultural values, and language ideologies of these communities and simple correlational responses drawn from myths linking schooling, literacy, and economic advancement in modernized societies will not apply' (Heath 1987, p. ix).

At a time when we are constantly urged to return to old values and old practices, it is crucial that professional educators understand the history of the close links between literacy, reading and social control of the masses in nineteenth-century England and Wales. We cannot rely on these same 'basic literacy skills' of reading and writing to equip children for survival in the twenty-first century, let alone for democracy and self-fulfilment. Something closer to 'literate behaviours' which foster independent problem-solving and knowledge-creating are required (*op. cit.*, p. vii), as is an understanding that there are many forms of literacy: alphabetic, mathematic, graphic, visual, musical, physical . . . (Graff 1987, p. 8).

Ironically, it is the undervalued early years practitioners who are most likely to understand such critiques of the literacy myth, because they are in constant daily contact with children and communities who 'read' the world in diverse ways (Freire and Macedo, 1987) and communicate in a variety of modes.

The misleading literacy myth of simple unchanging homogeneity is a pertinent symbol for the National Curriculum critique at the heart of this chapter and, indeed, this book. Just as literacy is more than basic reading and writing skills, so language development in the early years of education is more than National Curriculum English. The sections which follow will look at current policies and their likely outcomes, as well as at what might have been. 'The road not taken' is a broad overview of the emergence of National Curriculum English. This is followed by sections which focus on talking, reading, literature and writing in the early years.

'THE ROAD NOT TAKEN'

Before embarking on a brief version of the story of National Curriculum English, a few words about narrative form might be helpful. One of the most powerful aspects of narrative is the notion of choice: every story has nodal points from which new branches sprout. These are the points at which characters, or tellers and authors, choose one path or course of action rather than another. This element of choices to be made endows literature and folk tales with the powerful illusion of freedom of choice: Pandora deliberately opens the box, Cinderella dances until the clock strikes twelve, and John Brown finally accepts the Midnight Cat. These kinds of choices built in to narratives also produce the haunting 'what if' appeal of literature: what if Juliet had woken sooner from her drugged sleep, or Max had stayed with the Wild Things? As in literature, so in life, the 'what ifs' haunt us and this is particularly true of the recent history of education reports and legislation. So the story of National Curriculum English is best told as a tale of roads not taken and opportunities missed, a tale of 'what ifs'.

One particular book, in its original and new editions, straddles the period under discussion and was also a major influence on the first of the several 'English' reports which have been produced in the last twenty years. The book is James Britton's *Language and Learning*, first published in 1970 and republished in a new edition in 1992, and the report is the 1975 Bullock Committee Report, *A Language for Life* (DES, 1975). The story of the years between the two editions of the Britton publication is in essence an account of a radical and scholarly breakthrough in knowledge about language and its implications for education, and its subsequent rejection in the

1980s in favour of resurrecting a half-remembered but potent mythology of selective schooling, unquestioned privilege, centralized power and social stability. We are all increasingly familiar with the characteristics of the road we are now on, but the road not chosen had features which remain in the memory of many teachers in England and Wales and can still inspire good language teaching, despite the darkening landscape ahead. Furthermore, the road not taken, and now barred to British teachers, is still the route preferred by many professional teachers in other countries.

Britton's writings and his crucial influence on the Bullock Committee introduced the work of L. S. Vygotsky, A. R. Luria and J. S. Bruner to a wide audience of British educators, and also gave considerable impetus to the critical re-evaluation of Piaget's writings and influence on education. Most significantly, perhaps, language and learning were put at the heart of the educational enterprise and the very earliest preschool stages of language and social development were given pre-eminence. These priorities were rooted in the scholarly approach to linguistics which is the hallmark of Britton's work and has introduced many teachers to innovative studies of child language, as exemplified by the writings of Vygotsky, Luria, Brown, Halliday, Weir, Bruner and Britton himself. Suddenly everyone was child-watching and child-listening and the years before school and the early years of education were taken as the models for good practice in education generally, as well as in high-status research. The spirit of the age is captured in the title and the focus of the report on all aspects of the teaching of reading commissioned by the Secretary of State for Education: *A Language for Life* (DES, 1975). One can only speculate on the surprise this gave the minister who asked for a reading report and was given a major review of modern linguistic theory and its radical implications for educational practice, from birth through to teacher education!

Some enduring themes from this period have continued to inform research and good practice and leave traces in the current legislation. The primacy of spoken language, its close relationship with the development of verbal and abstract modes of thinking, and its role in generating literacy, is a perspective of incalculable significance. So much so, that it still provides the foundation for the increasingly rickety structure of National Curriculum English. Language in education work in the 1970s and early 1980s built on Vygotsky's insight that the infant's earliest language for social communication turned inwards to become innner speech and the basis of verbal thinking (Vygotsky, 1986).

Research studies have increasingly focused on the social context of adult and child partnership in which these important developments occur. It was

Vygotsky who pointed out that 'What the child can do in cooperation today he can do alone tomorrow' (*op. cit.*, p. 188). Britton updates his book (1992) with an example of this taken from Bruner: a mother and infant evolve the appropriate language forms for the management of playful giving and taking routines as they pass a ball back and forth (Britton, 1992, p. 276–7). We have in this observation some early indicators of the ways in which grammatical cases may originate in the meaningful use of language to communciate and to get things done. We also have the source of such notions as language learning being a kind of apprenticeship in which the older and wiser initiate the younger and least experienced into the ways of the language tribe, or club (Smith, 1988).

This theoretical model of apprenticeship was also applied to early literacy learning and it continues to challenge the simple transmission model of education imposed by the Education Reform Act. Modern psychological studies of learning in childhood have emphasized the social situations in which language and learning are negotiated and provide examples of children not just using the language but also acting out in play the social practices embodied in the languages of their communities (Beveridge, 1982; Walkerdine, 1988). In terms of recent proposals to make young children speak Standard English on the school premises, this is not just a different road, it is a different country!

Britton's original publication was deeply imbued with a love of literature and, just like Vygotsky many years before him, he used quotations and situations from poems, novels and plays to illuminate complex and multi-layered concepts and emotions. This tradition has been continued in the work of Wells (1987) and Bruner (1986) focused on narrative. More recently it has surfaced in studies of the power of 'folk psychology' (Bruner, 1990), in which we use our everyday autobiographical stories, gossip and beliefs to order and make sense of life.

These approaches have inspired a far more literary approach to the teaching and learning of reading and encouraged some degree of critical awareness of the linguistic and literary qualities of the texts which beginning readers are expected to use. In the new edition of *Language and Learning* the author's concern for the language of literature and for its power to operate at the extreme limits of our feelings and perceptions is undiminished. We are introduced to Vygotsky's inspirational claim that literature has always been a 'long range program for changing our behavior and our organism' (Vygotsky, 1971, p. 253), and reminded that literature preserves our awareness of the ineffable, the non-logical, the playful, the sub-verbal and the limits of language. All qualities to be treasured at a time when the purposes of education are increasingly 'read off in terms of a market economy' (Britton, 1992, p. 316).

But all this has been possible on the road not taken, although the first steps along the route chosen by central government were fairly reassuring, as we seemed to travel similar terrain and the two roads even appeared to run parallel at times. Our early guides looked back to the Bullock Report (DES, 1975) for models of good practice to be developed and still understood the teaching of literature and respected the insights about language offered by professional linguists and teachers (DES, 1988a; 1988b; 1989b). What we did not fully appreciate at the time is that some of these sensible procedures were already fatally weakened by government interference (Cox, 1991) and that the input from modern linguistics would eventually be embargoed (Carter, 1990).

Given the tightness of its remit, the Cox Report (DES, 1988b; 1989b) could not be perfect, but it is now possible to see that of all the National Curriculum subject reports it was arguably the most flexible and professionally useful. It is quite deliberately vague and undogmatic on those issues which are matters of complexity and variability and which must, therefore, be left to the judgement of professionals. A brief reminder of some of the strong moments in 'Cox' indicates that this kind of curriculum legislation is at its best when it provides 'attractive possibilities of a take-it-or-leave-it kind' (Britton, 1992, p. 8), leaving teachers with the responsibility for making educational and pedagogic decisions.

Talk as a means of learning was established as the basis of the curriculum, not just the English curriculum, and given high status as the first profile component in English. Teachers, particularly early years practitioners, who had valued and encouraged speaking and listening in their classrooms, now had a document which strengthened and legitimated their practices and asserted that oral work should continue to be developed, even in the later phases of education.

This concern for spoken language was expressed in terms of its variety, appropriateness and stylistic range and sensitivity; clearly a reflection of the linguistic, or 'knowledge about language', element which ran through the report. Knowledge about language, for pupils and for teachers, was focused on opening up for discussion the contentious issues of standard English dialect, other dialects, accents and multilingualism in a multiethnic society with a long history of assumed monolingualism. These issues are addressed elsewhere in the context of modern linguistics (Whitehead, 1990) and will be focused on in Eve Gregory's discussion of bilingualism in a later chapter.

However, the report's approach to literature also introduced a richly pluralist theme:

> We have taken within our remit literature from all parts of the English speaking world. Children whose families come, for example, from the Caribbean, from countries in Africa or from the Indian sub-continent can greatly enrich discussion about English as a world language and about literature and drama as world concepts.
>
> (DES, 1989b, para. 10.15)

To this enriched world view of literature we could also add the requirement that all teachers understand the significance of narrative and provide their pupils with some experiences of pre-twentieth-century literature (DES, 1988b, para. 6.2). This does not prove to be difficult for early years professionals who continue to use the traditional material of nursery rhymes, myths, legends and folk and fairy tales in their daily teaching.

There has been constant criticism of the reading requirements set out in the Cox report and it is true that they demonstrate a level of blessed unprescriptiveness which we have recently had cause to appreciate! Arguments over conflicting methodologies and materials for the initial teaching of reading are properly a matter for research and academic and professional debate. These complex issues can only be codified in prescriptive legislation at the risk of stifling research and development and fossilizing errors and misunderstandings, as has already become apparent with respect to 'real books' and 'phonics'.

The area of writing was tackled with a lightness of touch in the first report (DES, 1988b), covering the years 5–11, which still cheers the embattled educator. Suddenly, and quite unexpectedly, we were leafing through a government document containing an appendix full of examples of young children's work, annotated with a powerful developmental focus (Appendix 6). Furthermore, the main section of the report was quite clear in its claim that learning to write was not a simple linear process, but a recursive developmental matter of steadily refining features already in use and partly understood (*op. cit.*). Finally, the voice of the educator and teacher could still be heard in the frank admission that the 'best writing is vigorous, committed, honest and interesting' and cannot be mapped on to levels (*op. cit.*, para. 10.19).

The constant tinkering and skirmishing with all aspects of the National Curriculum finally settled on English in 1992, with the advice to the Secretary of State for Education that the English order should be revised (NCC, 1992a). The advice was a request for increased prescriptivism in the definitions and requirements for speaking, reading and writing, plus a strong hint that literature was to be valued mainly as a form of moral and spiritual training. The proposals which emerged in April 1993 are as tight and as traditional in their focus on the surface features of spoken and written language as had been expected. Listening and responding receive great emphasis, as does the use of reading schemes with a strong phonic approach. The official priorities are listed as standard English vocabulary and grammar, spelling and punctuation, all aspects of the teaching of initial reading and the literary heritage (DFE, 1993a, p. 6). Of course the literary heritage had already been safeguarded, first by the set Shakespeare texts, allocated according to age and ability of pupils, with specific questions to be answered; and, second, by the English literature anthology for all pupils at KS3 (DFE/SEAC, 1993a), with its ill-used bits of poetry, drama and prose to be learnt.

It is now certain that the proposed changes to the English order will be postponed for a period of two years (NCC/SEAC, 1993), but we should not forget that the proposals for a full 'nostalgia curriculum' are only on hold and certainly not withdrawn.

TALKING AND THINKING

For more than twenty years there has been a broad agreement in Britain and much of the English-speaking world that spoken language is the basis from which all areas of learning, including learning and teaching in schools, develop. This broad and positive agreement is particularly well exemplified in the work and publications of the National Oracy Project (NOP) set up in 1987 to promote oral work in all the phases of schooling and across all the curriculum subjects, and also to enhance teachers' skills and practices. A measure of agreement on the essentially twofold nature of talk is found in both linguistic and educational studies. In brief, it is clear that spoken language has an outward function which is communicative and social. Talk also has an inward function which is cognitive and concerned with understanding and thinking. These broad functions are clearly central to life and to learning and, although they may be subdivided in different ways for the purposes of different arguments and emphases, their unity and interconnectedness is indisputable. This fact alone accounts for both the educative power of oral work in the early years curriculum and for its problems when it is forced into a prescriptive National Curriculum straitjacket.

The NOP treats the communicative and social aspects of talk separately, defining communication as 'transferring meaning between people' and the social as 'getting along with people' (NCC/NOP, 1990, p. 8). These are powerful and valid definitions, but many experienced early years practitioners would be likely to share my reluctance to separate young children's communications from the 'social cement' kind of talk which binds them to their families, peers, carers and teachers. The examples of young children talking in this chapter are not easily categorized, but the 'getting along with you', or not, is woven in with the 'sharing what I do or do not know and understand'.

The inward aspect of talk has an essentially cognitive function and is concerned with the mulling over and ordering of experiences and feelings, in order to understand them. Such important activities are not limited to childhood, or to internalized talk and thinking: they are the stuff of playing, drama, narrative and literature and the driving concerns of a lifetime. However, they have their origins in the development of thinking and language in infancy and are frequently verbalized by the young child in egocentric talk-for-the-self and in communication with others. The cognitive function of internalized talk is not necessarily a silent or hidden process; it can, for instance, emerge in written communications in early and later childhood and it powers the writings of adult thinkers and writers. When very young children initially verbalize their thinking we have something akin to a window on the mind which reveals the child's insights, misunderstandings and unique concerns, as the spoken and the written examples from Natalie, at age 6, in the following sections will demonstrate. But even at 3 years, Natalie was engaged on the task of sorting out and evaluating such major experiences as starting kindergarten and having birthday parties, by means of talking aloud:

> Natalie (eating birthday cake): What is this for? whose is this cassette? this is for another day . . . the music [teacher] was there . . . inside a little bit and then I was outside later . . . I don't want this piece.
>
> (Engel and Whitehead, 1993)

This example feels very like verbal thinking with its complex clustering of questions, thematic links, temporal references and recalled events and people. However, the intellectual power of young children's talking and thinking is not only underestimated, it is frequently missed altogether, despite the work of Tizard and Hughes (1984) and Wells (1987) in the UK, and Vivian Paley in the USA:

> Lisa: (Pouring [pretend] tea.) My daddy says black people come from Africa.
> Wally: I come from Chicago.
> Lisa: White people are born in America.
> Wally: I'm black and I was born in Chicago.
>
> (Paley, 1981, p. 47)

Lisa and Wally are just 5-years-old, but in this duet in which t̶
adult claims is tested against the facts of individual experience anɑ
wanting, they socialize, they think and they unwittingly echo Americ
literary themes from Harper Lee to Alice Walker.

This powerful thinking in the early years is highly personal and reflects a fusion of unique life chances with cultural styles. When it is brought to bear on the business of schooling in the early years it has great educational potential. A potential which is best realized by activities and curricular approaches which are collaborative and active and engage children fully in talking, reflecting and doing:

> *C:* Do you know what colour sky is?
> *W:* Yeah – blue.
> *C:* Well, I done it on night time.
> *W:* Do some more blue on that side.
> *C:* 'Cos mine's – you're on the nother side of the world and I'm on this side of the world.
> *W:* And that's the path.
> *C:* So it's night on my world and it's morning on your world.
>
> (NCC/NOP, 1990, p. 9)

Now this is what should be meant by learning through talking, allied with the symbolic power of drawn representations, and it is certainly what we should mean when we contemplate exploring geographical concepts with young children. There is no way in which we can give children the facts or concepts of subject knowledge by a kind of compulsory injection. We can, however, provide the settings, the stories, the materials, the situations and the supportive adult partnerships which enable young children to talk the new and the unknown into the meaningful framework of recalled and known features of their lives.

The first section of this chapter referred to choices and alternative roads and provides a reminder that even the positive features of having a profile component for speaking and listening can be undermined by the direction taken. It is now apparent that there is a downside to all the positive points discussed above. The remainder of this section will focus on a set of problems and dangers in the current approach to speaking and listening in the early years curriculum.

First, the inevitable effect of making oral work a school curriculum 'subject' is to expose it to the demands and pressures for assessment and evidence in a curriculum which is driven by testing. No matter how well intentioned teachers and other early years professionals are, no matter how determined they are to concentrate on formative and diagnostic assessment, summative demands will be made and they will come to distort good practices in oral work. This is dangerous in the later years of education, but it is disastrous in the early years because it can undermine and devalue young children's self-esteem and their principal means of making sense of experience and relating themselves to their cultures and their communities.

Furthermore, any summative assessments of young children's speaking and listening competence are highly problematic, if not dubious. This is because of all the uncontrollable and even unknowable variables which can have their effects on talking and listening. For example, speaking and listening normally occur in social settings and are affected by, and are sensitive to, such things as conversational context, atmosphere, personalities, gender, race, emotion and even smells and furnishings. If the interior designers of restaurants, public houses and television studios know this, professional educators should at least remember it when assessment time comes round! Ironically, if there continue to be no formal requirements for the testing of talk at KS1 we are in the 'Catch 22' situation of no kudos and no priority time for the untestable and, therefore, unvalued elements of the curriculum.

Yet another factor in the assessment of oracy skills is the intriguing matter of speaker and listener choice. We can all choose to speak or to remain silent, to 'switch off' to another's speech, or to settle for minimal grunts and monosyllabic responses. Even apparently willing communication is only ever a partial reflection of the speaker/listener's linguistic competence. This is because language is not a one-off measurable unit held in some linguistic container in the head; it is a capacity which develops, changes and atrophies in complex interactions with life, languages and other people.

The situation of the bi- and multilingual child is relevant here, for the young speaker of more than one language does not simply translate in a straightforward one-to-one way between languages, even if that were possible, but evolves a kind of mixed staging-post or 'interlanguage' (Selinker, 1992). This facilitates between-languages movement in the early stages of bilingualism: the structures and even some words of a known language are incorporated into initial attempts at using the new target language. In the past these strategies were mistakenly called errors or 'interference', but the facts seem to be more complex than was once realized.

The constant underestimating of the skills of young bilinguals is compounded by a widespread failure to recognize the difference between productive and receptive language skills. Babies listen before they verbalize and we all understand more of a foreign language than we can speak, particularly if we learnt it in a formal way and have no need to use it on a daily basis. There is growing evidence that many of the young underestimated bilingual pupils in our schools actually function outside the school assessment situation as highly competent and linguistically sophisticated family and community interpreters (Mills and Mills, 1993).

The recent story of National Curriculum English has featured a retreat from any serious concern with modern linguistic knowledge and a retrenchment of old prejudices about proper standard English and prescriptive grammar. General ignorance and confusion about spoken and written grammars are being written into recommended classroom practices and testing and assessment procedures. Yet it is clear to any recorder and observer of spontaneous spoken utterances that language in action is, like the 'interlanguage' of bilingualism referred to above, a complex reflection of thinking being 'shaped at the point of utterance' (Britton, 1992, p. 296). We really should be able to reject the negative stance of describing what we find difficult to understand as 'mistakes' and pursue the notion that very young children's, and even adults', free-wheeling improvisations in speech are intellectual achievements.

As evidence of this, we can cite the research of Ruth Weir in 1962 and Katherine Nelson in 1989, who collated and analysed the presleep monologues of a 2-year-old boy (Weir, 1962) and a 2-year-old girl (Nelson, 1989). These studies, separated by more than two decades, provide evidence that while alone in bed and on the edge of sleep, some little children go over the events of their day, play and experiment with the sounds of language, practise linguistic structures, borrow and try out adult utterances and create episodic narratives about their experiences. All this research was recorded in family homes, but linguistic improvisation still goes on in supportive nursery settings:

> Mollie is brought to school everyday before eight. In the empty rooms, her large vocabulary pours out in search of time and place.
> 'I'm not too big to reach that,' she says, trying to hang up her jacket. 'But my already birthday is going to come now. Then I can be big to reach it.'
> 'When is your birthday, Mollie?'
> 'Tomorrow. It's called October ninth.'
>
> (Paley, 1986, p. 4)

The syntax of spoken language is pushed hard here as 3-year-old Mollie expresses her passion for making sense of school and adults, for locating herself in this new world and for preserving her own self-esteem.

In contrast, the grammar of written language is stabilized by the processes of writing and especially by the retention of standard usages over time. It is less subject to change and idiosyncratic forms (novelists and poets being honourable exceptions to this, of course), and more amenable to reflection, alteration and 'polishing up'. Written language grammars are different, not better, and they are not the perfect state to which all spoken grammars aspire. We do not aim to talk like a book in our daily personal and professional conversations and even the most formal delivery of a written paper or speech will be disastrous if the speaker fails to address and acknowledge his or her audience by eye contact and a few 'spoken' asides.

The recent proposal (DFE, 1993a) to force children to speak in standard English dialect by the end of KS2 is not defensible and not even achievable. This is because of all the complex variables discussed above. Vigorous and thoughtful language reflects personality, social context, upbringing and culture, emotional judgements and aspirations. We start by speaking in the linguistic forms and accents of those who nurture us; later we may choose to speak like others we admire, or at least wish to be associated with; and we are quite likely to keep our options open and become bidialectal. In the past, attempts at linguistic coercion have always failed but they have left a legacy of contempt and personal humiliation, for coercers and coerced. Children and young people can explore and discuss the social and economic influences of certain dialects and the nature of accents; they can model their own speaking on other dialects if they judge this to be desirable or useful. They can also be taught to write the structures of standard written English when they are appropriate, because that is how formal communications are written. Writing is always more fixed and less personal than speech, although even this judgement is challenged by a small child's note to granny, or an adult's incoherent letter of grief and loss. What is certain is that how we speak is far too closely bound up with our own sense of self-worth to be legislated for by civil servants and central government committees. Any further steps taken down this road can only result in large numbers of already disadvantaged children being 'made tongue-tied by authority' (NATE, 1992).

Young children talking and thinking in partnership with supportive adults are operating at the leading edge of their potential, in a zone of proximal development (Vygosky, 1978). At this level they are enabled to go well beyond the limitations of what they can do alone and unaided. This discussion has been a demonstration of the power and complexity of language taking children beyond themselves, so to speak, and it stands in sharp contrast to anything in the attainment targets and tests we have seen suggested and used in schools. The 1993 proposals for English may well be shelved for now, but they evade all the complex issues of language learning and teaching by emphasizing communication in spoken standard English (whose or which SE is not made clear) and listening and responding. This latter change in priorities is very disturbing, it hints at a return to 'the good old days' when children listened, teachers talked and children responded, in clear diction, with answers which their teachers knew already!

READING AND LITERATURE

Reading and literature have been linked together in the legislation for National Curriculum English and this not unreasonable arrangement can be used to explore the 'road not taken', as well as the likely direction early years teachers will be required to take. Writing about the teaching of initial reading is, like Shakespeare criticism, a major industry, but stern discipline will be exercised by this writer in order to restrict herself to a small set of issues! The discussion will begin with an eccentric review of 'basics' and then consider some recent reading debates. Any suggestion that a degree of subversive levity permeates the discussion is entirely intentional.

The start of this chapter set out to debunk the myth of the 'one agreed literacy' for schools to transmit and this has a corollary: why not alternative notions of the 'basics'? A non-standard set of basics for reading and literature would include: language play and metalinguistic awareness; narrative; and life's big questions. This list may not seem as straightforward and sensible as the conventional literacy checklists, such as sounds, spelling, punctuation and handwriting, but it is arguably more fundamental and closer to the nature of early learning.

Metalinguistic awareness, for example, involves sensitivity to the nature of language itself and includes all kinds of knowledge about language: its forms, varieties and its sounds. It has been generally assumed in the past that such sophisticated knowledge could only be expected to develop after considerable exposure to learning to read and write. However, there is widespread evidence from research with very young children who are pre-literate that they can be remarkably articulate about the sounds and even the structures of languages. The studies by Weir (1962), Nelson (1989) and Britton (1992), already referred to in this chapter, are rich in examples, as are those which focus on children's love of nonsense and rhymes, for example, Chukovsky (1963), Bryant and Bradley (1985) and Opie (1993). These are all very different kinds of studies, but they are picking up similar phenomena to that surfacing in Vivian Paley's nursery as the children exploit the alliteration and onomatopoeia of funny names:

'My name is Strawberry Shortcake.'
'My name is Lemon Meringue.'
'Mine is bumpety-bump down the stairs.'
'Mine is lumpety-lump down the stairs.'

(Paley, 1986, p. 43)

Or engage in the ancient language game of riddling:

'It's something dark purple in a red can.'
'Apple juice.'
'That's not purple. I said purple.'
'Purple juice. Cranapple.'
'No, it's Cranapple, the kind my mother buys.'

(*Ibid.*, p. 143)

Playing with rhymes and transposing letter sounds can soon lead to those subversively 'rude' forms which worry so many adults who regard literacy as no joking matter! This becomes clear when children escape from the confines of the classroom (Opie, 1993), or when an adventurous reading scheme introduces a book of Spoonerisms (Yorke, 1986) and is severely criticized by over-anxious parents some years later, when solemn National Curriculum English prevails! Once you go to big school and start to learn to read you leave stories about 'a dormal nay in the life of Smim Jith' in the playground and jettison yet another support for early literacy!

Narrative remains the crucial support which enables children to engage with the sense and the pleasure of early reading and sustains them through the inevitable slowing-down patches which occur as they tackle individual word recognition and phonological patterns. Narrative also provides a bridge from fictive stories to those stories we call 'true' or factual, helping children to handle history, astronomy and geology with the sense-making tools of narrative. This narrative ordering and evaluating which enables children, and adults, to sort out the new by putting it in the context of the known was recently demonstrated in a conversation with my grand-daughter, Natalie, aged 6:

Natalie: Do you know about Shakespeare?
M.W.: Yes, I think so, why?
Natalie: We're doing Shakespeare things at school.
M.W.: Really?
Natalie: Mm . . . Did you know that he wrote lots of poems and stories for boys and girls?
M.W.: Well, he wrote exciting plays for acting – and poems.
Natalie: Did he have a real name like me, like I'm called Natalie?
M.W.: Oh yes. Shakespeare was his surname. You know, the name of his family. His first name was William.
Natalie: Oh good – like I'm Natalie and Daniel's Daniel. [her brother].

Good indeed in terms of going for the nub of sorting out this Shakespeare business: if he was a real person he must be properly named and enter the human arena with the rest of us! The poetry and the drama will follow.

This is a reminder that children are better guides to the basics in terms of lesson planning and curriculum projects than ring-binders. The fragments of a conversation or a carefully observed and recorded piece of behaviour must remain at the heart of the early years curriculum; without these windows on children's minds we work in the dark.

Natalie's questions were also in the area of the 'big questions' about life which literature poses. This same concern is expressed with stunning simplicity, and attributed to Harold Loukes, in a recent discussion about good teaching and religious education: they are 'A conversation between older and younger alike on the simple question, "What is life like?"' (Broadbent, 1993, p. 14).

The simple questions of young children are often as unnerving and challenging as this and are the stuff of literature and of moral and religious education. They do not sit comfortably with narrow and reductive notions about the canon of literature or the 'good' books we must all read. Indeed, the good things of poetry and stories are usually those nasty moments when we are faced with greed, lust, cruelty and betrayal, or the dilemmas of conflicting interests and the pain of growing up and letting go. These difficult issues are as common in literature for young children as are humour, slapstick and subversion: 'the most thoroughgoing satirical attacks in the Alice books are directed at education. All the adults, especially those who resemble governesses or professors, are foolish, arbitrary, cruel, or mad' (Lurie, 1990, p. 6). Until recently we could possibly shrug off this as a dated and wildly exaggerated satire on the world of education seen 'Through the Looking-Glass', but now it has an alarming familiarity.

The reading debates which rage on, despite helpful case studies and research reports which confirm that in the early stages of literacy most teachers use a variety of methods and approaches (Cato *et al.*, 1992), seem to have a life of their own. They barely touch the realities of classroom life and yet they do great harm by undermining serious professional discussions and giving many hostages to fortune. I have in mind here the erroneous assumptions throughout the National Curriculum documentation that, for example, teachers do not use reading schemes, do not develop children's phonic skills and do not encourage children to read widely. The current state of play in the professional debates about reading are increasingly focused on getting the balance of the different perspectives right (Beard, 1993). To this end, early years educators must clarify what is important in the all-important early stages of literacy. And at this point in the discussion, it is increasingly difficult to sustain a tight distinction between reading and writing, but that is no bad thing.

Many misunderstandings about the use of reading materials such as 'real books' have led to quite unwarranted assertions about reading methodologies and appear to assume that materials and teaching methods are one and the same thing. Yet there is absolutely nothing in the reading of genuine narrative, poetic or information texts which precludes detailed focusing on new words, particular language structures or new ways of using known forms. There is, however, the bonus that the quality text will be a reflection of genuine concerns which the young reader can engage with and a source of the kind of richness and complexity which promotes talk and imaginative representations and recall. It may well be that a quality picture book also extends the reading of images and links with the human passion for creating forms and marks which stand for whole ranges of feeling and thinking.

The current pressure on teachers to depend even more on simplified and controlled initial reading texts, or reading schemes, is in danger of persuading us all that complexity, unpredictability and variety in texts for young children is a bad thing. Yet children do need to experience both variety and predictability in their language and literacy encounters. Supportive teaching will enable them to develop strategies for tackling the off-beat yet rhythmically predictable pages of *Each Peach Pear Plum* (Ahlberg and Ahlberg, 1977) and the almost boring safety of Rosie the Hen's walk round the farmyard before tea (Hutchins, 1968). There may, of course, be more to this latter book than I have noticed, but I shall check with the children! We must also bear in mind that the texts we make available to beginning readers are potential models for their own writing development and the same balance of predictable forms and challenging variations is essential.

The importance of phonological playfulness, sensitivity to rhyme and all the sound-based chiming qualities of language has been raised earlier in this chapter. There is at present a renewed professional interest in the role of early phonological awareness and rhyme in initial reading success (Whitehead, 1993) and this is coinciding with a demand from the National Curriculum Council and government ministers for the teaching of phonic skills (DFE, 1993a). The danger in this collision of concerns is that the richness of the properly tentative research-based work on phonology, phonemics, alphabetic systems and rhyme will stay outside the classroom, while 'knowing your sounds' and doing this week's phonic family will swamp reading approaches in schools.

As we enter the inevitable next phase of reappraising the teaching of initial reading and literacy there are misleading myths which early years teachers must counter. Among these are the assertions that teachers who put meaning before discrete skills and the pleasures of literature before spelling tests, cling to some idea that literacy is as natural as walking and requires little, if any, teaching. These calumnies have dogged all of us who have attempted to teach initial literacy in developmentally sensitive and linguistically aware ways and advocated these approaches in professional discussions (Whitehead, 1992a).

Early years professionals are probably as aware as any teachers can be that young children come from cultures and social groups which have evolved many and various ways of representing language in graphical forms. Some children may well speak languages which do not have written codes, but which are still complex and subtle systems for the purposes of communicating and thinking. Furthermore, close involvement with very young children who frequently ask about writing in packages, books, the home and the wider environment, or ask for help to do writing themselves, soon convinces early years professionals and parents that writing is not in the genes.

However, it is deeply embedded in most contemporary cultures and in the social worlds of children and it has very high status, and children always pick up the hidden messages about 'what counts' in our adult world. So, naturally, they do need to find out what is in it for them; failure to connect the curriculum with this search in the early years of education is likely to undermine the chidren's literacy learning. So we come to the issue of teaching literacy, for undoubtedly literacy is learnt and taught, although when the teaching is skilled, appropriate and successful the learning seems almost magical. However, reading and writing are not natural and effortless, but neither are they well taught by being structured to the point of stupidity. Just as literacy serves such crucial human needs as communicating across space and time, preserving records, expanding thinking and expressing our responses to life itself, so its teaching must be rooted in these same purposes from the start.

WRITING AND LEARNING

One day I got out of bed and my name is Lady Natalie I live in Battel Castle. and my friend invited me for tea She lived in Sea Castle then my maid packed my bags. then I went in my carriage I was wearing my red dress and my red slippers. on the way I saw a hill we went up the hill then the carriage stopped I

saw water I got out of the carriage then I had a drink of water. then I got in
my carriage then it went down the hill in the distance I saw Sea Castle then I
went in the castle my friend made tea. then I got in my carriage and went
home when I got home my maid unpacked my bags then I went to bed.

This is the first long story written by 6-year-old bilingual Natalie after nine
months of residence in the UK and attendance at an English infant school.
The text is long in format too, as it is written on a piece of paper 17 cm wide
and 59 cm long and rolled up into a scroll and tied with a red ribbon. The
text has bold full stops which mark the start of every line on the *left* hand
side (26 lines), in addition to the stops reproduced above, and is illustrated
by four tiny vignette-like coloured drawings of the two castles, Lady
Natalie in her red dress and slippers, and Lady Natalie back home in bed at
the end. The story was written at home during a half-term holiday and the
spelling of some words was dictated by an adult, as and when Natalie
asked. The long strip of paper was a fortuitous discovery in a pack of scraps
for drawing and painting.

It is important to have 'real' texts like this in front of us when we
contemplate the complexities and the joys of learning to write in the early
years. It is absolutely essential to be able to refer to such examples of
young children's struggles and strategies as they make the written language
their own and use it to make sense of school 'subjects'. The current order
(DES, 1989b) was commended in the earlier part of this chapter for its
sensitivity to the developmental aspects of learning to write, and it is worth
noting at this point that it is very clear on the importance of keeping the
secretarial and the compositional skills of writing separate in the early
stages. This is because each requires different kinds of teaching support;
the creative and cognitive aspect described as composition must have the
highest priority, because forcing young children to go for secretarial polish
from the start is a recipe for defeat and despair. Unfortunately, the latter
recipe is exactly what we find in the 'deferred' proposals for English (DES
1993a), with a strong emphasis at KS1 on the use of conventional spelling,
punctuation, grammatical organization and legible and accurately formed
handwriting.

As a matter of fact, Natalie does meet many of these criteria in this, her
personal response to a school project on 'The Age of Castles', but she also
does many other far more interesting and 'writerly' things which serve to
underline the superficial nature of the path chosen for National Curriculum
English.

In responding to Natalie's writing the professional early years educator
would note her skill in making sense of mediaeval life in terms of her own

experiences of much travelling between countries, reflected in the emphasis on packing and unpacking bags, as well as visiting places of historic interest, and going to tea with friends. There is no doubt that a strong sense of narrative form has been internalized by the young writer, as this 'day in the life of' account demonstrates, reflecting some substantial input from traditional and contemporary stories which always get the protagonist back home and safely into bed. The formulaic going up and down hills may be an echo of the phonic-based reading scheme in use throughout Natalie's school. There is also a delightful 'quirkiness' in this genuine kind of engagement with writing and history, from the inspired response to a long scroll-like piece of paper and the search for a ribbon seal, to the experimental play with the full stops which march down the left-hand side of the text. Perhaps these act as markers for the start of each line, but they are a reminder that Natalie's other language is modern Hebrew which is written from right to left, so Hebrew lines of text would tend to terminate on the left, with a high proportion of stops on that side. There are some interesting tense changes in the piece as the writer is drawn into the present reality of her narrative, 'my name is . . .', 'I live in . . .', and momentarily slips out of the story-teller's traditional past tense. This latter convention is still reasserted for much of the story, as in 'then my maid packed my bags'. The total silence on the nature of the socializing at Sea Castle, apart from the brewing of tea, contrasted with the great emphasis put on stopping for water is intriguing. Is the drink of water just a gesture towards historical authenticity? Or a reflection of this particular child's life experiences of living for her first six years in the great heat of the eastern Mediterranean, where a drink of water really matters?

The complexity, richness and uncertainty of what we can learn from young writers like Natalie must be central to our approaches to early literacy, although such qualities are not acknowledged in recent proposals, as Armstrong (1993, p. 16) points out: 'The distinctiveness of young children's punctuation, the subtle inconsistency of their treatment of tense, the novelty of their narrative forms, are unrecognised.'

The powerful dynamic of young children's desire to know about things does not follow easily predicted paths, as I was reminded on my next visit to Natalie. Suddenly she was into handwriting and I was required to teach her 'joined up'. Of course I did my best and this particular young writer is now experimenting with the loops and tails which eventually lead to cursive script.

Children 'teach their teachers' (Meek, 1991), they also teach their grannies, and the particular egg I am now sucking on is the renewed interest in handwriting in the early years! Recent research (Sassoon, 1990a, 1990b) may offer a way out of the dreary impasse which left teachers and children practising the low-level cosmetics of letter formation, but with no sustaining rationale which linked handwriting to other aspects of children's development and social experience. The work of Sassoon is empowering in its emphasis on developing a comfortable and flowing hand which is not divorced from the affective and aesthetic pleasures of movement, drawing and art. The approach is apparently free from much of the dogma of 'ball and stick' print in the early years and 'real joined-up' writing for the junior-school years, and no sensible links (literally!) between the two experiences. Just as good reading teachers encourage and support children who begin to read silently, no matter how young they are, so this research appears to recommend support for children who move to a flowing cursive at an early stage.

The only note of reservation I would make is that enthusiasm for the approach involves some lack of respect and understanding for what young writers are doing (Sassoon, 1993, p. 187) when they experiment with marks and letter-like forms and create 'pretend', but fully intentional, messages and statements. The zeal to intervene in very young children's developmental writing, so as to prevent the development of bad writing habits, could be as unwise as 'correcting' left-handed writers and insisting on universal spoken standard English dialect on the school premises.

Professional early years teachers should always be ready to evaluate and learn from research, but they must make sense of it in terms of their expertise in child development, language development and child observations. The decision to implement any research findings in the classroom is a professional one and subject to the practitioner's knowledge of children in general and these children in particular.

SUMMARY AND CONCLUSIONS

The central claim of this chapter has been that language development in the early years is far more than National Curriculum English, as we now have it or as it is likely to be. This could not be otherwise when we take seriously the common-sense fact that language, or languages, develop long before formal schooling and KS1 begins. If we add to the power of common sense the indisputable research evidence from twentieth-century psychology and linguistics, we have a picture of language development which is rooted in early nurturing and socialization, long before recognizable words appear, and bound up with thinking and cultural ways of making life meaningful. An achievement of this complexity must over-shadow the minor concerns of the English orders for England and Wales. For this reason, an attempt was made to dismantle some prevalent but unhelpful myths about primary teachers and about language and literacy.

In attempting to review the road we have followed and predict the nature of the way ahead in language and English teaching, an account of some crucial educational debates and publications which span the past twenty-five years was set down. This exercise in remembering and predicting resulted in regrets for the road not taken and serious reservations about the current direction of English in the early years.

The discussions of talking and thinking, reading and literature, and writing and learning were closely focused on young learners in order to highlight the nature and extent of their achievements before formal schooling, as well as outside school settings. These sections also indicated the kinds of teacher interventions which could develop and extend young children's language and literacy.

Any conclusion to a chapter on the challenges and the joys of coming to understand young children as emergent persons and linguists must reiterate the importance of respecting idiosyncrasies, complexity, difficulties and the not-known. We are regularly bludgeoned by the simple claims of the simple-minded who come up with simple solutions for educational issues which would tax the strongest minds! It is not surprising that gifted children frequently underachieve in educational systems which dampen playfulness, discourage quirkiness and take thinking to be synonymous with 'facts'. Yet these open-ended characteristics are typical of the thinking of very young children who have not yet entered a system driven by the 'measurement' of skills and mastery. Schools still fail the gifted as well as the less able, and this institutionalized loss of potential challenges all of us to question the curriculum we are given and renew our struggles to make it negotiable and, therefore, meaningful to the children we teach.

Teachers of young children must be the intellectuals who are at the forefront of nursery and classroom-based research, constantly trying to find out what is really going on. It is not easy: 'The first duty of an intellectual is to know what's going on and it's very hard work' (Cockburn, 1992, p. x). But it guarantees far more job satisfaction than can ever be found in doing what we are told.

6
MATHEMATICS IN THE NATIONAL CURRICULUM: IMPLICATIONS FOR LEARNING IN THE EARLY YEARS

Gillian Thumpston

Mathematics is not only taught because it is useful. It should also be a source of delight and wonder, offering pupils intellectual excitement, for example in the discovery of relationships, the pursuit of rigour and the achievement of elegant solutions. Pupils should also appreciate the essential creativity of mathematics: it is a live subject which is continuously evolving as technology and the needs of society evolve.

(DES, 1988, para. 2.2)

Mathematics has an important part to play in the education of all children and early years educators are committed to developing children's mathematical understanding, knowledge and skills. Mathematics is constantly evolving, the modes of representation and the ways they are used are constantly changing. There can, therefore, be no one correct form of mathematics, mathematics learning or teaching. This implies that we must continually evaluate the values and theories that underlie our practice, as well as the practice itself. Such evaluation enables us to analyse theoretical perspectives offered by others and challenge external influences which move us away from the processes essential to education.

Early years teachers have worked hard to implement National Curriculum mathematics so it would be natural to assume that assertions of raised standards could be seen as a positive outcome of their efforts. Assessment of mathematics in the National Curriculum is having a significant influence upon the mathematics curriculum offered to young children (Ofsted, 1993a; 1993b) and the effects of these influences are causing concern. The continual assertions that the National Curriculum has raised standards in mathematics leads to a situation in which external influences are placing

110

pressure on teachers to adopt teaching methods which are producing 'successful' short-term outcomes at the expense of true mathematics education.

Two years after the introduction of mathematics in the National Curriculum in 1989, a major revision took place and it is informative to return to the original proposals, not only to see what has been retained but also what has been omitted. Issues discussed in the document relating to the mathematics curriculum, to the teaching and learning of mathematics and the assessment of that learning have significance for the dilemma in which many early years mathematics educators now find themselves. With hindsight it would appear that the working group identified areas of the mathematics curriculum which continue to give rise to debate and concern. These include the nature of mathematics, standards of arithmetic skills, the needs of the work place and the role of calculators and computers. These issues have significance here as they contribute to the discussion of the impact of National Curriculum mathematics upon the teaching and learning of mathematics in the early years.

The National Curriculum view of mathematics learning is exemplified in the assessment and testing arrangements for this area of the curriculum. The central purpose of assessment in an educational context is to support the development of the learner. Assessment is an integral part of teaching which informs the teaching and learning process and educational decision-making. It is not fundamentally about providing information for others, although National Curriculum assessment of mathematics is very much about provision of such information. Indeed, the reasons for the 1991 revision of the statutory orders for mathematics appeared to be that the structure of the 14 attainment targets made mathematics in the National Curriculum difficult to test, reporting to parents was too complicated and the consistency and continuity of GCSE standards would be at risk unless the number of attainment targets was reduced. The objective was to simplify the structure so as to make the assessment arrangements more manageable (NCC, 1991b). There is a real danger of assessment leading the mathematics curriculum and where assessment is driven by tightly defined objectives (DES, 1988c) this is particularly worrying (Stenhouse, 1975).

The provision of information concerning children's mathematics learning is important for parents and other teachers, but the link between the publication of 'league tables' and meeting the needs of individual learners is tenuous. Furthermore it would appear that assessment of mathematics in the National Curriculum, particularly in the form of standard assessment tasks (SATs), is promoting forms of teaching mathematics which run counter to that which research evidence shows to be ways of ensuring that young children realize their potential (Morgan, 1992; Threlfall, 1992; Gray and Tall, 1993).

The constructive feedback about KS1 SATs received from HMI, teachers and independent evaluators by the Schools Examinations and Assessment Council (SEAC) has led to the assumption by some that KS1 SATs are of high quality. However, for example, Morgan (1992) has shown that the SAT for the old mathematics Attainment Target 3 (Ma3), concerned with number operations, does not give a true measure of mathematical ability, nor does it measure potential mathematical ability.

CHILDREN LEARNING MATHEMATICS – 'IS IT AN ADD, MISS?'

For many adults mathematics is identified as arithmetic and, while number pervades the mathematics curriculum and is an important aspect of the young child's mathematical thinking, mathematics itself is much broader than counting and calculating. Mathematics is a powerful means of communication, a way of solving problems, it is a search for patterns and relationships, it is a creative activity which involves imagination, intuition, exploration and should involve enjoyment.

Too often in mathematics the affective domain is ignored. Eisner (1982) and Donaldson (1978) highlight the importance of sense and feeling in cognition and argue that recognition must be given to the affective factors including the context of personal relationships in learning. All learners, whether children or adults, learn best when they enjoy and are motivated by what they are doing. It is enlightening to reflect upon our own experience and endeavour to discover the 'delight and wonder' in our mathematics education.

The influence of interpersonal and emotional factors upon mathematics learning can be seen if we recognize that learners are actively trying to make sense of their mathematical experience. When children are presented with material that is not intelligible they still attempt to assimilate it. They are aware that they cannot find meaning in the material but do not realize that the fault is not theirs. This can create an anxiety in the learner that can lead to negative attitudes towards mathematics. Anxiety itself may increase the difficulty of understanding; the more anxious the learner becomes the harder he or she tries, which leads to even less understanding (Skemp, 1971; Buxton, 1981). How did children make sense of the bizarre 'sums' that required, for example, the answer to 6 + 2 to be written in the outline shape of a pineapple and 4 + 1 in the plum, which formed part of the 1992 mathematics SAT?

The working group (DES, 1988c) defined five broad areas of mathematics: number, algebra, measurement, shape and space and data handling, but emphasized that while it is convenient to group mathematics in these areas they cannot be considered in isolation from each other. Mandatory national tests that focus upon one aspect of mathematics, in this case number, together with the proposal that the 'principal task' of the Key Stage 1 teacher is to 'ensure that pupils master the basic skills of reading, writing and number' (NCC/SEAC, 1993, p. 29) is unlikely to foster a broad mathematics curriculum which takes account of what children already know and supports their overall development as learners.

It must not be forgotten that children come to school with a variety of understandings, misunderstandings, methods and problem-solving strategies which they have constructed for themselves and which may be different from those taught. Mathematics learners are actively attempting to construct mathematics for themselves on the basis of their personal experience. Young children, for example, often demonstrate their knowledge of and fascination with large numbers that have meaning for them, the number on their front door, a bus number, their telepone number. This does not mean that they have a secure grasp of the numbers that lead up to these numbers, or an understanding of place value of the individual digits but they are developing their ways of thinking as their experience broadens, building on meaningful knowledge which has already been constructed (Shuard, 1986). Importance must be given to the children's mathematical background in order to build on the informal and untaught strategies they possess when they start school and should not be limited by ceilings placed upon learning by arbitrary levels such as only working with numbers up to ten. Their strategies may not be totally reliable, but they are meaningful to children (*op. cit.*), and should be the basis from which mathematical education starts. The notion of children's potential in mathematics demands that teachers use their professional judgement to provide appropriate learning experiences not just those that fall within the required levels of the attainment targets.

In contexts which make sense to them and allow them to deploy the skills they possess, young children are highly competent (Donaldson, 1978). There is now substantial evidence to show that young children start school with considerable mathematical abilities in the area of addition and subtraction provided the numbers involved are small and involve specific objects or events (Gelman and Gallistel, 1978; Hughes, 1983). Hughes (1986) argues that it is the formal codes of mathematics not the concepts that cause children confusion and difficulty. While the children may have an abstract understanding of number in the sense that they can apply their knowledge to new situations, they cannot express this knowledge in the abstract formal language of mathematics. Children have to learn to translate from a mode of representation that takes a real form, 'Three people can work with the sand, there are two of us now, so one more person can join in', their meaningful personal mathematics, to one that uses the formal code of mathematics such as 'one and three makes four, or $3 - 1 = 2$'.

Hughes considers that it is the 'translation procedures', the strategies that children develop for translating from one form of representation to another that are vital to success in understanding arithmetic. The concept of 'translation' provides an important way of thinking about mathematical understanding. The ability to translate fluently between different modes of representation is of paramount importance, yet it is the source of many difficulties which children have with mathematical problems. Children need to see that there is a reason for these translations, that they can help them to solve problems. While we as adults can see the advantages of making translations, children may not.

The work of Martin Hughes highlights the importance of formal manipulation of symbols and concrete experience and the disadvantage of the learner having one without the other. Children need help to form links between formal and concrete understanding, building on their informal methods of calculation and their invented symbolism in order to develop, understand and use more powerful formal modes of representation. Unfortunately children who do not easily make such connections are often given more paper and pencil work instead of talk and explanation. Learning to do arithmetic to set routines with no recognition of their own methods can lead children to perceive mathematics as a set of meaningless procedures.

Skemp (1989) identifies two categories of understanding in mathematics, relational and instrumental understanding. Relational understanding is not only knowing what to do but why, as it includes rationalization of the underlying mathematical relationships and properties. Instrumental understanding takes place when pupils and their teachers think they have understood something, because they get the answer right, but without knowing why their method works.

HMI (Ofsted, 1993a) report that the majority of pupils of all ages could perform calculations adequately *if they knew which operation was required*. Problems arose when the pupil was required to decide which operation to use. Mathematics is not about being given a page of sums and being told to do it. Competence in arithmetic requires relational understanding in order that learners are able to use number operations in order to solve their problems, not just perform a routine to obtain an answer which will be judged right or wrong by someone else. Consider the experience of the child who, when questioned about some addition and subtraction work he had done commented, 'I can do "adds" and "take aways" but I don't always do the right one. But it don't always matter 'cos you got a half and half chance you get it right', demonstrating a mathematical understanding that could not be perceived from his written work. The simplifying of National Curriculum assessment in mathematics at Key Stage 1 (KS1) is increasing pressure on teachers to concentrate on the practice of standard formal algorithms at the expense of developing children's understanding.

The ability to apply mathematics appropriately to unfamiliar problems is an essential element of mathematics. The link between mathematical knowledge and skills and their practical use is not obvious to all children and has to be learnt. HMI (Ofsted, 1993a) report that pupils whose understanding of number was most secure were those taught in classes where they encountered a variety of experiences which helped them to appreciate mathematical relationships. A model of mathematics learning that suggests techniques are learnt in isolation first and applied later cannot be countenanced; applications provide conceptual support and motivation for learning. Mathematics learning cannot be said to have taken place unless the understanding is transferable to other contexts and situations.

Using and applying mathematics is concerned with children's communication of mathematical thinking. Learning to communicate with and about mathematics is an important aspect of this area of the curriculum, and developing the ability and confidence to use mathematics in this way will also foster other important qualities such as perseverance, self-discipline, co-operation with others, imagination and flexibility. Provision for such learning must involve children working together co-operatively and talking about their work in order to share their knowledge, skills and understanding. It has been suggested that such activities promote mathematics learning but do not contribute to assessment of individual children (Shorrocks *et al.*, 1993). Many early years educators would argue that observation of such activities is essential in order to be able to make assessments of individual children (Lally, 1991; Hurst, 1992). The SEAC decision not to test Ma1 formally reinforces the contention that only knowledge, skills and understanding that are easy to test will shape National Curriculum mathematics. Curriculum priorities will be those identified as measurable (Eisner, 1985).

Children's mathematical ideas develop alongside an increasing awareness of language. However, the precise meaning of a word used in mathematics may be very different from the child's understanding of that word in an everyday situation. Certainly a difference between the numerals 7 and 9 is that one is composed of straight lines and the other curved lines. Children take time to learn the language of mathematics and will need to develop strategies to grasp the precise mathematical meaning of words such as 'difference', 'take away', 'equals'. For many children the first step towards solving a problem is to try to put it into a language that makes sense to them – using everyday language to clarify their thoughts. By describing mathematical relationships in different ways children can begin to understand the connections between mathematical ideas. Discussing the difference between the numbers 7 and 3, what is the sum of 4 and 3? How many more is 7 than 3? All are different ways of exploring the relationship between 4, 3 and 7 and, I would suggest, tell more about the child's understanding than a page of sums.

The starting-point for developing a more formal mathematical vocabulary is the child's own language. The learner needs to build upon his or her familiar use of words such as 'times' or 'share' to develop an understanding of the use of these words in a mathematical context and begin to use the more formal language of multiply and divide. Children who have wide experience of using language will be more confident at attempting to express ideas.

Assessing what children have achieved in a discussion session is not simple and straightforward; it involves the use of sophisticated observation skills and analysis of such observations. Such assessment takes time. However, the insights gained into the mathematical understanding of the children involved will be richer and more informative than, for example, the information obtained from the standard test purported to determine whether the children understand the language associated with number Ma 2/1. In this instance children were given 20 counters divided into two unequal piles and the teacher had to ask *either* 'Which pile has more?' *or* 'Which pile has fewer?' Apart from the obvious advantage of asking the first question rather than the second (which would you choose to ask the children in your class?), this highlights the absurdity of attempting to evaluate learning with 'simple straightforward' tests. All this activity can do is show whether the child can respond correctly to the word more or fewer in that situation.

The structure of assessment for mathematics in the National Curriculum is focused on reporting individual attainment which militates against collaborative work. Teachers may consider that children who are used to genuine group work could be disadvantaged when assessed in such a highly individualized way, even though collaborative activities which encourage discussion are among those experiences identified by HMI (Ofsted, 1993a) as supporting the acquisition of the mathematical language needed to develop understanding. An appropriate balance of whole-class, individual and group work, which is also a characteristic of good practice, may be jeopardized by this assessment format.

Mathematics is a network of ideas which are inter-related, and to concentrate unduly on one aspect of mathematics would be detrimental to the development of mathematical understanding, knowledge and skills (DES, 1982; 1988c). The potential contribution of mathematics to other areas of the curriculum, such as history, where census data may be analysed and represented through graphs and charts, science, which includes the use of measuring instruments, estimation, making and testing predictions, systematic recording, and design and technology, using modelling techniques such as drawings, scale models, recognizing the relationships between two-dimensional representation and three-dimensional shapes, as well as the significant contribution to communication, problem-solving and reasoning skills, supports the unique place of mathematics within the curriculum. In these ways mathematics can be seen to have a valuable contribution to make to the personal, social and intellectual development of every child.

THE TOOLS AND TECHNIQUES OF MATHEMATICS

A broad mathematical education is essential for all pupils if they are to recognize their true potential. However, one of the key issues that continues to be seen as central to mathematics is in the area of number, and involves traditional paper-and-pencil practices of skills and techniques, the place of calculators in the classroom and the need to ensure that all pupils are equipped with a 'basic' numerical competence. For some considerable length of time, at least one hundred years, there have been demands for improvements in the standards of number work in primary schools (McIntosh, 1977). Suggestions for such improvements have included the use of materials, practical activities, developing children's own methods of solving problems, encouraging discussion and aiming for understanding as well as a return to the 'basics'.

It would be interesting to discover when mathematics educators abandoned the basics. In 1965 the Schools Council observed that the mathematics curriculum in primary schools had remained virtually unchanged since the Education Act 1944. It suffered from a rigid approach and was divorced from everyday life; teachers clung to textbooks which transmitted content rather than aims and principles (Howson, 1983). In 1979 in response to public anxiety, the Secretary of State for Education and Science set up an inquiry into the teaching of mathematics. The results of this inquiry, *Mathematics Counts* (DES, 1982) supported broadening the curriculum, believing this would have 'a beneficial effect in improving attitudes towards mathematics and laying the foundations for better understanding' (*op. cit.*, para. 286).

> An excessive concentration on the purely mechanical skills of arithmetic for their own sake will not assist the development of understanding in these other areas. It follows that the results of the 'back to basics' approach (as we understand the words) are most unlikely to be those which its proponents wish to see, and we can in no way support or recommend an approach of this kind.
>
> (*op. cit.*, para. 278)

The Cockcroft Report (DES, 1982) drew attention to the importance of using mathematics to solve problems, mathematics arising from other curricular areas and the learner's attitude towards mathematics. Although the availability of calculators and computers was not as great as it is today, the implications for the mathematics curriculum were considered. The members of the comittee considered that the use of calculators and computers should be seen as a valuable aid to the teaching and learning of mathematics in the primary school. They indicated that the arithmetical aspects of the mathematics curriculum might need to be modified in the light of this development. Hughes (1986) raises the problem of the need to introduce children to the tools and techniques of mathematics which form part of our culture and which will help them solve problems. The impact of information technology on the primary mathematics curriculum has still to be fully realized. The technology of calculation is the biggest challenge to the content of school mathematics and it must be tackled if primary mathematics is not to consist of activities which are only done in school and have nothing to do with life (Shuard, 1986). Yet the use of a calculator is explicitly excluded in Ma 2/4 and non-calculator methods required to multiply or divide at Ma2/5 (DES, 1991b).

Mathematics in the National Curriculum would appear to be promoting the 'flat-iron curriculum' described by Anita Straker (1987). In her presidential address to the Mathematical Association Conference, Straker compares the use of a calculator in a mathematics lesson with the use of an electric iron in home economics. She argues that pupils are taught to use an electric iron – effective use of an up-to-date tool – they are not taught to use a flat iron nor to stretch clothes when they are wet in order to remove the creases. Compare this with the demand that pupils should calculate using appropriate pencil-and-paper methods without the use of a calculator. The abacus, Napier's rods, logarithm tables have all been used in the past as an aid to calculation and now we have calculators and computers. The requirement for initial primary-teacher education courses to include at least 50 hours of 'arithmetic' as part of the 150 hours of mathematics curriculum studies is presumably not to be wasted on a return to such a curriculum? 'Contrary to popular opinion calculators do not constitute a threat to mathematics education. Used sensibly they will make pupils better at mathematics, not worse' (DES, 1985, 3.16).

Straker questions whether we seriously believe that 'long multiplication trains the mind' and that 'calculators make children lazy'. Surely for children to be able to use a calculator or computer they must have a better understanding of mathematics in order to be able to make the correct choice of operation, ensure the result is appropriate and translate the display. The 'sensible' use of calculators takes place when calculations are needed with numbers that are too large or awkward for a child to handle mentally. The availability of calculators does not mean that they will be used for every calculation. With the use of calculators there is stress on the importance and power of mental calculation (Shuard, 1986).

'IT CAN'T BE MATHS, WE HAVEN'T DONE ANY HARD SUMS'

Attainment Target 2: Number
Pupils should understand and use number; including estimation and approximation, interpreting results and checking for reasonableness.

(DES, 1991b)

Formal assessment of Ma2 appears to take a very limited view of the understanding and use of number. With the present emphasis on the young child's acquisition of the 'basic skills', this view is of increasing concern. All those involved with the education of young children have a particular responsibility for addressing this issue in order to turn anxieties and misunderstandings into knowledge about the ways in which teachers teach and children learn about number.

Research (Gelman and Gallistel, 1978; Tizard and Hughes, 1984; Hughes, 1986; Threlfall, 1992) suggests that children generally pass through several stages in their acquisition of number bonds. They learn about numbers by handling and looking at sets of items and learning number names, comparing sets of things, learning the counting sequence and combining and partitioning sets of items in various ways. Children progress from counting out all the objects represented by an addition sum, through counting on from the first number given, to counting on from the larger of the two numbers to be added. This requires keeping track of the count, perhaps on their fingers, head nodding or using a mental image of a number line.

For the third year, teachers have been required to assess the child's ability to add and subtract using recall of number facts only, not by counting or computation (DFE, 1993b). Evidence of attainment could only be shown if the number facts were produced without using counting or calculating in any obvious way to arrive at an answer and within a five-second time limit. This is contributing to the pressure upon teachers to resort to strategies which ignore the wealth of available research evidence concerning the acquisition of mathematical concepts by young children and will not raise standards.

Counting is one of the early mathematical skills learnt and one in which children may have had a great deal of practice. It is only when the child realizes that the number of elements is independent of the way in which the elements are arranged and of the order in which they are counted that a number can become a mental 'object' that can be manipulated. Many young children use counting in calculation at least some of the time and some count all of the time. Young children can become very good at counting quickly and it is difficult to make a judgement as to whether a child is using an image of a number line (or some other means of counting) rather than recall when asked to give the answer to 4 + 5. When faced with a calculation they find threatening, there is evidence to suggest that young children resort to counting procedures (Gray and Tall, 1993). Children who can count quickly can succeed in achieving Ma2/2a, but this may lead to the development of a method that gives short-term success in the test and long-term failure in mathematics.

This form of testing would seem to encourage the development of rigid procedures rather than flexible procepts (Gray and Tall, 1993). Children are more likely to build number facts in a meaningful way if they see number as a flexible procept, as they are able to derive new facts from old. Children do not learn their number bonds just by rote. A child who has developed a knowledge of number in a flexible meaningful way has a powerful strategy for solving problems, whereas the child who retreats to the safety of familiar, but rigid, counting practices has to develop long sequences of counting to deal with more complex problems.

The non-statutory guidance (DES/WO, 1989) states that mathematics in the National Curriculum requires pupils to develop a range of methods for calculating; at every stage pupils should be encouraged to develop their own methods for doing calculations. It is a message welcomed and supported by mathematics educators. However, if these methods are not flexible, nor able to be generalized, this can lead to the development of a procedural approach that bodes ill for future mathematics learning. From the earliest stages, teachers encourage children to explore different strategies for calculation, and help them to build upon their informal and untaught methods to develop a range of more powerful and efficient strategies. Children and adults commonly use a mixture of methods when calculating, but neither children nor adults will always choose the most efficient strategy to try, especially in a test.

As previously noted, children are likely to resort to counting when faced with a calculation they find threatening, and indeed there is increasing evidence to suggest that children will 'play it safe' in response to SATs. Ceri Morgan (1992) found that the level children obtained in Ma 2 largely depended on how quickly they could count, but her greater concern is for those children who were attempting to use more sophisticated strategies for calculation. Children failed to answer questions they could have solved easily if they had restricted themselves to counting. Those who were using potentially more powerful and creative strategies could not be given recognition for this. The ability to derive mathematical facts from other knowledge is fundamental for successful mathematics learning. However children who demonstrated a higher level of mathematical thinking when asked for explanations of what they were trying to do in the SAT failed to gain a level which reflected their ability either as a result of the time limit or because their method of calculation was not as reliable as counting. A significant number of children attained levels which did not reflect their mathematical ability or potential. If what is wanted is a test of recall then any answer taking longer than about two seconds is very likely to have been generated by other methods. Allowing five seconds for a response would appear to be legitimizing these alternative methods. It is possible to train children to remember facts and give skilled performance, but if this is at the cost of future mathematical development it is a bad strategy. Schools can train children to become skilful operators, to perform well in the short term but this does not develop the network of connections, symbolic representations and meanings which extends the power of thinking and hypothesizing. It is training not educating.

An increasing number of teachers, headteachers and advisers are voicing concern that children are not demonstrating their true mathematical ability in the mathematics SATs. In order to remedy this situation some teachers have been directed to undertake professional development in mathematics so that they may develop styles of teaching that will enable the children in their class to produce the required results. There does not seem to be any consideration given to questioning the reliability or validity of the tests, an issue which must be raised, not only on in-service courses.

Giving children access to more powerful proceptual mathematics will involve using the mathematical tools we now have available. Calculators and computers allow children to explore how numbers work, to use larger numbers that allow patterns and relationships to become more obvious, to work with negative numbers and decimals, and they remove the emphasis from rigid counting strategies. Often the use of calculators allows children to demonstrate knowledge and understanding that challenges our assessment of their mathematical ability (PriME, 1991). Encouraging children to reflect upon their work and giving them time to do so will enable them to evaluate and refine their own strategies (Davis, 1983). A view of mathematics which focuses on instant recall of number facts and the ability to perform standard written algorithms will not encourage young learners to see themselves as mathematically competent and able to extend their mathematical understanding. Learning mathematics requires developing modes of understanding which incorporate strategies for self-evaluation and reflection, not learning tricks which are tested by someone else.

If children are to develop as independent mathematical thinkers teachers need to know what processes of mathematical thinking are and how children learn to use them. Teachers need to be consciously aware of the processes involved in mathematical activity and how they are embodied in activities in order to ensure that children are developing these processes. A logical analysis of mathematics does not provide us with a helpful focus for developing our understanding of how children learn mathematics, but an understanding of concept formation and the development of conceptual structures and schemas will enable the teacher to provide appropriate mathematical experiences (Skemp, 1971).

There is a significant difference between teaching mathematics and teaching children to learn mathematics. What mathematics is appropriate for children who will be adults in the twenty-first century? Can a subject which is 'essentially creative' and 'continuously evolving' (DES, 1988c) be determined by attainment targets defined by precise objectives and assessed by centralized testing?

The pace of change and the variety of ways in which mathematics may be used would seem to make it impossible to predict the challenges learners of mathematics will have to face. Mathematics is one of the ways of making sense of the world, of developing understanding. Mathematicians are not employed to practise old mathematics but to develop ways of solving new problems. Mathematics should have an important role in developing the learner's ability to live in a world of change (Shuard, 1986). Supporting and developing young children's active mathematical thinking will be an effective contribution to their ability to use mathematics now and in their future lives, in contrast to the large number of adults who are unable to use the mathematics they were taught in school (DES, 1982).

Professional educators working with young children have a particular responsibility to address issues concerning mathematical competence. Children bring a wealth of mathematical knowledge, skills and understanding with them when they begin formal education and we must build upon that foundation to enhance children's development through mathematics. By developing the young child's already existing knowledge, understanding and skills in the widest sense, we will enable the child to become an active investigator, to do mathematics (Metz, 1988). How can teachers develop styles of teaching which value children's mathematical thinking and enable them to think independently with enjoyment when the current emphasis on basic arithmetic skills ignores not only the need to make general sense of a situation first but also the importance of reflecting on the solution?

The young child's awareness of his or her movement through space, of sound patterns, of order and sequence is the foundation upon which mathematical skills are built. A child's numerical skills are develped through activities which encourage sorting, grouping, matching, counting and measuring. It is vital that early years classrooms are appropriately resourced in order to stimulate and extend mathematical thinking. A lack of access to practical apparatus can have long-term detrimental effects on mathematical understanding (Briggs, 1993). If children are to be able to 'select the materials and mathematics to use for a practical task' (Ma1/2a), they must have opportunities for making choices about which resources to use.

There must be recognition of quality and richness of resources for mathematics learning in all areas of the classroom; imaginative and role play provides opportunities for sorting and classifying as tables are laid for tea or 'babies' put to bed; blocks and construction materials allow children to experiment with three-dimensional shapes; the outdoor environment offers a wealth of opportunity for estimation ('How many leaves are on the playground? Will we all fit on this plank?'); many books have exciting mathematical content; and music provides opportunities for exploration of sound patterns. Resources for mathematics include the use of the everyday items which enable children to use mathematics to make sense of the real world. The desire to 'slim down' the curriculum must not lead to resources for mathematics being limited to interlocking cubes, counters and pencil and paper. Most adults identify mathematics with arithmetic and number is a very important dimension in mathematics. However, such a restricted view will limit understanding of what mathematics is and its role in the development of the child's understanding. A vital part of the professional educator's role is to identify and explain the full range of mathematics in school. An appropriate language for articulating professional practice must be developed in order that parents and others in the community can make sense of provision and we may begin to counter the myth that mathematics consists only of arithmetic (Pound *et al.*, 1992).

Mathematics has an important part to play in the education of all children and the National Curriculum is portrayed as an entitlement curriculum: the right of every child. However there is evidence that the outcomes of assessment of the National Curriculum are having an adverse effect on groups of children (Shorrocks *et al.*, 1993). Young children scored consistently lower than older children in the same year group, children from lower status neighbourhoods and children whose first language is not English obtained significantly lower scores. There is also concern in that an increase in narrowly based assessment procedures in mathematics will disadvantage girls.

Parents do not want their children to be forced to do written tests which assess progress on how many answers they get right with no regard for the quality and creativity of their thought. How can parents and teachers be reconciled to reporting children's achievement as 'W, 1, 2, 3 or 4'? Mathematics education must be seen as a means of increasing the quality of life not as training to know one's place in a society which does not recognize the worth of individuals who are not part of the educational élite.

SUMMARY AND CONCLUSIONS

The contention that the National Curriculum has raised standards and brought with it changes to teachers' planning and teaching and benefits for pupils and staff is discussed in Chapter 4. The acceptance of this contention is, however, worrying when it forms the basis for further change. Mathematics in the National Curriculum has already undergone one major revision. The effects of this revision have been discussed with reference to their implication for the mathematics education of young children.

Further 'slimming down' of the curriculum is now proposed for KS1 with formal testing in mathematics reduced to 'a single test in mathematics, based on the Number attainment target, and sufficient in length to offer the possibility of finer grading' (NCC/SEAC, 1993, p. 80). The tightly prescriptive definition of mathematics in the National Curriculum is unlikely to be eased as the teaching of 'numeracy' is considered to be so fundamentally important. This, together with the smallest time margin allowed for 'optional studies' in KS1 and increased interest in a value-added approach, would indicate that the Dearing review should be welcomed with caution by early years educators (NCC/SEAC, 1993).

Forms of assessment are many and varied, necessarily so; ways that are effective in some contexts are not effective in others. The current dogma that formal pencil-and-paper tests give objective and reliable measures of children's levels of attainment in mathematics has been shown to be false. As the purpose of the assessment structure in mathematics is to systematize the reporting of achievement (Shorrocks *et al.*, 1993), it is crucial that the unreliability of such reports is made known. This crude and simplistic form of assessment denies children the opportunity to make use of wide forms of knowing, by deliberately restricting mathematics to that which is easy to assess.

The instruments used to measure attainment are having a profound effect upon mathematics teaching and learning. For many young children mathematics has been reduced to remembering number bonds and multiplication tables and practising basic computation. This experience is unlikely to raise standards of number work. HMI report that exploration of number patterns leads to a sound knowledge of multiplication tables in a more positive way than learning by rote, and that 'overemphasis on written recording and computation, or the reluctance to allow pupils to omit written calculations which they could successfully compute mentally, or the excessive practice of skills already mastered' (Ofsted, 1993a, para. 24) contribute to low levels of achievement.

Recognition must be given to the contribution mathematics can make to the child's overall development. This involves much more than contributing a number which represents attainment in one area of the mathematics curriculum. Teaching mathematics is a difficult and complex task and involves making judgements about the quality of what has or is taking place. It is not just about outcomes or levels of attainment but how those are achieved. Eisner (1985) likens this to the difference between just knowing the score and knowing how the game was played. It is hard to apply a similar metaphor to mathematics in the National Curriculum, but in this 'game', although there are rules, that does not mean the game is fair.

Mathematics education must do justice to the learner and recognize the wide forms of knowing and learning. The central role of assessment in mathematics teaching and learning demands a positive approach which enhances the quality of teaching and learning. An over-riding concern is that teachers take a holistic approach, to strive to understand the whole child and his or her development and from this 'big-picture' focus more closely to identify particular strengths, weaknesses, developmental needs and the steps to be taken to move the child forward (Stables, 1992c). We must work towards improving what we have and not allow current inconsistencies to distort the view of mathematics which supports the development of the whole child. Mathematics education must be founded in what children need to know in mathematics and how they may learn, not driven by political dogma that focuses on a view of mathematics as a mechanistic, hierarchical body of knowledge.

7
SCIENTIFIC AND TECHNOLOGICAL DEVELOPMENT IN THE EARLY YEARS

Pat Gura

The advent of the National Curriculum has made it necessary for early childhood educators to decentre; to examine the familiar in the light of the unfamiliar and the unfamiliar in the light of the familiar. Necessity makes heavy work of decentration. Anxiety can reach levels which cloud judgement and induce ostrich-like responses. This chapter is not intended to add to existing anxieties but to flag issues which early childhood educators may want to draw to the attention of others, should the opportunity present itself.

THE NATIONAL CURRICULUM

The systems of education which Froebel and Montessori devised were taken apart and put together again by practitioners to suit their own purposes, often losing the spirit of the original. In the UK, the recent history of curriculum change, prior to the National Curriculum, is peppered with examples of this tendency for practitioners to customize curriculum packages which they did not help to develop (Kelly, 1989). In order to prevent the reordering of the National Curriculum by individual teachers and schools, a very detailed legal structure, dictating what must be taught to all children and when, interpenetrates the National Curriculum subject orders. As we saw in Chapter 1, loopholes are plugged as quickly as they are discovered. For example, considerable variability has been reported nationally in teacher assessment and the marking of the compulsory standard attainment tasks (SATs) in English, mathematics and science. Stricter controls of assessment and testing procedures are, therefore, to be put in place to ensure greater standardization of, within and between teacher assessment.

Filer (1993) doubts if this will lead to the 'objective' assessment required by legislation for the marketing of schools, so long as different pedagogies continue to operate with the same materials. Classrooms, she argues, are 'social and cultural contexts which are neither neutral nor uniform in their impact' (p. 3).

Almost inevitably, there have been calls for tighter control of teaching methods (Alexander, Rose and Woodhead, 1992; NCC, 1993). In response, Harlen (1993) has attacked the apparent reneging on the undertaking given in the National Curriculum consultation document (DES, 1987), that teachers would be free to decide on curriculum detail within the general frameworks of the programmes of study as well as on pedagogy. She quotes the NCC:

> Some schools have simply overlaid the requirements of the National Curriculum onto systems of curriculum organisation based largely on topic work. There is often a reluctance in such schools to dispense with familiar topics and themes which lie outside the National Curriculum so as to focus sharply and clearly on the requirements of the Orders.
>
> (NCC, 1993, para. 4.12)

It is less practicable, in the context of compulsory science and technology, for whole-school and year-group plans to be based on topics with *possible* lines of development, involving *possible* subject-matter, lightly pencilled in. I have seen much evidence suggesting that, to satisfy the continuity and progression dimension of the subject orders on a whole-school basis, topic 'development' is likely to be spelt out in permanent ink at the beginning of the school year.

It is not a simple matter to assimilate specific content from a range of subject areas to general topics. On the other hand, topics offer contexts for learning to which children can relate. Stories are particularly valued as starting points, for their characters and plots and because they offer common points of reference or 'scripts' (Nelson and Seidman, 1984) which facilitate collaboration. The narrative form itself is employed by children in their make-believe play and so they readily enter the story context (Stables, 1992a). Within this they are able to decentre, a process which liberates the mind and makes it possible for ideas to be considered at more complex levels than are available to them in the literal world.

One experienced and reflective early years teacher told me about the teaching of National Curriculum science to her Year-2 children (6- and 7-year-olds). The science levels, as she says, do not develop naturally and attainment is determined in subject-knowledge-based terms. She describes her determination, at the beginning of one term, to try not to let the

National Curriculum completely govern the conduct of teaching and learning in her classroom. She calculated that the topic of 'pirates' would be an appealing and fruitful starting-point, with plenty of scope for exploring ideas spanning the curriculum, including science and technology:

> The children developed a scenario, in which a pirate decided to bury his lunch along with his treasure, so that he could have a snack when he dug it up again. They buried marmite sandwiches, hard-boiled eggs and such, in flower pots. Assessing the children's understanding of decay, as required by the National Curriculum, presented few problems but the topic I had provided did not prepare them in any way to deal with questions relating to the earth in space, which might not have mattered except that it turned up as a compulsory science SAT. Some children were able to make connections between the work we had done and the questions they were asked, but that level of abstraction was beyond others and one child cried over it, which upset me greatly.

Pressure to 'cover' the syllabus holds a certain irony, in terms of scientific and technological development. The alternative suggested by Duckworth (1978), of 'uncovering' it, might lead us to question the value of 'getting children through the levels' as one teacher described what may be a growing tendency to teach to the statements of attainment.

THE IMPORTANCE OF LOVING

According to practitioners I have spoken with, the arrangement of attainment targets as a series of 10 levels of knowledge/competence is leading to an increase in specific subject teaching and ability grouping for science and technology in Year 2 where a teacher may be addressing children at Levels 1, 2 and 3. Ability grouping is seen by many teachers as the only certain way of ensuring that all children receive their statutory 'entitlement'. It satisfies the requirement to 'differentiate' individual learning.

Where ability grouping is practised, a child can theoretically move between groups, according to spurts or reverses in attainment. Experience, anecdotal evidence and research (Hart, 1992) indicate this seldom happens. Ability groups tend to become self-fulfilling. They also become social reference groups and, as such, can be socially divisive.

The principle of entitlement, enshrined in the National Curriculum, should include access to a range of other minds, including those of classmates, regardless of age and level of attainment. In the past couple of decades the crucial importance of the social context of learning has become increasingly apparent (Blenkin and Whitehead, 1988). Our understandings become increasingly elaborated as much through informal social interaction as by being given facts and shown how to do things. Max de Bóo (1991) conducted some research into reception-age children's ideas about food and growing and found a wide and fascinating range of answers to questions like 'How do we grow?' and 'When do we grow?' Viewed as 'starting-points', de Bóo comments that few of the answers could be empirically tested. She concludes that in some things, more experience of living is what is needed, coupled with opportunity to hear and talk with friends about what they think: 'sharing my opinion with you, and listening to what your experience has taught you, is likely to get us both a little further than we could manage on our own' (*op. cit.*, p. 24).

Harris (1988) nominates 'loving' as a key element of learning in successful scientific and technological development. Loving, described as 'the learning how to work with other learners', is the most likely of all the key elements to be neglected, he suggests (p. 49). The separation of learners on the questionable basis of ability can be seen as a threat to such loving. This is not a criticism of teachers but of the underlying causes.

In order for the social context to become a positive contributing feature of teaching and learning, steps need to be taken to create, and/or maintain, a climate of mutual trust and respect between adults and children, children and children. All need to feel confident about offering comments and suggestions; challenging and being challenged; questioning and being questioned.

Several teachers of 5–7-year-olds have commented to me about the amount of talking *at* children they now engage in. Teacher talk (McAuley, 1990) has always tended to dominate in the classroom, often unconsciously, as a means of controlling the pace and content of teaching and learning. The indication that this is increasing is disturbing and may be put down to pressures to cover the syllabus at the designated levels and times.

About half of all adult–child interactions in school are in the form of adult questions (Wood, 1986; Cassidy, 1989), with the majority of these aimed at getting children to recall *what* they know rather than encouraging them to develop their ideas by thinking *about* what they know.

Much has been written about the art of effective questioning, especially in relation to scientific and technological development. Feasey and Thompson (1992) stress the importance of teachers' using a wide range of question types on which children can model their own questioning. They also draw attention to the need for a pause after asking a question, to give children time to think. Research cited by Wood (1986) found that teachers tended to leave about one second before resuming control of an interaction. With a three-second wait, there was a subsequent increase in the level of children's replies. In order to develop their range, Wragg (1992) recommends teachers become aware of the research on questioning as a basis for examining and developing their own practice. Wasserman (1991) advises that a question can appear more or less threatening, more or less like an invitation to reflect, depending on the tone of voice adopted as well as phrasing.

The individual statements of attainment, within the attainment targets of the National Curriculum, are stated in terms of behavioural objectives. When behavioural objectives become the basis of teaching, Wasserman suggests, they create the conditions in which questioning about trivial details flourishes, while the 'big ideas', e.g. that 'machines allow us to do more work with less expenditure of human energy', are neglected. In concentrating on details, she argues, children learn that these represent what is worth knowing. To find the big ideas in the subject orders of the National Curriculum, the programmes of study are more useful than the statements of attainment.

Where the social context is accepted as a necessary dimension of teaching and learning, with all contributions valued, there is an understanding that conclusions reached in discussion may vary widely from conventional ones. This makes ongoing dialogue between teachers and learners essential, so that, in time, differences can be resolved or better understood. Sometimes it is necessary to acknowledge the legitimacy of different perspectives – an issue to be dealt with more fully later. Arguably, by encouraging the sharing of ideas and opinions, it is more likely that conventional wisdom, represented by teachers, parents and others, will eventually find its place in children's interests and understandings. The Association for Science Education (ASE, 1992a), thinking along similar lines, has produced a very useful science familiarization pack aimed collectively at children, parents and teachers.

SCIENCE AND TECHNOLOGY IN PRIMARY SCHOOLS

Science

Very little science was taught in primary schools at the time of the HMI National Primary Survey (DES, 1978a). That which did exist was taught on an *ad hoc* basis through general topic work, rather than systematically at the whole-school level. The present concerns of the National Curriculum with differentiation, continuity and progression can be traced back to this survey. Children were either insufficiently challenged or plunged out of their depth by the tasks set and there was much repetition of content, at the same level, within schools, regardless of year-group. There appeared to be no provision for the development of ideas. These problems were diagnosed as stemming from 'teachers' lack of subject knowledge' (DES, 1989c, p. 6).

There was a marked concentration on the biological sciences and this mostly involved observation, description and recording with very little exploratory and investigative work. Physical sciences were poorly represented and likely to be integrated through general topic work with mathematics, art, craft and design. In relation to these, the range of materials and tools offered for children to explore and use was more likely to lead to the creation of two- rather than three-dimensional artifacts, i.e. paint, paper, card, glue, scissors, rather than wood, clay, plastics and appropriate tools with which to transform them. Such a range can be seen as restricting the consideration of ideas which could be explored through modelling.

The teaching and learning of science in primary schools has steadily improved since this survey, especially at the level of the individual class, according to HMI (DES, 1989c). Lack of co-ordination at whole-school level has been a more persistent problem, indicating uncertainty about how to develop ideas from a scientific perspective.

Given this background, it is possible to see that the *form* of the National Curriculum was inevitable: it had to be a 'whole'. The test of a whole is whether it adds up to more than the sum of its parts and this one does not seem even to be trying. Subjects ensure separation, otherwise why bother having subjects? As we have seen, there is growing opposition to general topic work and much talk of specialist teachers for young children.

Despite this, according to recent reports, 3–7-year-olds are doing well in science (Revell, 1993). One study indicates, as we saw in Chapter 3, that attainment at age 7, of children who have attended a nursery school or class is greater than that of children without this nursery experience. The difference was not great and related to knowledge of scientific facts (Shorrocks, 1992a). This is interesting given the reported weakness of teachers' subject knowledge.

The introduction of the National Curriculum overlapped with the steady improvements in primary science described by HMI. Yet in official statements credit appears to be given to the National Curriculum. However, investment in school science at central government and local authority levels has declined steadily since its introduction and it can be argued that the continued maintenance of the number of primary schools reported to be offering science at satisfactory levels has occurred in spite of rather than because of it.

It is important that the real reasons for the steady improvement of science teaching and learning from 3 to 11 years be understood, otherwise the goal of universal scientific literacy, and in turn a steady increase in the numbers of professional scientists, will be difficult to sustain. There is a need for massive investment in staff development and advisory support. This will be discussed in more detail in a later section.

Equally important, as already suggested, is the need for learning to be situated in contexts which offer worthwhile experience, in accessible forms from children's as well as adult's perspectives. An own goal, in this respect, in terms of National Curriculum science, is the change in the form of the compulsory, external SATs from practical, investigatory, activities, to paper-and-pencil tests.

According to an evaluation of these early, practical SATs by Gipps (Kirkman, 1992), some teachers had never actually taught in this way and were experiencing practical work with 7-year-olds for the first time. Their subsequent comments frequently indicate that in these practical contexts they discovered unsuspected strengths in the children. They also gained valuable insights about teaching and learning and in general found they positively enjoyed this way of working with children. As a result, they were determined to adopt a more active, practical approach to their teaching.

This model of teaching and learning can be seen from this experience to make sense of the concept of 'entitlement' from the children's perspective. It is also apparent from the experience of these practical science SATs that the teaching and learning involved cannot be rushed. Time taken over the practical tests, which were additional to teachers' own compulsory for-mative assessment, when added to that taken up by English and mathematics, proved too much for the system in primary schools. The official response was to commission pencil-and-paper tests, adequate, if that is the word, only for the testing of certain kinds of knowledge. This trivializes science. It exchanges internal for external motivation and is not in the interests of scientific and technological development.

Technology

Many of the activities contained in the statutory orders for National Curriculum technology, which came into effect in 1990, were familiar to primary teachers as an aspect of science, or in association with craft and design (DES, 1991c). What is new and initially more difficult to grasp is the fusion of these into a new whole. A near relation, in some respects, to technology prior to the National Curriculum was the 'problem-solving' which had begun to appear on the timetable. The idea behind the allocation of time to problem-solving was to give children the opportunity to co-ordinate and apply knowledge and skills. This involved a temporary shift in emphasis from dealing with collections of facts and skills for their own sake which, according to various HMI reports, tended to dominate the primary curriculum, to using them in meaningful contexts. Another reason was to help children become conscious of problem-solving as a process by making this explicit (Fisher, 1987; Gilbert, 1989; Watts, 1991).

Practice at problem-solving is believed by its advocates to result in a general problem-solving capability. Critics dispute this, suggesting that problem-solving is context specific (Hennessy, McCormick and Murphy, 1993). Timetabled problem-solving imposes its own constraints and often means that the problems tackled are suggested by the teacher. In these circumstances children do not always have the necessary internal motivation to respond imaginatively and creatively. This can be even further reduced by the adoption of a rigid problem-solving drill, which does not match the non-linear reality of problem-solving (Stables, 1992b). It is perhaps against this background that many practitioners perceive technology as problem-solving.

The committee which produced the original draft orders for technology made no attempt to specify a knowledge base for the subject, seeing it as a central and co-ordinating feature of the curriculum, drawing on knowledge from all areas. This lack of prescription appears singularly out of character with other subject orders, which have been criticized for their over-prescriptiveness. Perhaps because so much has been spelt out elsewhere, leaving little scope for teacher initiative, this relative absence causes uncertainty and anxiety. Later in the chapter, a story is told of what happened when a teacher of 7-year-olds decided to stop telling the children what to do and when. The confusion has not been confined to primary teachers. It has also affected the secondary stage, where the identity of technology has implications for vocational and higher education. There are also concerns at secondary level about the subject identities that have been assimilated to it and the legitimacy of its constituency.

It was these problems in the secondary sector, in the main, which after only five terms of implementation, called forth a highly critical report commissioned by the Engineering Council (Smithers and Robinson, 1992). This contributed, more than the concerns of primary teachers, to a government decision to conduct a fundamental review of National Curriculum technology. At the time of writing, no final decision has been taken but it seems likely that there will be two rather than four inter-related attainment targets, one for designing and one for making. There is widespread agreement that the order is easier to understand in this form. However, champions of the existing Orders believe the heart has been ripped out of technology with the identification of needs and opportunities and evaluation assimilated to designing and making.

As in the case of National Curriculum science, there has been insufficient investment in staff development and support and in ensuring that schools have adequate resources for technology. Instead, there have been repeated calls for primary teachers to be replaced by subject specialists – an argument which cannot be sustained in the light of the difficulties the specialists are having. Technology is a new and visionary subject with genuine pretensions to entitlement: the right to be enabled to learn that the way things are can be changed to something better by the efforts of human beings.

Primary school teachers who piloted the optional SATs for technology (SEAC,1992) learnt to appreciate technology as a whole and to approach its holistic assessment through attending workshops. As with the early, practical science SATs, these were intended to model good practice. Carrying out the assessments was seen as enjoyable and worthwhile by adults and children alike, with enough ideas generated by the SATs themselves to fuel several weeks of voluntary activity. This is the kind of assessment which advances children's education. Learning to use it should be a priority for in-service funding. These technology SATs were, like those for science, extremely time-consuming and therefore threatening to the statutory curriculum balance.

VISIONS AND REVISIONS OF NATIONAL CURRICULUM SCIENCE AND TECHNOLOGY

The official response to dealing with a difficulty, at one key stage, as in science, has tended to be towards tinkering and cutting across all key stages, or all attainment targets. This, presumably, is seen as safeguarding the whole and seems to be an overgeneralization of the mathematical formula which says what you do to one side of an equation you must do to the other. By following this rule, you can solve your problem without really changing anything. Crowe (1983) has speculated on the possibility that there is an intuitive tendency, particularly in childhood, to apply this rule to a range of problem situations, and cites numerous delightful examples: an adult recalls taking an illicit bite from one of the tomatoes in a bowl, then panicking, unable to take a second bite. Suddenly, a wonderful idea occurs to her and she knows exactly what she must do:

> I put it back and took a bite out of another one – then put that back and took a bite out of the next one. I knew if only I had time to take a bite out of each they would all be the same and no one would ever know. (*op. cit.* p. 82).

The problems for primary schools with technology were different from those of secondary schools, but in order to keep the curriculum whole, the same changes, whether or not appropriate or necessary, must be made across the board.

The systematic nibbling at the 1989 version of National Curriculum science culminated in a complete rewrite of the orders, taking effect from August 1992. A newcomer to the teaching of science in the early years and unaware of the contents of the original orders would tend to underemphasize the quintessential 'scientific' character of the subject, i.e. the nature and processes of science. After strenuous searching, the chairperson of the original working group found fragments of the old orders, buried in the new (Thompson, 1993). Enthusiasts have also discovered that 'it's still there if you know what you're looking for'. One teacher of 7-year-olds I spoke with was determined to hang on to her 'obsolete' 1989 copy of the science orders. She may come to feel the same about retaining the 1990 technology orders which have suffered a similar fate with the identification of needs and opportunities and evaluation being assimilated to designing and making. As resources for personal and professional development, these documents are invaluable.

It is salutary to note that according to several sources the introduction of scientific investigation at Key Stage 1 has been 'one of the outstanding achievements so far in the implementation of National Curriculum science' (Revell, 1993).

Some thoughts about specialists

The number of students of A-level science continues to be significantly lower than for arts subjects, according to recent reports. Commenting on this fact, the director of the museum of the chemical industry, Dr Gordon Rintoul, blames the Green movement for giving science a bad name and primary teachers for making the Green movement so popular. He suggests that primary teachers opt for environmental issues in their science teaching, as these allow for a 'descriptive' rather than an 'understanding' approach for which they lack the necessary 'scientific' gifts. He is optimistic that the situation will improve with the introduction of science specialists into primary schools (Dore, 1993). There is no hint of a suggestion that primary teachers might actually *care* about the environment. The Association for Science Education itself embraces environmental education (ASE, 1992b) and condemns professional élitism such as that expressed by Dr Rintoul. The demystification of science was high on the agenda of the 1993 ASE annual conference (Nash, 1993).

Some professionals display a refreshing candour and flexibility of approach to their speciality and occasionally spill the beans about what the less knowing are taught to regard as holy writ. In his *Advice to a Young Scientist* (1979, p. 93), Medawar writes: 'Most scientists . . . have received no formal instruction in scientific method, and those who have seem to do no better than those who have not'. (See also Medway, 1992; Hennessy, McCormick and Murphy, 1993; Swatton, 1993.)

Predetermined bodies of knowledge increasingly dominate the National Curriculum and discovering gaps in primary teachers' knowledge has become a National Curriculum sport. Take astronomy, for example. Some primary school teachers do not know the relative distances between planets, according to one source, while another reports that some of the ideas they have about the Earth in space are inaccurate. Other research shows that, in this respect, these teachers are much the same as the bulk of the population (Durant, Evans and Thomas, 1989; Nash, 1992; Baxter, 1993; Mane and Summers, 1993).

Those of us who are not professional scientists tend to go about our everyday affairs using 'common-sense' explanations of the world around us, partly because we do not need to think like professional scientists and also because there is often very little in our immediate perceptual field to help us hold on to scientific ideas, e.g. the earth is 'round' and revolves on its own axis. These are not immediately obvious facts. Gardner (1991) suggests that although we may meet with scientific explanations for natural phenomena during our schooldays, our earlier common-sense versions re-emerge in the years after school, as those which guide our everyday thinking and behaving. This is not intended as an anti-science argument, but offered as an indication that the having of a prescribed body of knowledge, by teachers or children, in itself, changes nothing.

Given all of this, what intrigues is the fact that some people do become professional scientists. The mind, according to Gardner and his associates (Malkus, Feldman and Gardner, 1988), is a multiple phenomenon, with 'relatively separate realms of functioning' each with its own line of development (*op. cit.* p. 28). This could account for the fact that an individual may be particularly competent in some realms, and barely adequate in others. Individual genetic make-up may predispose towards biases in the strength of our development in different realms, e.g. some people are innately more likely to become scientists than they are to become dancers or architects. Whether this predisposition is realized seems to depend very much on circumstance.

An important one in the lives of many creative individuals, including scientists and inventors, according to Wasserman (1992), is the extent to which, in childhood, their creative play was positively encouraged. Apparently, with their mother's permission, instead of going to school, the Wright brothers engaged for several years in much 'tinkering' in the backyard of their home. Thomas Edison, Frank Lloyd Wright, Richard Feynman are also cited as examples of innovative thinkers and doers, who explored and experimented for sheer enjoyment. It could be argued from this that to create the conditions in which scientific and technological development is most likely to flourish it may be more important for teachers of young children to know how to encourage and support playful, innovative thinking and attitudes to learning than to have predetermined bodies of knowledge to impart.

Since the launching of the subject-led National Curriculum, the projection of a deficit view of primary school teachers has been a major preoccupation of a number of commentators, such as, for example, Alexander (1992), who is currently backing a call for more equitable funding for primary schools relative to secondary, so that they can buy the services of subject specialists.

Where were these critics of primary teachers when funds ran out for advisory support and professional development for all teachers? This was, by all accounts, a major contributing factor in the steady improvement in science repeatedly noted by HMI. Invaluable insights were gained by science advisory teachers about the nature of their role, which evolved, by negotiation, with teachers in schools (de Bóo, 1990). There has been a lack of non-contact time for subject curriculum co-ordinators, many of whom have taken the opportunity for professional development. According to DES (1989c; 1991c), best practice in primary science and technology occurs where co-ordinators have worked with colleagues to produce whole-school policies. Co-ordinators often have a combined science and technology brief and need non-contact time pro rata. A co-ordinator may be the strongest teacher of the subject on the staff team, but has little opportunity to learn how to handle the personal–social dimension of the co-ordinator role and is therefore unsure of how best to fulfil it (Moore, 1993). A worthy case for funding, surely?

Instead of rubbishing the science which primary teachers do well, it should be seen as a strong starting-point on which to build, perhaps through the adoption of an action-research perspective with professional tutorial and financial support (Ovens, 1993). Teachers confident about subject-matter can get to the heart of it. They have no problems with the idea of cutting up the attainment targets and statements of attainment for the whole curriculum and rearranging them, as suggested by NCC (1990). The less confident would not dream of it and have spent vast amounts of time and energy addressing every statement of attainment, in turn. It will not help primary teachers to achieve the confidence needed to reorder the curriculum within the programmes of study, if the proposed slimming down of the curriculum is done *for*, rather than *with* them. It seems whenever there is a choice between cutting and clarifying, the cuts win every time.

Should teaching by subject specialists become a reality in primary schools, this would mean the end of approaches which span the curriculum through general topic work. It is likely that specialist teacher–child relationships would be more neutral and less 'intense' (Katz, 1977) than those which exist between teachers and groups of children in the early years, who spend most of their time together in school. They know what to read into each other's behaviour and have a history of shared experiences to draw on when communicating with each other. As a class teacher, Paley (1986) likens her role to that of a Greek chorus, commenting on events and providing continuity. Elsewhere (1990) she writes of her ambition to connect everything which happens in the group. She uses knowledge gained from listening to children, to refer them to each other, as well as to past events. Subject-specialist teaching in the context of the National Curriculum would be concerned about connecting children with the subject orders.

Early childhood educators have important understandings about how children learn. This is the specialism which *they* are able to contribute to scientific and technological development in the early years. They are able to recognize the validity of the tentative and constantly changing nature of children's understanding of the world around them. Scientists make no greater claim to their own truths. The sense that young children make of the world is both personal and *human*. It might also be *scientific* in the sense of reflecting a particular rational discourse. Failure to distinguish the personal and human sense a child is making from the scientific can lead to very different conclusions about a child's level of thinking and to the making of inappropriate responses. At best this can waste a lot of valuable time and at worst cause alienation (Barrett, 1989; Kelly, 1989).

An example springs to mind from the field of experimental cognitive psychology, which uses the scientific investigative approach.

The study of children's theories of the workings of 'mind' is an expanding field of research. The definitive questions are to do with false belief: when does the child begin to differentiate between what something seems like and what it is really like? When does the ability emerge to recognize that someone else holds a mistaken belief and predict what they are likely to do because of this? 'False belief' research stems from the study of the development of rational thought of the kind adopted by scientists.

In one particular experiment about one's own false belief (Harris *et al.*, 1991), it was first established that the children, aged 4–6 years, understood the word *pretend* and the difference between *virtual* objects, like a photograph or a picture of an everyday object, and *fantasy* creations like witches, ghosts and monsters. They were then shown two boxes and told they were empty. Next, they were asked to pretend there was a big, scary monster in one, which would bite off any finger poked through the hole in its box, and a puppy in the other, which would lick any proffered finger. Next they were invited to poke a finger, or stick if preferred, into the hole in the box of their choice.

The experiment was rerun numerous times to try to establish why the majority of children were reluctant to poke anything into the box containing the imaginary monster, even after they had established that the boxes were indeed empty.

The conclusion was that the children's behaviour suggested a conceptual deficit. The legitimacy of a non-rational, affective response is ruled out by the discourse of rationality, which accordingly labels the children's responses as immature. Casual observation of children playing monsters indicates that they prefer to control the comings and goings of monsters for themselves, and that the gratuitous introduction of one, in a sense, broke with their convention.

The Department of Education and Science (DES, 1989c) is critical of the tendency for primary teachers to regard 'investigation' as a science activity, whether or not the focus is a scientific idea. Paley (1981) demonstrates that children's thinking does not automatically shift into scientific mode because the focus is identifiable as 'scientific'. The question of whether stones can melt surfaced in play, after a telling of the folk-tale *Stone Soup*. Later, in group discussion, Paley first checked the children's own theories, including one which held that stones melt if you boil them. They decided to investigate, and she gradually steered them towards increasingly more sophisticated ways of checking the truth of their statement, including weighing before and after boiling. Although everyone agreed the stones weighed two pounds, *according to the scales*, each time, they held on to the view that they had lost weight because 'the scale can't *see* the stones' (*op. cit.*, p. 18).

None of this is to deny the importance of ideas about scientific phenomena, or that sensitivity to the scientific possibilities of children's actions and comments is irrelevant, or the need for children to be helped to develop increasingly more scientific understandings about certain phenomena. What is being suggested is that knowledge cannot always determine the teaching of science, at any stage, but particularly in the early years.

To respond appropriately to children, early childhood educators need an understanding of the processes of science and technology so that they are able to recognize and encourage the intuitively scientific and technological behaviours of young children, as they try to describe, make sense and gain control of aspects of the world around them. Research indicates that in addition to encouraging these behaviours which include observing, questioning, exploring, taking things apart, mixing things together, making things happen, speculating, ordering and reordering, imagining, experimenting and investigating, early childhood educators need to encourage children to reflect on *how* as well as *what* they are doing, so that they become increasingly able to choose one course of action as being more likely to lead to success than another (Froebel Blockplay Research Group, 1992).

DIFFERENTIATION

Differentiation is the current euphemism for ability grouping. In the vocabulary of early childhood education, however, it refers to the detailing of understanding and is a continuous, active mental process. A related process is that of 'integration' or the co-ordinating of understandings. The two processes of differentiating and co-ordinating relate to each other reciprocally. As the store of detail expands, new co-ordinations can occur, which make possible the discovery of more detail and so on. The statements of attainment in the subject orders of the National Curriculum and the corresponding attainment targets can be seen as crude concrete analogies of these cognitive processes. As such they do not correspond to a single real mind and can work only on a hit-or-miss basis. This represents a shocking waste of human potential. It is far better to go about the organization of learning experiences in the form of projects and topics with learners doing their own differentiating and co-ordinating in co-operation with the teacher and other learners as suggested by de Bóo (1991), using formative assessment to organize for *cognitive* continuity and progression, which are neither linear nor evenly paced dimensions of learning. It does not preclude the introduction by teachers of material the children have not yet thought about.

In the everyday world outside schools, children and adults often meet situations they cannot immediately connect with but, if they are lucky, there will be someone around who knows them well enough to be able to help them connect meaningfully to the new. In schools, the arbitrary introduction of subject-matter can be made palatable, even enjoyable, provided teachers have time to partner children when they need it, tuning and retuning their own contribution according to need. This turns the answering of particular questions or solving particular problems into a joint creative struggle. Successful partnering depends on an understanding by the teacher, who could be another child, of the nature of the task in hand, and the relationship of various aspects of it to the whole.

Knowledge and understanding of individuals is also needed so that reference to previous experience, which is similar or analogous to the present situation, can be used to help the learning process. Analogy can be a very powerful communicative device in both science and technology. A history of diverse events and experiences shared by teachers and groups of children is its raw material. Young children who have had a rich experience of make-believe play and stories have fewer problems in understanding complex ideas when they are asked to 'imagine' or 'pretend' that one thing represents another, which is the basis of analogy.

This kind of teaching *takes time*, and it is what teachers of 6- and 7-year-olds have been doing with class sizes of thirty plus in some cases and countless attainment targets to get through. If more money is to be allocated to primary schools, an obvious investment would be to reduce class size. The Association for Science Education insists that twenty is the maximum class size for 5–16-year-olds for the effective teaching of science (ASE, 1992b).

PLAY

A teacher friend and I were looking at some photographs. 'They're all there', she said, 'eighty one, eighty three, eighty two.' Baffled, I looked again at the photos. They were of blockplay. 'I don't understand.' It turned out she was referring to ATs (attainment targets). She had not noticed the play.

The National Curriculum may be changing our perceptions in important and disturbing ways about children's self-directed exploration, problem-solving and play. These can make an important contribution to the refining and elaborating of ideas, but only if we respect the children's own intentions and try to reflect this in our assessments.

As a participant in the Froebel Blockplay Project (Gura, 1992), I receive more invitations to offer talks and workshops on the teaching and learning of mathematics, science and technology through the 'use' of blockplay than for talks on blockplay, as such. The difference between these two ways of looking at blockplay is *radical*, as I shall try to explain.

My suspicion that perceptions of play are being negatively influenced by the National Curriculum, even in nursery schools and classes, is prompted by the labelling of resources, especially of 'areas' and equipment, in terms of the core and foundation subjects. This results in sand and water being filed under 'science' and blocks and other construction kits under 'technology'. Inevitably this must influence the general character of what is planned in terms of those materials. If not, why the labels? Where this labelling is practised, particularly in nursery schools, staff may be rotated from subject area to subject area. The length of a subject 'residency' may vary from one day to a week, although I have come across instances of longer periods being involved. Practitioners with whom I have discussed this see the labelling and supervision of activities in terms of National Curriculum subjects as a good way to ensure balance and of providing opportunities for all members of staff to develop subject expertise across the curriculum. It sometimes looks a little bit like the emergence of specialist teaching for the under-5s. These changes, which are not universal, were appearing prior to the National Curriculum, and represent radical shifts away from the holistic frameworks which have informed my own teaching and development as a professional early childhood educator.

Play, like technology, is more than the sum of its parts and, like technology, it needs to be assessed holistically. It is essential, therefore, that we try to understand play on its own terms and use this understanding as the basis of our assessments. We need to become 'connoisseurs' and 'critics' of play.

Eisner (1985) defines connoisseurship as the 'art of appreciation' and criticism as the 'art of disclosure', i.e. assessment. Appreciation, he suggests, implies experience in a particular field. It involves detailed knowledge of what to attend to and what to ignore; a heightened awareness of the unique attributes of particular phenomena; discernment, enabling connoisseurs to recognize how different instances relate to and compare with each other. It may also involve knowledge and understanding of sociocultural and ecological influences. Criticism combines connoisseurship with interpretation and the art of communicating this in ways which suggest the quintessential qualities of the original (*op. cit.*).

Becoming connoisseurs and critics of play involves hours of observation and interaction between particular people so that the nuances which give behaviour its meaning can be understood. Geertz (1973), an interpretive anthropologist, writes of the need to describe behaviours 'thickly'. This is contrasted with 'thin' description which leaves no scope for interpretation and appreciation. The Froebel Blockplay Research Project (Gura, 1992) used thick description of blockplay, which enabled practitioners to understand the different meanings of almost identical structures. Examples of thin description can be found in Hutt *et al.* (1988). These writers leave the behaving person out of their account and describe children's play with clay, for example, strictly in terms of motor behaviour: squash, squeeze, brush, scrape, rub, smooth, move, lump, etc.

The assessment of play in terms of mathematics, science, technology, etc., can be done only if our thick descriptions permit these interpretations of particular instances.

Thick descriptions of play, carried out by those who work with young children, reveal the social constructedness of activities like blockplay and waterplay. There is no pre-existent reality called blockplay or waterplay. Blocks and water-trays are cultural inventions which can both enable and constrain behaviour and thinking in particular ways. The way in which children use these inventions reflects not only what is within themselves and the physical attributes of the situation but also the culture of particular classrooms, schools and communities. This is why we need to reflect on the effects it may be having on children's play when we start calling it something else. We may think we are 'working in the spaces' of the National Curriculum (Whitehead, 1992b) when we adapt play to it and it to play, as suggested by the Early Years Curriculum Group (1989). In reality we may be going over the lines with a different coloured crayon.

As suggested in an earlier section, there appears to be a high correlation between play in childhood and the creativity associated with important scientific and technological developments. Players must be free from having to do things out of necessity, or to produce particular results; free to wonder and have what Duckworth (1987) calls 'wonderful' rather than right ideas; free to imagine alternative realities. In this mode novel connections can be tried out and new understandings arrived at. It is obvious from this that the more pressure adults and children are under to produce particular results the more play will suffer – even though it may be an important key to scientific and technological development.

MOTIVATION

Reviewing the National Curriculum on its own terms is a fairer test than doing it from a constructivist perspective. On its own terms it could succeed in achieving all that it sets out to do by adopting the strategies suggested by Alexander (1992), Alexander, Rose and Woodhead (1992) and NCC (DES, 1987). These relate to the organization of learning from a behavioural perspective. It may even succeed, by its own standards and definitions, in raising levels of attainment. A distinction needs to be made, however, according to Katz and Chard (1989) between what children are able to do and seem to like doing and whether they should, in our professional opinion, be doing them. It is necessary, they argue, to take the long-term view of the effects of what children are obliged to do in school. Evidence that young children often do well on standardized tests may draw attention away from the possibility that their attitudes or 'dispositions' towards science and technology, for instance, may be damaged in the long term. Test results of children in early years settings, where such attributes as interest, persistence, curiosity and initiative are encouraged, have, according to Katz and Chard, been unimpressive in the short term but considerable benefits are indicated long term.

The search for the most important variables leading to successful outcomes long term of early childhood education are beginning to indicate the importance of an individual's attribution of personal achievement to self-directed effort (Sylva, 1992b). Where children (and adults) see progress as something which develops over time and is related to practice and effort, they are able to concentrate on mastery of the task in hand and not be dependent on external approval. They encourage and guide themselves as they go along and appraise themselves in terms of their own past performance (Thomas, 1989). The converse of this applies where children and teachers are obliged to concentrate on outcomes, as in the National Curriculum, rather than immersing themselves in satisfying and cognitively challenging activities, for their own sake. Under these circumstances, teachers and learners are likely to feel more pressured, learning tends to be less thorough, they feel less in control of the situation and children become dependent on their teacher (Deci and Ryan, 1982). The process is described by Holt (1984) in terms of 'learning to be stupid'.

For many children this could be the long-term outcome of the National Curriculum if what I heard from one teacher of 7-year-olds is any indication. This year she taught children raised on the National Curriculum from the age of 5. When she attempted to introduce a degree of informality into the organization of teaching and learning, shifting the familiar subject boundaries to give the children some freedom for the decision-making and creativity she felt ought to be part of the business of schools, the children were at first immobilized. As the days went by they became very naughty. Complaints about her class, involving normally well behaved children, came in thick and fast. In class they were anxious about what they were supposed to be doing and became very dependent on her for instruction. The children had learnt particular pupil roles only too well and could not operate outside of them.

None of this is very surprising and things may have settled down in time, only there was no time. The curriculum was not being covered and colleagues were beginning to wonder what was going on. The status quo was restored, with one important change agreed to, after the experiences of the past few weeks had been thoroughly discussed with the children. A collective decision was taken to set aside certain times when a less formal set of rules and relationships would apply. The children used this time on a technology project involving the production of a puppet show and displayed a range of positive, creative behaviours not previously suspected. One idea they developed arose out of a feeling some of the children had that they did not want to operate their puppets from below and out of sight of the audience or from above and be seen. The solution they arrived at was to wear masks, designed to make them unrecognizable.

This general idea of quality time cropped up in several different guises, when the pressures of the National Curriculum were temporarily lifted and children could engage playfully and collaboratively in activities of their choice or to do with an ongoing project.

In one infant school a spare classroom had been equipped to high nursery education standards and was used by all classes on a turn-taking basis. Perhaps these are the beginnings of the way forward, with the benefit of lessons learnt.

SUMMARY AND CONCLUSIONS

What has struck me most in the effort to decentre is the radically different meanings given to terms like 'whole', 'differentiate', 'continuity', 'progression', depending on whether one is using the behavioural discourse or, as we saw in Chapter 1, the rhetoric of the National Curriculum or the constructivist discourse of early childhood education. Does this similarity serve to fuse or confuse? Play could prove to be a testing ground.

The issues flagged in this chapter could be seen to apply across the board and not just as they affect scientific and technological development: the social divisiveness of ability grouping versus the need for loving in learning; the right of children to appropriate contexts for learning; the right of teachers to appropriate professional support and respect for what they know and do well; the need for professional early childhood educators to perceive play as a whole and look for its deep structure; the right of children and teachers to see themselves as makers of their own history. This last seems to me, at a most profound level, to have a particular bearing on scientific and technological development.

Acknowledgements

Many colleagues in primary and nursery schools and colleges of education were consulted during the preparation of this chapter: Jean Ainsworth-Smith, Janet Barnes, Max de Bóo, Ann Bridges, Cheryl Challoner, Jane Devereux, Jill Lee, Maureen Morris, Gwynne Paice, Pam Page, Vivien Spevock, Kay Stables and Jill Vereycken.

8
THE NATIONAL CURRICULUM AND NON-NATIVE SPEAKERS OF ENGLISH

Eve Gregory

The term 'equality of opportunity' is at the core of the Education Reform Act 1988 and is central to the various documents emerging from it. It was used by Kenneth Baker (1987, p. 8) when, as Secretary of State for Education, he claimed that the Act would 'open the doors of opportunity' for all children. It is reflected in the National Curriculum Council's initial promise (NCC, 1988, p. 4) that it 'will be taking account of ethnic and cultural diversity and ensuring that the curriculum provides equal opportunities for all pupils, regardless of ethnic origin or gender'. It is reiterated by the School Examinations and Assessment Council with the claim that the assessment development agencies would be making every effort to ensure that the SATs (standard assessment tasks) avoid race, culture or gender bias, that they should be amenable to translation into another language other than English or Welsh and that they would not contain material to put pupils from the ethnic minorities at a disadvantage (SEAC, 1989). Finally, its special status is fleshed out in two recent NCC documents *Curriculum Guidance 3: The Whole Curriculum* (1990) and *Starting out with the National Curriculum* (1992b). Here we learn that equal opportunities must become a cross-curricular dimension which underpins every area of the curriculum; that, as such, it must be an explicit part of the curriculum policy of every school and integral to the planning, development and evaluation of a school's curriculum.

The aim of this chapter is to illustrate the complexity of fulfilling the promise of equality of opportunity to those children who enter school unfamiliar with the English language and culture. In the first section, an example from the classroom is used as a means to unpick the implications of the promise in terms of the paradox it might present. The next section considers how far provision for cultural and linguistic difference made within the English curriculum is grounded in recent theories on how children learn a second language. The third section takes us outside England to consider briefly the curricula of other European countries in relation to non-native speakers, each with a very different approach to what counts as 'school knowledge' and how it should be presented. Finally, a practical section returns to the English classroom and suggests some ways towards promoting equality within the parameters of the current curriculum.

It is in the hub of classroom activity where the real test of equality takes place. In the section which follows, we need to ask how far a group of children is being given access to the concepts presented as well as the language in which to express them.

THE CLASSROOM CONTEXT

A group of 5–6-year-old Year-1 children are called to work with their teacher. They seem reluctant to leave their unfinished writing, yet start chattering as soon as they sit down together. The language they are speaking is Sylheti, the dialect of Sylhet, a region in north-eastern Bangladesh. This is the language they speak at home, at their evening community classes, in the school playground and in class when the teacher is not present. Consequently, although these six children were born in England, their grasp of English, like that of all their classmates, is still very limited. Yet each child's knowledge of the new language is very different: one child appears to understand a lot but will hardly speak; another understands little but strings long utterances together interspersing English and Sylheti; another seems neither to understand nor be able to say very much at all. In recognition of this, extra provision has been made by central government in the form of a second teacher to work in the classroom. But the work they must cover together is exactly the same as in any monolingual class.

The lesson is carefully prepared in terms of the content and concepts to be presented. Every week, the teacher (who is new to the class) has a long list of teaching points which must be completed if the children are to keep up with all the curriculum requirements. This leads her to designate a short period of time to each task, taking care not to exceed the limit. In order for records to be collected for their files, all the children attempt the same written task.

This particular lesson is maths and will be easily recognized by early years teachers. The group are doing investigations on measurement. The teacher has two identical bottles: one is filled with coloured water and one is empty. The teacher aims to introduce the concept of 'half' and to practise estimation and measurement. The task, then, is for the children to estimate how many cups are needed both to fill and half-fill the empty bottle, to measure these out from the full bottle, to discuss together and finally to record their findings on the sheet provided.

Name   My guess   Result   Am I right?

The children have difficulty in grasping what they are being asked to do. The teacher tries to help by starting to fill the empty bottle and asking again, 'How many cups go in here, do you think?' Finally, one of the three boys in the group shouts 'four!' The others copy him immediately. They are noisy and the girls have little chance to intervene – they are, in any case, reticent. The boy fills up the empty bottle which takes just under four cups. Trying to make it simpler, the teacher tells the children to 'round it up to four'. The children appear confused and the girls seem anxious to start their sheet. The task is repeated again just for counting purposes and the children record this finding by drawing the number of cups needed to fill the bottle. The teacher abandons the idea of introducing 'halves' as she feels it is too complex for the group.

Afterwards, the teacher agrees that what should have been a discovery for the children turned into merely an exercise of memory. Yet the activity itself fits well into different maths programmes of study (AT1 'Using and Applying Mathematics'; AT 2 'Number'; AT4 'Shape and Space') and the teacher has completed the same activity with monolingual children without difficulty. The teacher concludes that this particular task is probably beyond the children's conceptual level of comprehension.

What are the NCC requirements which ensure these children's access to the curriculum? As these are to be the responsibility of individual teachers, their precise formulation is important. NCC documents stress that equal opportunities and multicultural education should be a 'dimension' which is cross-curricular and should 'permeate' the curriculum (NCC, 1992b, p. 15). The promise offered is as follows:

Providing equal opportunities for *all* pupils means:

A   1)   treating pupils as individuals with their own abilities, difficulties, attitudes and experiences
    2)   challenging myths, stereotypes and misconceptions
    3)   ensuring that equal access to the curriculum means real opportunity to benefit

Educating pupils for life in a multicultural society means:

B   1)   extending pupils' knowledge and understanding of different cultures, languages and faiths

2) valuing cultural diversity by drawing on pupils' backgrounds and experiences
3) offering positive images and role models from all cultures

(*Ibid.*)

Referring to our maths lesson above, we realize how difficult fulfilling these requirements is likely to be. Without a common language, we are left unsure whether the children's apparent lack of understanding comes from their unfamiliarity with the English language, their difficulty in understanding the concepts presented, their cultural interpretation of the task or all three? For example, to fulfil points A1 'treating pupils as individuals . . .' and B2 '. . . drawing on pupils' backgrounds and experiences' the teacher would need to be able to answer the following: Are the children able to understand the teacher's use of lexis such as 'guess', 'same/different', 'cups', 'coloured', 'full', 'empty', etc.? Question forms such as 'How many?' 'What do you think?' etc. Do they understand the language but are unfamiliar with the mathematical concepts of measuring, comparison, halving, etc.? Might they understand both of the above, but be unable to interpret what is required of them as a 'valid' learning task within the classroom context? For example, might the idea of 'estimating' or 'guessing' be totally alien to methods of work they are accustomed to outside the English school?

The crux of the NCC requirement above is point A3, which promises 'equal access to the curriculum' and the 'real opportunity to benefit'. How far do these children have access to what is being offered and to what extent are they benefiting from it? The meaning of the promise is ambiguous. Do 'equal access' and 'equal opportunity' mean access to the 'same' curriculum as their monolingual peers? Could it be that, paradoxically, provision of the same curriculum for all might actually prevent some children from gaining access to it? The answer will lie in whether the present curriculum can make adequate provision for children learning English as a second language within its parameters. The next section turns to examine how far this is the case.

THE NATIONAL CURRICULUM IN RELATION TO CURRENT THEORIES ON BILINGUALISM AND SECOND LANGUAGE LEARNING

Although a range of definitions exists on what constitutes 'bilingualism' and, similarly, various opinions are held on the differences between first and second language learning and the cognitive, social and psychological effects of bilinguality on the individual (summarized in Skutnabb-Kangas, 1981; McLaughlin, 1987; Hamers and Blanc, 1989; Romaine, 1989), patterns of common agreement can be found across a span of research data and studies. From these patterns emerge certain key generalizations, referred to by Cummins (1991) as 'theoretical principles'. This is a useful term, for it draws our attention to the way the National Curriculum is based upon certain theoretical assumptions which inform its policy and which are ultimately reflected in pedagogic practice. The question asked in this section is: How far are the theoretical assumptions in the English National Curriculum grounded in generally accepted principles derived from recent research studies?

Each of the principles discussed below necessarily overlaps with others. Nevertheless, they are presented separately as they originate in different areas of research or groups of studies. The first principle is the most general in that it draws upon research from a number of different fields.

Principle 1: the principle of bilingualism as a multidimensional phenomenon

Like many children of immigrant parents, BS found herself in the situation of liaison between her minority language environment and the majority language community . . .

Father to BS (in Italian): Tell him he's a nit-wit.
BS to third party (in English): My father won't accept your offer.
Father angrily to BS (in Italian): Why didn't you tell him what I told you?
(Grosjean, 1982, p. 200)

Throughout this century, there has been a movement from viewing bilinguality primarily as a linguistic skill to regarding it as a multidimensional phenomenon, from believing it to be a negative hindrance to considering it a positive asset. In parallel, definitions of what is understood by the term 'bilingualism' have changed according to the centre of interest.

Early studies focused primarily on linguistic competence in terms of accuracy of grammatical use and breadth of lexis. 'Bilingualism' was understood in terms of 'ambilinguality' or 'balanced bilingualism' whereby an equal linguistic competence by the child was demanded in each language. Verbal intelligence tests (e.g. the Peabody vocabulary test, etc.) measured a child's bilinguality using monolingual norms. Perhaps unsurprisingly, examples from the 1920s and 1930s all showed children who spoke a different language outside school generally to score lower than monolingual children (Saer, 1924; Mead, 1927). It is worth noting that this view of bilingualism coincided with large numbers of immigrants of low socio-economic status arriving in the USA (Fishman, 1970), coupled with feelings of nationalism in Europe (Schmidt-Rohr, 1931).

By the 1950s and 1960s there was a movement away from viewing language in terms of grammatical and lexical competence towards an interest in language use, whereby a child was considered 'bilingual' 'as soon as he is able to make himself understood within his limited linguistic and social environment' (Rivers, 1969, pp. 35 6). The new definition marked a shift to focus on general communicative competence whereby bilinguality implied the ability to produce appropriate 'linguistic behaviour' (Macnamara, 1969) in different social situations. Nevertheless, interest at this time was still largely limited to linguistic and sociolinguistic studies.

Recent studies recognize bilingualism as a complex multidimensional feature (Skutnabb-Kangas, 1981; Grosjean, 1982; Hamers and Blanc, 1989; Romaine, 1989). 'Bilingualism' or languages used within a society is now more clearly distinguished from 'bilinguality' or the psychological state of an individual; both are understood as involving not just linguistic ability but also psychological, social and cultural issues, which can be viewed adequately only through a study of communication in intercultural contexts. A few of these issues which are most important for this discussion are outlined below.

The focus of psychology and social psychology in relation to bilingualism is generally on the powerful intra- and interpersonal linkage in language learning. Psychological studies investigate attitudes and feelings towards bilingualism by the individual and their possible effect on motivation to learn. Some studies investigate the 'liberation' of bilingualism on the individual, where words and phrases (swearing, use of familiar, e.g. *tu*, instead of polite, e.g. *vous*, form in French) simply do not touch the emotional identity in a second language.

One area of interest in social psychology is that of 'speech accommodation theory' (Giles, 1973; Tajfel, 1974), whereby success in speech interactions is seen broadly to depend upon similarity attraction in terms of personal and cultural attributes. Studies with Chinese children in the USA (Yang and Bond, 1980) revealed that the children needed to affirm their 'Chineseness' more when they felt themselves to be in a culturally threatening situation (in this case, where the teacher was American), but wanted to accommodate more in a situation which was congruent with their own cultural background. A second focus in these studies is on the role taken by the young bilingual learner in different language and literacy contexts and the extent to which a child's success might run parallel with recognition of the home language and culture and with being treated as an 'important learner' (Schieffelin and Cochran-Smith, 1984; Gregory, 1993).

Work in sociology and sociolinguistics in relation to bilingualism has emphasized the need to distinguish 'bilingualism' from 'diglossia'. This term was originally used to refer to the relationship between a 'high' and 'low' variety of the same language which were used for specific functions (Fishman, 1972). Recently, the term has been extended to describe two separate languages within a society, the important features being the precise domains in which each can be used and the different status of the two languages (Grosjean, 1982).

Finally, any current definition of bilingualism must include the realm of culture which may or may not be directly linked with language. Cultural studies focus on the possible contrast in interpretations or 'primary message systems' (Hall, 1959) by members of different cultural backgrounds, e.g. what constitutes 'learning', 'work' and 'play' in different cultures? The questions tackled by cultural studies are: If there is a contrast between home and school culture, how far must a child develop a *Doppelgänger* character? How can a harmonious bicultural identity be developed? Suggestions for balanced 'biculturality' have been: the child should identify positively with both cultural/ethnic communities; both languages should be equally valorized; the relative status of both cultural groups should be perceived as dynamic; and there should be no surmountable contradiction in membership of the two groups (Hamers and Blanc, 1989).

Official education policy documents over the past twenty-five years have shown some awareness of current research findings. The movement from viewing individual biliguality as a negative to a positive feature is clear from their changing terminology. The 'immigrant' or 'non-English-speaking' children suffering 'deprivation' of the Plowden Report (CACE, 1967) eight years later become the 'English second language' children whose first language should not be discounted of the Bullock Report (DES, 1975) and most recently are recognized in the Cox Report (DES, 1988b) as 'bilingual' children whose linguistic ability is an 'asset' to be drawn upon.

It is in the recognition of the multidimensional nature of bilingualism that the curriculum orders remain detached from current research studies. The promise of equal opportunity cited in full in the last section shows how 'culture' is viewed separately from language. Thus teachers are required to draw upon children's 'cultural background and experiences' (but not their language) and, significantly, the children's literature suggested from different cultures does not include dual language texts. At the same time, bilinguality is still viewed only in terms of linguistic competence. Although 'bilingualism' is referred to as an 'asset' (NCC, 1991c), children's first languages are to be used only where there is an inadequate mastery of English and there is no indication as to how a child's bilinguality can be developed.

Ironically, reference to young children of immigrant origin in England as 'bilingual' is misleading as it implies that 'bilinguality', i.e. both languages, are being developed in school. It may also do children a disservice in that it detracts from the need of those with inadequate mastery of English for specialized language programmes. In this sense, it may be argued that the terms often used in American studies, 'English second language' or 'non-native' speaker, are more honest. Where appropriate, the term 'non-native' speaker will be used in this chapter.

In what ways might a recognition of the multidimensional nature of bilingualism change the group lesson outlined in the last section? Acknowledgement of the inter-relationship between language and culture could have led the teacher to look more widely for the cause of the children's difficulty and to investigate closely what the children brought to the task from their lives outside school. She might then have found out that their problem did not lie in a lack of conceptual knowledge. In their community classes all the children were able to add and subtract numbers to 20; likewise, they were familiar with 'halves'. A closer look at their approach to work would have revealed to her that 'estimating' or 'guessing' is not considered appropriate to formal school learning; likewise, the recording of results in a pictorial form. Recognition of these factors may have enabled her to encourage the children in the role of important learners, able to teach as well as learn from her. This realization might have led her to focus on the language skills needed to understand the task. She would have understood that the children were learning a new prestigious language in a diglossic situation, where school may well be the only domain in which English is spoken. Finally, awareness of all these factors may have highlighted the need for a sharper, more systematic focus on the language itself. Ways in which she might go about this are described under Principle 2, below.

Principle 2: the additive enrichment principle

He who knows no other language does not truly know his own.
(Goethe quoted by Vygotsky, in John-Steiner, 1985, p. 368)

A considerable body of evidence has recently been collected pointing to the advanced development of specific types of linguistic and cognitive skills of bilinguals given certain conditions (summarized in Gregory and Kelly,

1992). Linguistic skills are expressed in a greater metalinguistic and analytic competence where attention can be focused on isolated components. Cognitive advantages are most obvious in areas such as conservation of measurement, classification according to shape, colour or size or manipulating and reorganizing visual patterns. The important question for classroom practice is: What are the conditions whereby these advantages accrue?

As early as the 1930s, when Western European research was pointing unambiguously to the negative effects of bilingualism, a very different direction was taken by Vygotsky (1935, trans. 1962). Vygotsky's thesis was that first and second language learning involved very different processes, whereby 'the child assimilates his/her native language unconsciously and unintentionally but acquires a foreign language with conscious realization and intention' (*op. cit.*, pp. 2–3). It is through gaining control over two languages involving different lexical, syntactic and semantic systems or, put simply, through learning that there are two ways of saying the same thing, that the individual gains this added analytical awareness which, argued Vygotsky, contributes to a more conscious understanding of linguistic patterns in general. Later research studies conducted in the West support Vygotsky's thesis that this awareness is particularly enhanced through literacy learning in two languages.

The key to gaining access to this consciousness is the effective mastery of two or more languages, whereby learning a second language is 'added' to the development of the first (Cummins, 1979; 1992). In contrast, for children learning in 'subtractive' contexts, where their first language is 'submerged' (Skutnabb-Kangas, 1981) and seen merely as an obstacle to be overcome, no cognitive or linguistic advantages are likely to accrue. Not only this: a widely accepted opinion finds that second language learning runs parallel with first language competence and that acquisition of a second language is, indeed, dependent upon the level of development of the native language (John-Steiner, 1985). This thesis has been termed the 'linguistic interdependence principle' which quite simply states that first and second language skills are interdependent.

A number of research studies also support the view of a common underlying cognitive proficiency across languages (Vygotsky, 1962; Cummins, 1981; Hamers and Blanc, 1989), which states that children are capable of transferring cognitive functioning in their first language at home to their second language in school and cognitive skills in their second language in school to their first language at home. Problems arise when no transfer is possible because a child has not acquired a certain cognitive functioning in the first language before school (Skutnabb-Kangas, 1981). In this case, the child has the difficult task of learning both the cognitive skill and the new language together.

The question so far unanswered is: What is meant by 'effective mastery' of the first language? This complex issue is the subject of considerable discussion (Skutnabb-Kangas, 1981; Cummins, 1980; 1991). A number of researchers point out that children's second language proficiency is often thought to be better than it really is. Cummins first distinguished between two different aspects of second language learning. The first he terms BISC (basic interpersonal communication skills), i.e. the skills of communication in everyday language, in concrete, cognitively undemanding situations, using contextual cues where understanding is not entirely verbal. Linguistically, BISC is distinguished by a 'surface fluency' of accent, fluency, basic vocabulary and syntax. The second aspect he terms CALP (cognitive/ academic language proficiency), i.e. a cognitive competence in addition to the communicative competence of BISC. This is distinguished by complex linguistic skills and is language as an instrument for thought. Cummins argues that BISC is learnt very quickly by young children, but that their use of CALP may lag behind native speakers for many years.

Our maths lesson in the last section initially presents a puzzle in the light of the studies discussed above. The children are already in the process of becoming literate and numerate in their first language at evening community classes. Yet their results in the English classroom suggest that they are not acquiring linguistic or cognitive advantages from their incipient bilingualism. It seems that the process of transfer of cognitive functioning from one domain and language to another is more complex than revealed in present studies and is context specific. Observation of this group reveals two major problems of transfer: the children's knowledge of English is insufficient for them to understand what is required and there is no opportunity for preliminary discussion in their first language; and the approach to learning in the English and community school is so different that the children do not know which cognitive skill to call upon, even if they are well familiar with it.

Recognizing the principle of additive enrichment and common underlying proficiency would entail the following: a more organized provision of bilingual education for children during their early years of schooling; a much closer link with the children's homes and community classes; a division of the lesson into 'content/concept' and 'language', so that the children are not trying to cope with both at once; and a separation and deliberate presentation of CALP language needed for the task, e.g. how many cups does the bottle *hold*? What might be the *capacity* of the bottle? These suggestions will be discussed in later sections of the chapter.

Principle 3: the 'comprehensible input' principle

Second language learners, like young children, remember best the items they can interpret.

(Ervin-Tripp, 1974, p. 116)

Most second language theorists (Krashen, 1982; Wong Fillmore, 1983; Cummins, 1991) currently endorse some form of 'input' hypothesis which states that second language learning depends upon access to input which is modified in various ways to make it comprehensible. Underlying this principle is the fact that a central function of language is meaningful communication. Factors influencing the comprehensibility of the input have to do with the child's level of cognitive functioning, linguistic proficiency in the target language, knowledge of the world and chance to infer from contextual cues. In addition, anxiety must be low, motivation and self-confidence high. The consensus of opinion is that these factors must exist in order for 'input' successfully to become 'intake'. Legaretta-Marcaida (1981) describes the difference between 'input' and 'intake' in a kindergarten with 14 Spanish speakers learning through the medium of English. The school programme, she says, was eradicating Spanish and teaching very little English – though the children were 'exposed' to it all day long.

The National Curriculum makes no special recognition of the special need of young non-native speakers for comprehensible input by providing circulars or appendices containing detailed guidelines for pedagogic practice. Our maths lesson not only contains a large number of new lexis and syntax ('full', 'empty', 'fill up', 'guess', 'round it up', etc.) but also asks the children to link the task with their knowledge of school learning (guessing, recording by drawing, etc.). Guidelines to ways of enabling 'input' to become 'intake' could have provided the teacher with the following: an understanding that a period of just listening and watching is necessary for many children before speaking and explaining are demanded; the explanation of 'key' vocabulary before a task (if possible, using a translation); and provision to the learner of as much knowledge about both school ways of learning and knowledge of the world outside school and the corresponding language for this through play and role-play experiences. Tuition in 'immersion' classes for both 'élite' bilinguals in international schools and for children of immigrant origin in Europe and the USA is based upon this principle. Curriculum areas are presented in deliberately simplified language which focuses on specific lexis and syntax (Byram and Leman, 1990; Bernhardt, 1992).

Principle 4: the language/experience and interlanguage principles

Language . . . does not . . . stand apart from or run parallel to direct experience but completely interpenetrates with it.

(Sapir, 1970, p. 8)

Although these represent two separate groups of studies, their implications for pedagogy with young learners is closely related. General agreement exists that second language learners pass through universal developmental stages, such as negation, phrase structure, word order, plurality, tense and aspect, determiners and possessives (Hatch, 1983; McLaughlin, 1988). From a wide-scale study of different first language speakers, Hatch, for example, concluded that the development of 'Wh-' questions was the same for all: the 'wh' word appears at the beginning of the question followed by the declarative word order, e.g. 'What you want?'; inversion appears, e.g. 'Who are you?'; and inversion and the 'do' support are correctly used, e.g. 'What do you want?' Within this general development, learners create and develop 'interlanguages' that have forms (and possibly meanings) which appear neither in the first language nor the target language. Significant to the construction of these interlanguages is the way the learner generalizes on syntactic forms in the second language and mixes these with the first language, e.g. 'Gestern (yesterday) we goed fishing' and the way in which interlanguages are domain specific, i.e. learners have different interlanguages for different domains according to the input.

There is also general agreement on the inter-relationship between language learning and experiences gained in the new language. For young children, the ideal way of gaining experiences in the target language is through social play. Language here has an optimal level of comprehensible input. It is context bound and provides the child with large chunks of language which can be built into the learner's interlanguage system for specific domains without a child necessarily completely understanding the words or syntax. The learner is also able to experiment in a non-threatening situation and motivation is high. Similarly, studies have shown that play with language itself is an important element in second language learning. Various examples are available which document clearly ways in which children experiment with lexis and syntax, mixing languages, until they reach the target language, e.g. 'necklace man' for mayor (5-year-old

Panjabi speaker); 'Can you desentie (untie) this?' (3-year-old Spanish speaker).

The group of children in our maths lesson sat at a table together, were introduced to the task in question, were expected to understand it conceptually and linguistically, to assimilate it culturally and to represent their understanding on paper, all at one short session. Owing to the large number of tasks to be covered, there has been no time for play or experimenting with the water in the bottles. Recognition of the importance of experience and the principles of interlanguage and developmental stages in the curriculum would have meant emphasizing the importance of play for the children to learn through talk together in their first language and (in the absence of English speakers) for the teacher to 'model' the task in a play situation, matching her actions with the words and syntax used.

This brief overview suggests that NCC documentation takes very little account of theoretical principles recognized in the body of work on second language learning and, consequently, neglects any principles for pedagogic practice which could be drawn from them. Consequently, the maths lesson, which is accordant with suggestions in the curriculum programmes of study, leaves children like those in our group literally in the dark. It is beginning to look as if provision of the same curriculum might not be adequate to give children equal access to it.

But is this the only way possible to cater for non-native speakers? The next section investigates briefly what might happen to our children if they were to attend school in three European countries.

CURRICULA IN EUROPE: LEARNING FROM DIFFERENCE

It is easy to forget that our European neighbours all have regional or national curricula and are all affected in some way by the current waves of migration from both within and outside Europe. This section considers briefly the implications of curricula in France, Baden-Württemberg (Germany) and Catalonia (Spain) for non-native children who embark on formal learning in a new language. Like the National Curriculum in the UK, all three are either new or in the process of change: France has recently reorganized its primary education into two-year cycles instead of a yearly change; Baden-Württemberg is currently rewriting its curriculum into interdisciplinary themes instead of traditional subject divisions; Catalonia has recently changed the formal medium of instruction from Castillian

(Spanish) to Catalan in all educational institutions which means that large numbers of children will be learning in a second language.

France

France's non-native speakers are largely from Morocco or Algeria, and thus speak Arabic, or from other European countries, notably from Portugal, Spain or Italy. Arabic speakers are economically the most deprived group and are concentrated in the poorer *banlieues* (suburbs) of Paris, Marseilles and other urban areas. Most primary-aged non-native speakers were born in France. The French National Curriculum is highly centralized and makes no special provisions for children entering school unfamiliar with the French language and culture. The Key Stage 1 equivalent curriculum focuses mainly on French and mathematics. Central features of the curriculum are record-keeping, teacher assessment and, eventually, the 'évaluation' or national test at age 8.

Precise record-keeping for each individual child is likely to begin as the child starts the *maternelle* (nursery) at 3 and continues throughout the primary school. A typical method is through the child's own exercise-book, where each page is marked off like a register, with separate columns for the day, date and each subject. By age 5–6, in the first cycle, subjects are likely to include *écriture* (writing); *lecture* (reading); *fichier de lecture* (reading work-book); *dictée* (dictation); *numeration* (maths); *fichier de numeration* (maths work-book). Each subject is coloured in daily according to the child's assessed progress, e.g. green = good; yellow = satisfactory; red- = needs more work. The exercise-book is taken home regularly for the parents to sign.

To assist teacher assessment, the nursery (*cycle premier*) and infant (*cycle des approfondissements*) curricula have copious documentation (200–300 pages), the '*Aide a l'Évaluation des élèves*' with oral and written assessment exercises in French and maths and detailed notes at the end of each to assist the teacher in analysing the child's progress. The introduction to these books uses familiar terminology. It stresses the importance of formative assessment and of providing teachers with 'tools' for this; of assessment as a 'mission' of the Ministry of Education and of developing a 'culture of assessment' which should be at the heart of the education system. Finally, assessment at a national level takes place at age 8, where a child sits two three-hour written tests in French and maths.

Children have their own thick maths and French reading books and an accompanying work-book which contains highly structured exercises reflecting both those in the teacher assessment book and the national 'evaluation'. These examples are taken from current exercises for Year-1 children: maths (an exercise on 'heavier than', 'as heavy as', 'less heavy than'). The sheet first gives an example to illustrate the concept, e.g. a picture of two children up or down on a see-saw, accompanied by the appropriate text. Underneath, the exercise is presented using a similar type of picture, e.g. objects on scales, and the child has to ring the appropriate text for each picture. Other maths work largely contains traditionally presented sums, e.g. 'tens and units' for addition and subtraction, always providing an example before the exercise. In reading (story-reading), a short text is read out loud by individual children who then complete the following exercises: separating a sentence written without a break into the individual words; highlighting words containing certain sounds, e.g. *ou*; cross-words; a cloze exercise; describing a picture using given words; practising prepositions through matching words to pictures.

At first glance, the French National Curriculum would appear not only to ignore the cultural and linguistic background of non-native speakers but also to contradict all the principles of second language learning outlined in the last section. It assumes that all young children learning in France must share a common language and a 'French' culture. The rigidly structured curriculum which emphasizes accuracy of expression in lexis and syntax makes no recognition of interlanguage or the link between language and experience and allows little scope for experimenting through play.

We might predict that our group of Sylheti speakers will experience even more problems than in their English classroom. Ironically, however, the structure and content of the French curriculum may hold advantages for non-native speakers in spite of serious weaknesses in its provision. First, the detailed record-keeping is a potential source of valuable diagnostic information for both teacher and parent. Second, the close match between the child's daily exercises in maths and French, the teacher assessment and the 'évaluation' means that the child is constantly practising what he or she will eventually be tested on. This is an approach which our Sylheti speakers would recognize and feel comfortable with from their community classes. The restricted nature of the exercises also means that far less complex linguistic and cultural knowledge will be demanded. Also, the exact grammatical nature of the French tests, e.g. prepositions, etc., could appeal to the analytic approach that bilinguals can score highly on. Nevertheless, without an acknowledgement of the child's first language, culture and 'knowledge of the world', it is questionable how many children would be in a position to take advantage of this skill.

Baden-Württemberg

Baden-Württemberg is one of 16 *Länder* (regions) in Germany, each of which has its own curriculum but is commonly subject to the national German law (*Grundgesetz*). Like other areas of Germany, Baden-Württemberg has recently become host to many non-native speakers (in early 1992, 150,000 were in Baden-Württemberg schools). These can be divided into three groups: guest workers (Gastarbeiter), largely from Europe and Turkey; ethnic Germans, largely from the Soviet Union (*Aussiedler*) and political asylum seekers. Most wish to remain in Germany. In contrast with the English and French curricula, the Baden-Württemberg curriculum (*Bildungsplan*) contains two separate annexes devoted entirely to the education of non-native children. These set out in detail the legal entitlement of families and the duties of the educational system and individual schools, which include: enabling children to integrate quickly into German classes through provision of the most efficient means to mastering German; and facilitating and encouraging additional tuition in the language and culture of the family's origin which can be taken on a voluntary basis but is part of the school's afternoon curriculum. This is viewed as vital, both for the child's cultural identity and for cognitive and emotional development.

Special provision for young non-native speakers is of three types: 'preparatory' or full-time immersion classes for up to one year, where structured language tuition following the ordinary curriculum provides the child with enough German to join the ordinary class as soon as possible; 'additional' classes of up to four hours per week to assist children in individual subject areas; and division of an ordinary class into two. There are no national or regional tests for young children in Germany. In addition, non-native speakers must be excluded from class tests in German until they are considered fluent. Detailed indications are also provided for tuition of the children's home language and culture. The consulate of each country provides a teacher and the German school must enable him or her to understand the German system. This is to be promoted through a yearly meeting between the head and the community teacher to discuss plans for collaboration; provision for the community teacher by the German school of accommodation, materials, telephone, etc.; the community teacher writes a comment on the child's German school report; the community teacher attends staff meetings, socials, etc.; and the community and the German teacher observe each other's classes, plan work together, discuss teaching approaches, assess individual children, etc.

These special provisions are grounded in the key principles underlying the primary curriculum, which are: to promote joy in learning; to ensure self-confidence and a feeling of success in learning; to further independence in learning; to enable a child to take responsibility for his or her work; and to provide a basis for formal school learning. The theoretical orientation section of the curriculum enlarges on these principles by drawing on research showing how early learning takes place through questioning, experimenting and discovery and explains the importance of the early years curriculum in building on this knowledge. From 1993, an integrated approach (*Ganzheitsunterricht*) is to be presented on the grounds that the child does not divide learning into 'subjects'. Themes such as 'I have a name . . .' will integrate the existing traditional subjects of German, maths, 'The World of the Child' (Environmental Studies), religion, arts and crafts, music and sport.

If we transplant our group of Sylheti speakers to Baden-Württemberg, we see that the classes they would attend heed most of the principles outlined in the last section. The 'additive enrichment principle' of bilingualism would be recognized through the close link between the first language class and the German school. The importance attached to learning through play and experimenting should provide scope for interlanguage and the opportunity to link language and experience. At the same time, structured immersion classes should supply 'comprehensible input' across the curriculum for beginners. Our group of children should do well. How far their culture and language will be recognized and understood by their monolingual peers is another matter; notably missing from the documentation is any reference to multicultural education for German children.

Catalonia

Catalonia's status as an autonomous province of Spain means that Catalan is now the formal language of instruction in all state schools and universities. In accordance with the Law of Linguistic Normalization, all children should know Catalan and Spanish by the end of Basic General Education at 14. As the Catalan language was banned for official use until the death of Franco in 1975, a considerable percentage of the population is unfamiliar with the local language. In addition, Catalonia has attracted a regular flow of guest workers from poorer parts of Spain (e.g. Andalusia), as well as immigrants, largely Arabic speakers, from Morocco and Algeria. This means that the teaching of the Catalan language and culture is a central task in all primary classes, which may contain from a few to 100 per cent non-Catalan speakers. Introduction to the language and culture takes place through immersion classes which mix structured tuition, e.g. through songs, rhymes, stories, drama and teaching of the curriculum areas in simplified language, with free sociodramatic play and construction.

The structure of the 'reformed' curriculum, whereby primary education will finish at 11 as opposed to 14, shares much with that of Baden Württemberg. Similarly, there are no national or regional tests. A detailed introduction sets out the theoretical basis for a movement from subject disciplines to themes (areas) which allows the child freedom to experiment, build upon experience and work independently and where the teachers' role is that of a partner in learning. The work of Piaget, Vygotsky and Bruner are referred to as providing a foundation for the curriculum. Different themes are suggested, e.g. avoidance of racial and social discrimination, to show how the traditional subjects of language, maths, social science, ethics, music, foreign languages, art and sport can be integrated. There is a strong emphasis on cultural and linguistic diversity throughout the curriculum.

Our group of Sylheti speakers would most probably find themselves in a Catalan immersion class, where most of the children would be learning in a second language. The curriculum would be presented in a simplified form and there would be plenty of play provision where the teacher would 'model' play situations in the early stages. Like the Arabic children, their language and culture would be much further away from Catalan than that of their Castillian-speaking peers. Feelings of local nationalism in parts of Catalonia run high and dealing with prejudice is an important part of in-service courses. Nevertheless, our group may feel confident in their work that linguistic and cultural diversity and provision for it is at the centre of present educational issues and likely to be so during their future school careers.

An investigation into other European curricula is important, for it highlights the arbitrary nature of how 'learning' is defined and what 'knowledge' is chosen as important for young children. Interestingly, the two curricula which are based on a thematic approach and individualized learning make detailed reference to theories on how children learn. Even the French curriculum, which is very subject based, has redesigned the cycles to give more scope for individualized learning. It may be that the unique combination in the National Curriculum in England and Wales of linguistically complex work in every subject, coupled with national tests for which no direct practice is given, leaves our group in the most unprotected position of all the countries considered above. Again, we are left asking how far 'equality of opportunity' is compatible with the 'same' curriculum for young non-native speakers in school.

THE NATIONAL CURRICULUM AND NON-NATIVE SPEAKERS: APPROACHES AND STRATEGIES

The final section of this chapter returns to the English classroom and our group of Sylheti speakers. Given the high linguistic demands coupled with the lack of provision for second language learners, is there any way that these children can gain access to the English National Curriculum?

What follows are brief notes on a series of lessons given to the same group by a teacher who is also new to the class and monolingual, but who is trying to combine her knowledge of how children go about learning a second language with the content requirements of the National Curriculum. It is not intended to be a template for lesson planning, but aims to highlight: the spiral nature of second language learning; the role of the teacher in 'modelling' an action or a situation in a deliberate way using appropriate language to accompany it (this takes place through rhymes, stories and songs or, where fluent English speakers are present, through play); the importance of teacher observation and record-keeping in order to know what next to teach; and the aim of the teacher to separate 'content' from 'language', 'conceptual' from 'linguistic' demands, for planning, recording and child assessment purposes. This is a basic principle in immersion classes and highlights the occasions when CALP arises and needs to be taught.

As in most early years classes, the teacher follows an integrated approach to learning, although 'knowledge' in the English orders is not divided in this way. The theme in focus is that of 'time' (see Table 8.1). The sequence of lessons shows us how one teacher tries to provide children with access to complex concepts through a new language. Teachers accustomed to working with fluent English speakers may be surprised by the number of turns in the spiral of learning. Understanding the concept is just the first step in the task of matching the English language to it and transferring passive understanding to active use. Adults who have struggled to understand CALP in a new language understand this very well. After participating both in sessions designed for first language speakers in Catalonia and specially simplified sessions for non-native speakers, a group of English students all begged for more of the latter on the grounds that 'it was the only way they could get through to the content'.

Table 8.1 Time

Focus and concepts	Material	Language	Principle
Session 1 Prediction: more sand in the top of a timer will take longer to pass through to the bottom than a small amount	Different conventional sand timers	*Ordinal nos* 1st 2nd last, etc.,; *adjs* big, small full, ½ full, empty, *comparatives*, more/less, bigger/smaller, emptier/fuller, *superlatives*, most	P1: link with comm. class P3: comp. input

Teacher learns: children can actively use only big/bigger; small/smaller but understand the concept. The other vocab. and structures are practised through games, stories and songs

Session 2 Introduction: use of play; sand passes faster through a large hole than a small one	Sand-tray; home-made sand-timers from yoghurt pots; cups to fill them; tapes	First language use; monolingual children 'model' appropriate chunks of language	P2: add. enrichment

Teacher learns: L1 competence of children using tapes which are discussed with bilingual staff. If English is used, tapes are analysed for error analysis purposes, i.e. to examine what lexis and structures the children can and cannot use

Session 3 Formal introduction to concept of session 2 by modelling and discussion in English	Child-made sand-timers and cups	See session 1; how far are these now used? fast/faster/fastest; slow/slower/slowest	P3: comp. input P4: lang. experience

Teacher learns: the children are able to use 'last, full, empty' but are unable to compare speed in English. They use the word 'late' instead of 'slow' to describe the pot with the largest hole. From this and the tape, she learns that they understand the concept. She prepares work using adjectives, comparatives and superlatives important to the task.

Session 4 Hare & Tortoise story; moral of overconfidence; 'slow & sure', etc.	Story-pack; magnet-board puppets; simplified book & tape (dual lang.)	Hare, tortoise; I can run faster than you; You are slower than me, etc.	P1: home culture P3: comp. input

Teacher learns: through role-play, the teacher learns how far the children can

Table 8.1   (cont.)

Focus and concepts	Material	Language	Principle

actively use the comparatives, etc. She knows that the story is familiar as it is in the children's community school work-book. Simple dual language versions of the story are taken home.

Session 5

Water evaporation; length of drying time relates to thickness of material	Different types of material; washing-line	*adjs.* dry, wet, damp; *comps.* drier, wetter, faster, slower	P3: comp. input P4: experience

Teacher learns: the children initially seem unable to explain why thick material might take longer to dry; it is unclear whether or not they understand the concept. Suddenly, one child takes the thickest piece (the felt), points to its side and shouts 'more' and 'fat!'

Session 6

The thin material is transparent and shows light through	2 washing-lines for thin and thick material	*adjs.* thin, thick; thinner, thicker; *adverbs* slowly/quickly	P3 P4

Teacher learns: children all quickly sort material and understand the concept. All the adjectives and use of adverbs need practising

Session 7

Hare & Tortoise		Repeat using adverbs, slowly/quickly	P4

Teacher learns: adverbs gradually transferred to different situations

Session 8

PE moving quickly/slowly		Fast, quickly, faster, fastest, running, jumping, skipping, tiptoe running; slow, slower, slowest, slowly; walking, creeping, etc.	P4

Teacher learns: the children are now beginning to use the above vocabulary confidently and in different situations

Session 9

Return to sand measurement through different-sized holes in yoghurt pots	Beads, pots, etc.	Practice of vocab. from earlier sessions	P4

Teacher learns: no hesitation with describing what they are doing using appropriate lexis

Table 8.1 Time

Focus and concepts	Material	Language	Principle
Session 10 Jelly-making; different setting time whether in fridge or outside	Jelly, water, fridge, etc.	*verbs* pulling, boiling, melting, pouring; *adjs.* sticky, slimy, hard, soft, wet; *noun* steam	P3 P4 P1

Teacher learns: this is only possible now the children are confident in understanding and using 'fast/slow', etc. All the above lexis appears new, although the children are familiar with the activity from home. One child refers to 'steam' as 'smoke'; another predicts that the jelly will 'grow' as boiling water is poured on to it

SUMMARY AND CONCLUSIONS

This chapter set out to investigate the nature of the promise made in the Education Reform Act of 'equal opportunity' and 'equal access' to the curriculum for children of all cultural and linguistic backgrounds. An excerpt from a maths lesson with a group of Sylheti speaking children, where the teacher was working within the framework of curriculum requirements, suggested that the promise equates 'equal access' with provision of 'the same' curriculum for all. The obvious question was: How 'equal' is the same curriculum for children who enter school with a limited knowledge of English?

To examine this question, a study was made to find out how far provision for non-native speakers in the present curriculum reflects generally accepted principles for successful second language learning. A brief overview showed that curriculum documents recognize very little current research and consequently neglect its implications for classroom practice. It suggested that even use of the term 'bilingual' is confusing, as it gives the idea that 'bilingualism' is regarded as an asset, but then provides no conditions for 'additive bilingualism' to take place and thus diverts attention from the children's need for extra help in English. For this reason, use of the term 'non-native speaker' was chosen as more appropriate in the English situation.

The third section of the chapter moved to other European countries and briefly compared what provision would be made for our group of children if they were starting school in France, Baden-Württemberg (Germany) or Catalonia (Spain). This review suggested that the two national curricula of France and the UK largely assume the learning of a second language and culture to be unproblematic, whereas the regional curricula of Baden-Württemberg and Catalonia both show a much greater awareness of 'difference' and 'diversity' and provide for these in their programmes of study. Finally, the last section returned to the English classroom and suggested ways in which monolingual teachers might begin to provide access to the language and content of the curriculum to children whose English is still very limited. The lesson notes provided serve to highlight the unequal situation for children deprived of either bilingual teaching or immersion classes.

Paradoxically, then, we see that 'equal access' is not necessarily given by entitling non-native speakers to the same curriculum 'delivered' in the same way as it would be to monolingual English children. This argument is by no means universally accepted. Even in Canada, where bilingual education and immersion classes are more widely available than in England, Duquette (1992, p. 14) reminds us that the case for difference still has to be fought for bilingual children with special needs:

> One also hears the claim, 'All children should be treated alike. There should be no discrimination'. It must be conceded that to overlook individual differences and cultural differences and to treat everyone as if they were the same, does, indeed, involve a lack of discrimination. Think about it, it certainly is not in the child's interest.

By the end of this chapter, the reader may well be left asking why a promise of equal opportunities was made if so little account was eventually to be taken of accepted principles for successful second language learning. After all, a number of educators were available and anxious to give advice on how the promise might be fulfilled. A task group was, indeed, set up in 1989 by the NCC as a response to the Secretary of State for Education to 'take account of ethnic and cultural diversity and the importance of the curriculum in promoting equal opportunities for all pupils, regardless of origin or gender' (Tomlinson, 1993, p. 21). This group provided five drafts over nine months, with detailed suggestions, the crux of which was the planning of a curriculum for bilingual and ethnic minority pupils. Unfortunately, the government decided not to publish the paper and the group was officially disbanded in January 1991. In a short piece, Tomlinson (*op. cit.*) details the stages of the work and neatly supplies its obituary in the title 'The multicultural task group: the group that never was'.

Teachers who work only with monolingual English speakers might read this chapter but believe it to have no relevance to themselves. A final point for anyone in this situation is offered by Fantini (1991, p. 116):

Understanding the interrelationship of language and culture provides new incentives . . . not only for limited-English-speakers, but for all children, especially the monolingual ones. Monlingual children indeed are most in need of dual language education to ensure that they too benefit from participating in dual visions of the world and to preclude the 'smug narrowness and narrow smugness' (Fishman 1976) of the ethnocentric being.

Learning a language can result in a change of the world. In Catalonia and Baden-Württemberg, there is a growing belief that the twenty-first century will see migration within Europe on a scale which will affect us all. It is a belief we cannot afford to ignore as we make the promise of 'equal opportunity' to those learning a second, third or even fifth language in school.

Acknowledgements

I should like to thank Herr Auberle (Oberstudienrat, Baden-Württemberg), Mercedes Roc (Autonomous University of Barcelona), Maica Bernal (University of Vic) and Jean Biarnès (Université Paris Nord) for their information and help. I am also grateful to Nasima Rashid and Elizabeth Weston for examples provided of classroom practice.

9

SPECIAL EDUCATIONAL NEEDS AND THE EARLY YEARS

Chris Lloyd

The purpose of this chapter is to review and discuss some of the pertinent, and indeed urgent, issues which have arisen as a result of the changes which have taken place in education in recent years, and which have given, and continue to give, cause for concern in the area of special educational needs, particularly in the early years of education. There is no doubt that the rapid pace of educational change over the past few years in the UK has led to considerable concern among teachers, educationalists and, indeed, parents too, about the welfare of the children currently engaged in the processes of education. Within the ensuing debate it is posible to explore special educational needs from a variety of perspectives.

This chapter will seek to investigate two major themes:

- The way in which pupils with special educational needs, in the early years, are identified, their needs addressed and answered in the current educational situation.
- The way in which the current changes in the system are in danger of exacerbating and indeed creating special educational needs in the early years.

It is not possible to address either issue effectively without first setting the whole discussion into some sort of context or framework. Nor is it reasonable to embark upon a discussion about special educational needs without first attempting to define and clarify what is meant by the concept of special educational need. Similarly, any discussion about special educational needs in the current scene requires some discussion about the changes which have taken place, and still continue to take place, in the system as a whole in order to reflect on their relevance and importance to early years education.

172

THE CONTEXT

In 1978 the Warnock Committee reported on their investigation into the education of handicapped children and young people (DES, 1978b). The report, though far reaching in its recommendations, has been greatly criticized for failing to address effectively the many issues raised by its inquiry. Indeed, in a recent BBC television programme (July 1993), Baroness Warnock herself admitted that the effects of the Warnock Report have been to concentrate too much attention on a small minority of children with special educational needs while the needs of the majority of children with difficulties have not been addressed, or in many cases even considered.

In spite of the many criticisms and its, now widely recognized, shortcomings, the Warnock Report played a very important part in redefining and reinterpreting educational provision for children with disabilities and difficulties. The clearly stated influence, which underpins all its recommendations, is that of the child-centred approach to education. The recognition that there is a continuum of need, which is not only to do with the chronological progress of the child but also to do with the rate and pace at which the child develops and the changing nature of the child's needs during that period of development, is a clear indication of this influence. Similarly the redefinition of handicap to the notion of special educational need is a demonstration of the view that the child is central and that his or her needs are seen as the starting-point for the planning of educational provision. There is a firm acknowledgement that a child's needs will change and develop during his or her progress towards maturity and also, of course, that the quality of the educational and social experience and the context will affect that growth and development.

The importance of the educational context is emphasized throughout the report, as is the approach to curriculum planning and assessment. If needs are constantly changing and the pupils' development is the aim and goal of education, then provision must be sensitive and flexible, it must enable and support. Assessment procedures similarly must be ongoing, flexible, sensitive and diagnostic and must take account of the different rates and paces of development. Recognition is also given to the potential for the educational context to exacerbate or even, in some cases, to cause special educational needs.

> Some handicapping conditions, particularly behaviour disorders, may be brought about or accentuated by factors at the school such as its premises, organisation or staff. In such cases assessment may need to focus on the

institution, the classroom setting or the teacher, as well as the individual child and his family if it is to encompass a full consideration of the child's problems and their educational implications.

(*op. cit.*, 4:33)

Perhaps the most well known of the Warnock Report's claims is the assertion that as many as 20 per cent of pupils in the education system may, at any one time, be experiencing special educational needs. The recognition of this point alerts us to the need to look at the mainstream of educational provision in the light of this finding and to reappraise and redefine the approach in order to begin to address the needs of all pupils effectively. In the Warnock Report's assertion that the aims and goals of education are the same for all children there is a clear recommendation that, while we need to recognize special educational needs, we also need to provide for the education of all children to continue to take place within the mainstream of educational provision. The mainstream of educational provision must take account of the needs of all children, irrespective of ability. While the report recognizes that a small percentage of children may need extra, specialist provision, the goal should be to provide for the maximum number of children in the mainstream.

What is clear is that the view of education, and within that of the learner and the learning process, is fundamentally informed by a developmental approach which sees an approach to the curriculum as 'one which can be tuned into at different levels and have different outcomes which are internally consistent with that particular child's needs and levels of cognition' (Gammage, 1992, p. 4).

While there is no doubt that the Warnock Report acted as a powerful consciousness-raising tool for many, and focused the debate about special educational needs, there is equally no doubt that it failed to address in any real terms any of the issues it raised. For example, while pointing to the deficiencies of the curriculum in mainstream schools and to the large number of children whom that curriculum may be seen to be failing, it failed to question why or satisfactorily to address the issue. Baroness Warnock herself admits 'We assumed that a special need would be defined in terms of the help a child might have if he was to gain access to the curriculum . . . only occasionally did we think that the curriculum must be changed to suit the child' (Warnock, 1986, p. 56).

The question of access to the curriculum is hardly addressed at all in the report, nor is the model or the role the curriculum and schools themselves can play in creating barriers to access for children considered a great deal. The creation, or, indeed, the construction (Tomlinson, 1982) of special educational need is for the most part ignored and the underlying social causes of special educational need only hinted at or suggested. There is in fact no recommendation for curriculum reform or reorganization, seen by many as a prerequisite for any real attempt at catering for all children in the mainstream of education.

The roles of professionals and of parents in the education of children with special educational needs are seen rather simplistically. There is a lack of any real recognition of the potentially problematic nature of this process. While not seeking to undervalue the importance of involving both groups there is a need for us to recognize that the procedure is neither straightforward nor without many problems.

This chapter is not the appropriate place to debate these failings further or in more detail, although some of them will be discussed further in relation to other issues. What is important to recognize is that the failure of the Warnock Report, and the subsequent Education Act 1981, to do more than raise awareness of the issues, has led to considerable confusion, obfuscation and to the centring of the debate around less important areas such as resourcing and organization. The Education Act 1981, coming as it did at a time of shrinking resources in education and with no sound financial backing, concentrated on the very small minority of children, identified as having special educational needs, requiring additional resourcing. The legislation concentrated on the implementation of the statementing procedure and on little of the wider recommendations of the Warnock Committee.

The implications for children with special educational needs in the early years can best be illustrated by looking a little more closely at Chapter 5 of the Warnock Report – 'Children Under Five'. The main themes raised in this chapter are:

- the vital importance of early educational opportunities for children showing signs of disability or difficulty;
- the role of parents as educators of their children and the need for skilled help and support in this role; and
- the need for close inter-professional co-operation and for good training for those professionals involved.

The chapter begins with the statement:

> The period between birth and four years of age is generally accepted to be that of the fastest intellectual development, while the years between one and three to four normally see a rapid development in language. Thereafter the rate of intellectual development progressively diminishes and the learning of

language becomes increasingly difficult. Education during the first five years
of life is thus of crucial importance.

(DES, 1978b, 5: 1)

The importance of positive early experience is recognized as even more
vital for children with disabilities or difficulties and a strong commitment is
made for legislation to ensure resourcing for such early experience for
these children. The joint role of parents and teachers as educators of children with disabilities is also discussed and the importance of creating effective, beneficial partnerships from an early age is stressed. Parents of
children with disabilities need understanding and support and must be
encouraged to take an active part in their education from as early a stage as
possible. Similarly the importance of early identification together with continuous and sensitive assessment and diagnosis of need are emphasized.
Here a multi-professional approach is suggested involving the development
of enabling partnerships.

Although the home is seen as the best place for the stimulation of early
development of children with disabilities or difficulties, there is also a
recognition that all parents may not be able to provide this stimulus without a great deal of support, and there is therefore the suggestion that
compensatory measures, such as the 'nurture groups' started up in some
London primary schools, should be provided for children approaching
school age who are recognized as being affected by deprivation or disadvantage in early childhood. These 'seek to provide, so far as possible, the
normal relationships and experiences of early childhood which these children have missed' (*op. cit.*, 5: 30).

The Warnock Report lays strong emphasis too on the importance of
'skilled' support for children and their parents in the early years:

> We therefore recommend that reinforcement and skilled support should be
> provided for parents of children with disabilities or significant difficulties in
> the early years.
>
> (*op. cit.*, 5: 31)

> We recommend that a range of different forms of skilled support for parents
> of children with special needs should be available in every area.
>
> (*op. cit.*, 5: 32)

> We recommend that there should be a comprehensive peripatetic teaching
> service which would cater, wherever possible, exclusively for children with
> disabilities or significant difficulties, below school age. It should cover every
> type of disability and disorder . . . We recommend that there should be scope
> for specialization within the service; in particular in view of the specific skills
> required for their teaching.
>
> (*op. cit.*, 5: 37)

The job of these peripatetic teachers should include

- sensitively assessing children's educational needs;
- working with parents on an educational programme for the children;
- working directly with the children; and
- working with other professionals to meet the needs of the children.

In addition there should be a conscious effort to encourage parental support groups and workshops for parents of children with disabilities. The teachers' job should also include putting parents in touch with resources such as toy libraries and preschool playgroups.

Significantly also there is a recommendation that teachers should receive properly organized in-service training and professional development, including inter-professional aspects of the work.

The immense value of nursery education is also stressed as 'it not only contributes to a child's early development but also provides opportunities for the early identification of signs of special needs and problems in young children' (*op. cit.*, 5: 49).

The Warnock Report recognizes clearly that the expansion of nursery education is not just important for children with special educational needs but is vital for all children: 'We recommend that the provision of nursery education for all children should be substantially increased as soon as possible, since this would have the consequence that opportunities for nursery education for young children with special needs would be correspondingly extended' (*op. cit.*, 5: 51).

For children with special needs to benefit from ordinary nursery classes, however, certain conditions should be met, according to the Warnock Committee:

- Attitudes of parents of all children and of staff must be positive.
- There must be suitable accommodation and equipment.
- There must be generous staffing ratios of teaching and non-teaching staff.
- Implications of encouraging the inclusion of all children irrespective of ability or disability must be considered and preparation made.
- Teachers need regular advice, support and specialist assistance.

In addition to the importance of nursery education, the value of playgroups is also stressed. Again the emphasis is on inclusion. That is, that children with disabilities should attend regular play and opportunity groups and that their parents should be encouraged, through these groups, to meet each other and to discuss with staff their children's progress and development. The importance of the availability of skilled specialist help for these groups is again reiterated, as is the need for good communication with all other professionals involved with the children. Day nurseries are seen as another means of ensuring early educational opportunity for children with special needs and the Warnock Report recommends better training for staff to encourage the provision of real educational opportunities.

The recommendations of this chapter highlight very effectively the failure of the Warnock Report to acknowledge fully the very problematic nature of some of the issues raised. The difficulties arising from the early involvement of parents in their children's education and assessment are either glossed over or avoided. It may well be very important to involve parents in the procedures of assessment and to encourage supportive partnerships, but it cannot be assumed that this will always work to the benefit of the child. It is possible that what the parent views as in the child's best interests might in fact result in additional stress, as in the case where parents are unable to come to terms with their child's disability and have unrealistic ambitions for him or her. Other parents may be overprotective and thus prevent full development. For some the involvement with professionals can be daunting and inhibiting. The whole structure and concept of family has changed in recent years. Single parents, who are unable to spare the time to involve themselves as much as they might want to, may as a result feel inadequate, causing further stress and tension.

Similarly the whole idea of early identification and assessment of special educational need is problematic. While many would agree that to identify and begin to address special needs at an early stage can be beneficial, it must also be recognized that early concerns and anxieties about the rate of a child's development can lead to the problem of labelling and of the 'self-fulfilling prophecy'.

The problems of resourcing have already been mentioned. The lack of funding meant that the recommendations of the Warnock Committee were never in any real sense fully addressed. Reporting as it did at a time of shrinking resources and cut-backs in public spending, there was little opportunity for the development of skilled peripatetic teaching teams supported by strong advisory services and specialists. In fact, developments in the area of special educational needs in the early years have been sporadic and dependent on local prioritizing procedures.

In answer to the strong recommendation for extra resourcing for special educational needs, the Education Act 1981 introduced the statement procedure, making local education authorities responsible for ensuring that policy in this area was developed. A lack of any clear national guidelines for this procedure, however, has resulted in the development of different criteria and processes for statementing, and a recent survey (HMI, 1989) shows that it can take anything from six months to two years for a child to be statemented. As already mentioned, the statementing process also concentrates on a very small percentage of children, approximately 2 per cent, totally ignoring the much larger percentage identified by the Warnock Committee as needing support and help. Baroness Warnock has repeatedly referred to the mistake the committee made in concentrating on the idea of statementing and has suggested recently (BBC television programme, July 1993) that it should be abandoned altogether as it fails to address the real needs of the large and growing number of children experiencing special needs and needing extra support in the mainstream of education.

It is important, however, not to dwell too long on the negative aspects of the developments in special educational needs in recent years. There is no doubt that the debate engendered by the Warnock Report has continued. The clear recognition of the importance of early support for parents and their children; the importance of parents as partners in their children's education; the importance of sensitive, skilled assessment/identification procedures; the vital recognition of the value of integrated nursery education for all children; and the need for effective training and professional development to assist teachers and other professionals in their work are all issues which continue to be as important and essential a focus for the debate as they were in 1978. A debate which, in the light of current changes and developments that will be discussed in more detail later, it is perhaps even more important than it was in 1978 to continue, so that these issues may be raised again and again.

THE CONCEPT OF SPECIAL EDUCATIONAL NEED

Before moving on to look at the effects of recent and current changes in the education system it is important to consider what the term special educational need means, and to rehearse some of the current arguments about disability and the rights of disabled persons to a full educational opportunity.

Traditionally the view of handicap and disability has been firmly rooted, and many would say still is (Oliver, 1992), in a medical model. The Warnock Committee made it clear that they wanted to see a change in understanding of what was meant by handicap and, in fact, to eliminate the distinction between handicapped and non-handicapped and to move towards a concept of special educational need 'seen not in terms of a particular disability which a child may be judged to have, but in relation to everything about him, his abilities as well as his disabilities – indeed all the factors which have a bearing on his educational progress' (DES, 1978b, 3: 6).

The traditional 'medical' model which regards disability as personal tragedy or trouble (Oliver, 1992) has led to the organization of educational provision based on criteria concerned with caring or even nursing rather than true educational criteria. This has resulted in a proliferation of different, and often segregated, educational provision where real educational opportunity for disabled persons has been a hit or miss affair. Any concept of integration based on this model has been concerned with normalization. That is, making the child fit into what is considered to be the 'normal' mainstream provision. Obviously the term 'normal' is extremely problematic in this context as the concept of the norm is subjective and open to manipulation and distortion in order to serve the purposes of resourcing, politics, marketing, etc., none of which have a great deal of relevance as educational criteria.

This model, then, is found by many to be totally inadequate and indeed unsuitable as a model for special educational provision (Tomlinson, 1982; Fulcher, 1989; Oliver, 1992). To categorize people as 'normal' or 'non-normal' is to engage in value judgements which are certainly open to question. Fulcher (1989, p. 24) points out that disability as a category 'is used to exclude rather than include and to oppress rather than enable'.

There is a danger too of the 'medical' model leading to the personalization of disability: 'A theme of professionalism pervades medical discourse and its associated discourses; psychology; social work; occupational therapy; counselling; physiotherapy and educational discourse. The phrase "in the best interest" [of the patient child etc.] instances this theme' (*op. cit.*, p. 27).

The Warnock Report claimed to be moving away from this model to a different view, but it can be seen from the recommendations made with regard to the under-5s and special educational need that these underlying problematic issues were not really addressed. Certainly there is a recognition of the need to consider the home and the family background of the child, and in the school years the curriculum and organization of the school itself are seen as possible factors influencing special educational need, but by failing to address sufficiently the issues raised above, concerned with attitudes and beliefs about disability, the report failed really to shift the debate into a different gear or to propose successfully an alternative model.

The assertion that nursery education should be expanded for all children, and that those with disabilities and difficulties should be included in that provision, is a positive acknowledgement of the need to expand and extend the mainstream of provision to address the need of all children, and of the positive benefits of that inclusion to all children. On the other hand, the discussions about early assessment and identification, and the emphasis on the role of skilled professionals, fails to tackle, or even to take account of, those problems concerning labelling and categorization raised above.

The idea of nursery education for all finds expression in the work of writers such as Tony Dessent (1987). He proposes a desegregationalist approach to all educational provision, which is not about fitting people in, or normalizing, but is about the expansion and enhancement of provision to enable the needs of all children to be met. This model can be seen to address some of the major inadequacies of the 'medical' model in that it acknowledges the responsibility of society, to a certain extent, for the exclusion of certain groups. It also shifts the onus from the individual to the context. What it still fails to do, however, is to address adequately those deep-rooted practices and attitudes of society which have led to the acceptance of segregation and exclusion in the first place. There is still within this model the notion that provision for special educational needs is dependent on the benevolent act of extra resourcing, and there is also the idea of the need to compensate in some way for disability. This model remains a 'deficit' model which takes no account of the fact that difference might provide enrichment and that disabled persons, given a voice, and indeed a choice, can add a valuable and important dimension.

In answer to the 'deficit' models of disability there has been, in recent years, a growing discourse around, what can be seen as, an 'equal opportunities', 'human rights' approach to disability. This approach, strongly supported by disability movements and disabled people themselves, is rooted in notions of self-reliance, independence and consumer rights rather than needs. It is an overtly political model which takes an equal opportunities stance which demands that the traditional models of disability should be rejected on the grounds that they have led to discrimination, exclusion and oppression both socially and educationally (Oliver, 1990; 1992). It rejects totally any ideas about normalization or compensation in provision for disabled persons and demands a voice and a place, by right, at all levels of policy-making. Educationally the demand is for an inclusive approach to all planning of provision. There is a recognition too of the value of celebrating and capitalizing on the enrichment of difference and diversity rather than the impoverishment of provision through the process of fitting it to a narrow set of artificially produced concepts of what is normal.

It is important to be aware of the issues raised by the discussion above before making any attempt to appraise the effects of recent educational developments on children with special educational needs. The lack of any clear conceptual definition or of a real understanding of the issues raised by the above debate is, unfortunately, all too apparent in current educational policy-making and reorganization. Assumptions are made; traditional attitudes and practices are reinforced; and the debate is centred around the less important, superficial resourcing and organizational issues. There is a lack of genuine insight, or of any sound theoretical underpinning to the discussion about educational opportunities for children with special educational needs. Indeed this may be said to be the case for all children (Kelly, 1990), but in the case of children with special educational needs the matter is further clouded by the lack of any consensus or even understanding of the fundamental concepts involved.

SPECIAL EDUCATIONAL NEEDS AND THE EARLY YEARS: A CURRENT PERSPECTIVE

In the introduction to this chapter the suggestion was made that it might be useful to examine the influences of current educational developments and change with regard to special educational needs in the early years from a dual perspective:

- The way in which children with special educational needs are assessed/identified and their needs addressed in the current scene.
- The way in which current changes in the education system can be seen to be responsible for exacerbating, or even creating, special educational needs in the early years.

These two perspectives are obviously not mutually exclusive and have great bearing and influence on each other. For the purposes of this discussion, however, it is useful to deal with each separately in order to see more clearly the issues of concern.

At the same time it is not possible within the scope of this chapter to cover all the factors influencing children with special educational needs, or indeed to cover any factors in great detail. It is therefore the intention to attempt to highlight some areas of concern in order to generate and stimulate some genuine, and very necessary, debate. Kelly (1990) points out that the whole area of special educational need has been, at best, scantily addressed in the recent debate and that what has been said has reflected a failure to take account of what has been learnt about the provision of education for pupils with special needs from both the experience and research of many years, in particular from the work that has been undertaken in the last decade or so since the publication of the Warnock Report in 1978.

(*op. cit.*, p. 100)

As has already been said, far from tackling the underlying principles, much of the debate about special educational need, even before the Education Act 1988, has centred around peripheral and often totally non-educational issues, leading to many misconceptions and much confusion about the whole area. It is to be hoped, therefore, that this examination will serve, at least, to raise some questions and point to some areas which are of real concern and which need urgently to be considered.

Provision for special educational needs: the current scene

To return then to the first theme proposed at the beginning of this section. Recent discussions with teachers working in early years education with children with special needs, and with parents and the children themselves, have pointed to a number of areas of concern about the current scene. As already mentioned it is not within the scope of this chapter to deal with all these issues or indeed to attempt to cover any in great detail. It will be useful, however, to illustrate some of the causes of concern by concentrating on the National Curriculum itself, some of the organizational changes which have come about as a result of delegated budgets to schools (LMS) and the whole area of teacher training and professional development. All three areas have far-reaching consequences for children with special educational needs and will provide a useful framework for the discussion.

There is no doubt that the National Curriculum is having a considerable influence on provision and procedures concerning children with special educational needs. The demands of the National Curriculum can be seen to be exerting pressure on educational provision even for the very youngest children. In a recent paper given at Nottingham University (1992), Philip Gammage (p. 3) states:

Britain seems to have misread the signs and sticks obstinately to its newly defined curriculum and its avowal that assessment is central to it. What frightens me even more than the delusion that centrally defined curriculum can be imposed on children is the new and rather dangerous tendency to let THAT curriculum press down upon the provision for even the youngest of children . . . It is here that many anxieties really begin to develop. Basically the argument beginning to be heard from the politicians is that since they are becoming more and more convinced that early education matters, then it should be a version of that which they deem appropriate for older children.

Certainly for colleagues working with children in the early years, and especially with children with disabilities and difficulties, it is becoming more and more difficult to retain the child-centred, developmental approach which they believe to be vital as they are forced to bow to the pressures of the subject-centred approach being pressed on the education system by central government.

Much has been written about the inadequacies of the National Curriculum as a curriculum for all (Lawton and Chitty, 1988; Kelly, 1990). For children with special educational needs, particularly in the early years, opportunities to play, to talk, to interact, to experience and to investigate, at their own pace, are especially vital. While there are procedures available under the Education Act 1988 to modify, or even in some cases disapply children with special needs from the National Curriculum, this can only be achieved through the statementing process, the shortcomings of which have already been discussed. Also there is an inherent contradiction in an entitlement curriculum, which is the claim made by the Education Act 1988, which has provision for disapplication. Does this not imply, one wonders, a lack of inclusive planning and an acknowledgement that the National Curriculum is not in fact a curriculum which is designed to make provision for all but one which is designed for those who can be fitted to it?

Discussions about this issue with an infant headteacher colleague highlighted certain problems she is facing. Since statementing is the only way of securing extra resourcing she is keen to have children statemented as early as possible in order to obtain extra support for them. While recognizing the dangers of early labelling in this way she feels, pragmatically, that it is the only way she can continue to retain children with difficulties and disabilities in her school. She also expressed fear and concern, as a great supporter of integration for children with special needs, that other colleagues might be using the statementing procedure as a means of removing children to segregated provision rather than continuing with them in the mainstream school. While this is obviously anecdotal, and therefore of limited value as evidence, there is no doubt that it raises serious issues for thought and concern.

The linear model of progression on which the National Curriculum is based also presents many problems. It totally ignores the different paces and rates at which children learn and develop and is related to norms which, as we saw in the previous section, can prove to be exclusive and problematic for children with disabilities or difficulties. Philip Gammage

(1990, p. 3) points out: 'because of the wide developmental range found in classrooms (I have known four year olds just starting to speak coherently while others were reading well), the notion of a uniform presentation of a CURRICULUM is very far from reality.'

He cites the work of educational writers and researchers such as Bredekamp (1987), Weikart (1987) and Bloom (1988) to support his view that curricula designed from a developmental perspective are more likely to prove beneficial for young children, or indeed for all chilldren. Certainly for children with disabilities and difficulties, a developmental, child-centred, differentiated approach is vital from the earliest years. Many need extra opportunities to play, to interact to experiment, to manipulate materials, to develop social skills. Discussions with colleagues working with children with special needs in the early years all highlight grave concerns about the pressure being put on the time available for these activities and about the inappropriateness of the levels of attainment and the activities suggested for those levels in the early years in the National Curriculum. Many expressed concerns about the wide range of subjects to be covered by children in the early years, again pointing to the need for more time to develop basic concepts.

The recent National Curriculum Council review of special educational needs in the National Curriculum brings together the views of teachers working with children with learning difficulties in the mainstream and in special schools. Their view supports the above concerns: 'the links between Key Stages and chronological ages are reported to be unrealistic for this group of pupils . . . priorities such as speech therapy, extra time on reading and mathematics and life skills mean that time available for National Curriculum subjects is reduced' (NCC, 1993, p. 5).

Certainly, to return to some of the issues raised in the previous section about the concept of special educational needs, a curriculum which is rooted in a developmental approach and which recognizes the different paces and rates of development, concentrating on the processes of education rather than the end-products, has more possibility of being inclusive and of offering an equal educational opportunity to children with disabilities. A curriculum matched to the needs and interests of the child is less likely to exert the kind of pressure on the early years being experienced at present and more likely to increase opportunities for inclusion in the mainstream of education from the beginning. In discussions, teachers working in special units express worries about the unwillingness of mainstream colleagues to integrate their pupils because of the current National Curriculum demands. Where in the past at least partial integration had been possible, mainstream colleagues are becoming more and more reluctant to take on additional pupils who would be unable to keep pace with the demands of Key Stage 1.

Another key area of increasing pressure on existing practice in the early years for children with special educational needs is the assessment procedures associated with the National Curriculum. The particularly narrow view of assessment and testing which is promoted by these procedures is potentially dangerous for all children, but even more so for children who are experiencing difficulties:

> Most people who work in or with education are fully cognizant of the dangers of assessment. They will know too that successful teaching requires careful diagnosis of where the particular learner is at that stage of the enterprise. Such diagnosis, even for the very young children, will of course often mean carefully recorded evaluation. Eventually such evaluation may well form part of a profile of the child, or of her development. But the danger of the 'tail wagging the dog' is real enough. Testing and certification can often pervert and alter the goals of education.
>
> (Gammage, 1990, p. 5)

There is no doubt that teachers in their recent refusal to carry out the tests and, in cases where testing took place, their refusal to report the results to the NCC (summer, 1993), have recognized these dangers. Ongoing, sensitive, diagnostic, formative assessment is an essential part of the effective teaching and learning process. There may also be a need at various points in a child's development for summative assessments which may need to be made public to genuinely interested parties such as parents. The National Curriculum standardized tests, however, have other, clearly stated purposes: to raise standards; to ensure teacher accountability; to encourage competition between schools, to name but a few. All these purposes are questionable and extremely controversial, at the same time as being highly problematic. The current rhetoric employed by politicians, however, ignores this and loudly proclaims that testing and the publication of test results, in the form of league tables, are a vital part of the procedure of raising educational standards. Kelly (1992) points out very effectively the lack of any coherent base or underpinning for these claims and highlights the danger of such rhetoric being absorbed into current thinking and accepted as fact.

For teachers working in the early years of education with children experiencing difficulties, the idea of chronologically linked, standardized testing with the publication of results is a matter of extreme concern. The linking of test results to competition and comparison between schools is even more worrying. The dilemma becomes immediately obvious. To keep these children within the system may distort or lower the test results. Extra time will be required for those children with difficulties and disabilities for the testing process, which may in turn disadvantage other children. Of course it is possible to turn again to the statementing procedure in order to secure extra support for this, but the dangers of this have already been discussed. In practice teachers find that the tests are daunting and time consuming enough for those children who are progressing at what may be considered to be a 'normal' rate.

An additional problem is that the tests, in many cases, seem to be designed to find out what children cannot do rather than what they can do. Teachers working with children with learning difficulties find that there is little scope in the testing procedures at 7 plus for recognition of the positive achievement and success of many of their charges. They would prefer to see a system which placed greater emphasis on the ongoing, teacher assessment which they already do, and which would give more opportunity to acknowledge success and achievement, however small, outside the narrow academic, subject base of the prescribed testing procedures.

The whole idea of standardized testing tied to chronological stages has questionable value if we take account of the large body of research available in the area of child development. While there is no doubt that the early years are a period of rapid growth and development, there is equally no doubt that progress differs from child to child. The whole question of the influence of home, social and economic factors must also be raised. Many children have impoverished and deprived early experience, materially and in terms of social development and relationships. The need to nurture and develop, to provide enriching and enhancing early experience will differ from child to child. While there is no doubt that stimulating, enriching early experience is vitally important for all children, it must be recognized that some may require a great deal more than others.

The orgnization and provision of the necessary experience for children in the early years is inevitably more difficult with the spectre of testing at 7 plus looming over the whole process. Indeed, discussions with colleagues point to this as one of the greatest areas of concern. For some children there is just not enough time to provide the vitally important opportunities to experience, to play, to develop social skills, before they are plunged into the formal assessment procedures. They are unable to understand, or to interpret, without a great deal of assistance, even what is being asked of them by the test questions in many cases.

An additional ogre is now also under discussion, the idea of testing at 5 plus. It is reasonable to expect that, if schools are to be held responsible, publicly for their pupils' progress at 7 plus, they should want some kind of evidence to prove just how much, or little, progress has been made. What does this mean, however, for the child experiencing difficulties, or who is disabled? Again there is the prospect of being excluded, of being categorized, of generally even more restricted opportunities from an earlier age. The possibilities are more than worrying.

While many headteachers welcome the flexibility that local management of schools (LMS) brings with it, there is no doubt that it has implications, not all positive, for children with special educational needs. Many schools have been forced to raise their class size, a factor not conducive to the inclusion of children with special needs. In some schools, in order to provide extra support and assistance in the classroom, the decision has been made to increase class size by not filling an empty teaching post and to employ extra classroom assistants, who are of course far less expensive than a fully qualified teacher. This may well provide an extra resource in the classroom but whether it will provide the most effective support for children with special needs is debatable.

LMS has also led to the depletion of centralized local authority advisory and support services. For many this has proved to be a great loss in terms of support for teachers in the form of in-service training (INSET) and in terms of support for the statementing and assessment procedures. The issue of professional development and training will be discussed more fully later but it is important perhaps to look back and reflect upon the Warnock Report recommendations about support teams for teachers and parents and to consider what possibilities there are for the future for these sorts of resources under current funding arrangements.

LMS in special schools and units may also lead to further segregation for children with special needs since in these establishments it is the number of places which is funded rather than the number of pupils. It would seem likely, therefore, that, having funded, say, 130 places in a special school, the local authority will be most anxious to have those places filled. Again the manipulation of the label 'special educational need' is possible.

These effects, and many others, are becoming of increasing concern as having far-reaching consequences for the future of special educational needs, but perhaps the most worrying professionally is the new way ahead being signalled for initial teacher training (ITT) and associated professional development. The Warnock Report laid heavy emphasis on the importance of good INSET and of effective ITT in the area of special educational needs, highlighting the fact that, if as many as one in five children can be said to be experiencing special needs, then it is clearly the responsibility of all teachers to cater for those needs. As previously mentioned, the report also makes very clear the importance of effective training for those working in the early years with children with special educational needs. In a series of recommendations in Chapter 12 about ITT and INSET, the message is made very clear:

> The procedures which we have recommended elsewhere in this report for recognising and meeting the needs of children who require special educational help will be of no avail unless all teachers have an insight into the special needs which many children have, and unless teachers with defined responsibilities for such children have the specialist expertise required to meet those needs. The necessary skills and expertise must be acquired through training. Our proposals for the future development of teacher training are therefore central to our report and should be acted upon as quickly as possible.
>
> (DES, 1978b, 12: 85)

As a result of these recommendations a special educational needs element has become a required part of ITT courses and many part-time special needs courses have been developed. This has in some ways begun to address the recommendations of the report, but there is no doubt that they still leave a great deal to be desired in terms of achieving Warnock's aims.

Recent proposals for school-based ITT and for the reduction of INSET monies, as a result of LMS, have extremely worrying implications for the future development of effective teacher training for special educational needs. Where will teachers find the sort of support and professional development they need to cope with the demands of the special needs of their pupils? Where will they be able to go to develop the expertise, discussed in the Warnock Report? Colleagues at present attending part-time diploma courses in special needs find the process of meeting with other colleagues, to discuss renewing and updating information and developing a sound theoretical base which enables them to articulate more fully what they are attempting to achieve, to be vitally important to the development of their practice. They, among others, are extremely concerned about the future.

Many issues raised above are areas of growing concern for the whole area of special educational needs. There are, of course many others, but what becomes obvious from the discussion above, brief and superficial though it may be, is that for children with disabilities and difficulties in the early years, and indeed throughout their education, the effects of the Education Act 1988 and the subsequent developments, are adding further problems and concerns to what was already an area of considerable confusion.

Current policies and the creation of special educational needs

To turn now to the second theme, the creation of special educational needs through the current developments and changes in education. Again, the points to be made can best be illustrated by looking at the same factors: the National Curriculum and its assessment procedures; LMS and its implications; and teacher training and professional development.

The concern, already raised, about the prescriptive, academic nature of the National Curriculum, and its growing downward pressure on the early years of education, is of particular relevance here. There is no doubt that in the early years children grow and develop at a rapid pace. Given an irrelevant, ill-matched, over-prescriptive curriculum which does not reflect the development of the child him or herself, disaffection, boredom and lack of interest will inevitably set in – that alienation we noted in Chapters 1 and 2. This can be the beginning of a range of difficulties, or special needs.

> To be among such a group (young children aged roughly 3–10 years) for any reasonable length of time, makes one aware of the danger of seeing curricula or programmes of learning as somehow best fashioned outside the children. Rather there is an undeniable pressure that forces one to acknowledge that such children demonstrate vastly different perceptions which greet processes, internalize and make anew any ideas 'provided' by the teacher. This means that the teacher cannot wholly structure, deliver or create the precise chains of knowledge. It means that she may have to link ideas with great subtlety, to follow 'red herrings', to play alongside, to observe carefully, to abandon certain threads of exposition and to search for others.
>
> (Gammage, 1992, pp. 3–4)

The damage that can potentially be caused by imposing, at too early an age, a totally inappropriate approach to teaching and learning is immeasurable. Certainly discussions with teacher colleagues lead to the same conclusion as Philip Gammage's. Children need time to play, to develop, to explore, to interact, to inquire and to experience. Certainly, then, there is a real danger that the prescriptive curriculum being imposed at present will at least exacerbate difficulties being experienced by children with special needs, if not create a range of special needs: 'Teachers point out that for all pupils with special educational needs the National Curriculum provides only a part of the curriculum. Access to developmental work across the curriculum, personal and social education and enrichment activities in particular should be given equal status with access to National Curriculum subjects' (NCC, 1992b, p. 2).

There is also a growing concern about the number of children, even at the earliest stages, being statemented as having emotional and behavioural difficulties (BBC Television, May 1991). Perhaps one of the causes of this is disaffection with what is being offered in terms of curriculum. Certainly there are other factors which can be cited, but the mismatch between the child's needs and attempts to address them must surely be regarded as at least an area of concern and an issue for further research:

> What dangers then can be seen in the assessment procedures currently being imposed on children in our education system. At the close of the 20th Century we seem obsessed by qualifications, by hurdles jumped, honours amassed, certificates gained, skills achieved. This attitude does enormous damage to the process of being educated, since it puts the emphasis on crudely measured outputs rather than emphasizing the worth of what is going on. It is, by its very nature, designed to produce gradings, lists, stratification of the population, so that while there may be joyful winners there are innumerable losers, and these latter may be turned off the real educative possibilities for the rest of their lives.
>
> (Gammage, 1992, p. 5)

It seems impossible that after such a short time the lessons about branding children as failures, made so clear by the 11-plus examination, should have been forgotten – so much so that testing at 7 plus, 11 plus, 14 and 16 plus are considered, by the politicians at least, to be key elements of educational provision. What will happen to children who repeatedly fail these tests, the shortcomings of which have already been mentioned? Indeed, what will happen, if testing at 5 is introduced, to those children who are labelled at that tender and very formative age with the tag 'failure'?

There is no doubt that positive early experience of success leads to the development of a good self-image and to strong foundations for future learning. The converse is also patently true. Children in the early stages will not be encouraged or enabled by the experience of failure.

One of the most important arguments in the debate about integrating children with special educational needs into the mainstream of education, made by the disability movements and by those calling for equal opportunities for disabled persons, is that we need to expand and enhance our concepts of success and achievement to include more people. The work of Eisner and Bruner points to the value and benefit which can be gained from extending our understanding and the value we place on achievements beyond literacy and numeracy. Wilson and Cowell (1986) discuss the need to develop new criteria for assessing children so that what we consider to be 'normal' development can be expanded to become more inclusive. They criticize (p. 57) the emphasis on academic achievement to the detriment of other qualities and abilities:

If we could imagine an education regime in which the development of character, the handling of emotions and personal interaction were genuinely valued
as central, in which plenty of time was devoted to them and in which a serious
attempt was made to foster and assess them, then what we count as normal
. . . would turn out very differently from what we do today.

In the current educational climate, with its constant emphasis on testing
and raising academic standards, there is a real danger that other qualities will
be excluded, or at least undervalued. The narrow view being promoted, of
assessment as standardized testing of children's abilities to read, write and
cope with number, is potentially a process for expanding the number of
children we brand as failures, or as having special educational needs. By
developing more sensitive, responsive, teacher-led assessment procedures, it
is possible to credit more children with more success. It is possible to see
that, while a child may be struggling with the formal processes of reading or
writing, he or she may be at an advanced stage of creative development. The
careful nurturing of self-esteem through the process of achievement and
success can reduce children's special needs considerably. At the same time
by widening the concept of what we understand by success, and by valuing
diversity and difference, we can make a very real reduction in the number of
children we regard as having special educational needs.

The effects of the reorganization of funding in education have already
been discussed to some extent in the previous section. In terms of their
potential to exacerbate and create special needs there is no doubt that
teachers are concerned about the growing need to place financial considerations before educational considerations, indeed to make educational decisions based on economic criteria. Increasing class size has already been
cited as an example of this. The question of balancing the budget means
that, often, priorities must be made and that special needs considerations
cannot be made. Extra support for children with special needs is expensive
and is becoming an increasingly difficult issue to resolve. There is, also, a
need to attract pupils, as funding comes with pupils in the mainstream
school. Headteachers with whom this matter was discussed confessed to
growing concerns about the sort of 'image' projected by the school. 'Marketing' an infant school effectively means presenting an orderly, quiet,
trouble-free environment. For one headteacher who has previously worked
hard to promote the integration and inclusion of children with emotional
and behavioural difficulties the problem is a real dilemma. She is being
forced to bow to pressures from parents and prospective parents which
will, in the long term, mean that she will find it increasingly difficult to
include these children.

ITT and INSET have already been discussed in the previous section. Recently the amazing suggestion has been made by the government that teachers in the early years do not need to be qualified or to receive the same level of training as teachers of older children. John Patten, the Education Secretary, has suggested the idea of non-graduates becoming infant teachers after one year of training 'on the job'. There is a clear lack of recognition here of the vital importance of the early years in a child's development.

Many colleagues working in this area with full professional qualifications and several years of experience feel inadequate to the task of sensitive assessment and diagnosis of, and response to, children's needs. It is hard to imagine many people allowing anyone to work on their teeth after a year's apprenticeship and the dubious credential that they had had their own teeth treated before. How then can we even consider the possibility of allowing the precious early years of education to be handed over to untrained, unskilled people? Mr Patten would do well to listen to the words of Plato, quoted earlier in Chapter 2: 'Don't you know that in every task the most important thing is the beginning and especially when we deal with anything young and tender.'

We know that to grow strong and sturdy and healthy children need a good start in life. To develop intellectually, a good start educationally is also vital. The value of early years education must not be underestimated. Poor early experience can create what will later become recognized as special educational needs. Surely it is our task to reduce and minimize the handicapping effects of disability and difficulty for children, not to exacerbate them through poor ineffective experience. A guiding influence for the early years might be the following statement from Philip Gammage (1992, p. 10):

> By any account, and looking back over a long line of research, early childhood education certainly PAYS OFF handsomely. It very often provides the meaningful opportunities for play, for social response, for burgeoning confidence to operate. It lays a foundation for the pro-social and possibly for cognitive behaviour necessary in later schooling and may, we are told, have considerably more lasting effects than that . . . Early childhood education must be of high enough quality to be more than mere child minding. Teachers should be properly trained . . . early childhood education needs to be resistant to claims that it should simply provide a watered down version of elementary education . . . Practice should be based on a thorough appreciation of child development; the balance of process and content properly understood and matched to the needs of the child.

SUMMARY AND CONCLUSIONS

In seeking to explore the influences of current educational changes and developments on special educational needs in the early years it was useful first to look briefly at the recommendations in the Warnock Report concerning this area. These recommendations have proved useful in illustrating some of the important issues raised by the report but also in highlighting some of its shortcomings. Perhaps the most important influence of the Warnock Report was to attempt to redefine the whole concept of handicap and disability and to establish a new concept of special educational need. As a result, however, there have arisen a number of misconceptions and a great deal of confusion about the whole area. A brief discussion has therefore been included in an attempt to make clearer an understanding of the concept of special educational need. This discussion raises a number of issues and in particular highlights the lack of any clear understanding or conceptual underpinning which can be seen to be guiding current change and development in the area of special educational needs.

The final part of the chapter looked at some of the current developments which have occurred since the Education Act 1988. Two themes have been examined: the effects of recent change on special educational needs and the potential for current developments to exacerbate and create special educational needs in the early years.

It has been central to the aim of this chapter to highlight what must be considered to be some of the areas of growing concern for all children in the early years, but especially for those with special educational needs. There is a great danger in the current political manipulation of the education system that the voice of those who cannot compete, or are unable to even enter the 'contest', will not be heard or that some kind of lip service will be paid to their needs.

Sir Ron Dearing has recently been given the task of reviewing the National Curriculum and already we have been promised changes with regard to the weighting of time spent on the compulsory subject areas of the curriculum. Although this is, of course, a welcome development, and it is hoped, one among many more which will make the task of teachers less onerous and allow them to get on with the job of educating their pupils, it is at the level of organization. The fundamental issues, the model of curriculum, real educational balance, the need for theoretical underpinning are once again, it seems, being ignored. Unless these are tackled genuinely, the future for children with special educational needs remains an unhappy one.

The Education Act 1988 introduced, for the first time, a positive entitlement to a full education for all irrespective of ability or disability. To offer entitlement without access is a hollow gift. It is therefore vitally important that we consider with great care the opportunities that we provide for all children from the beginning for real access. Early years education can provide an important key to that access but only if the issues raised in this chapter, and many others which could not be explored within the scope of this work, are genuinely debated and considered.

10
IN CONCLUSION: NO IMPROVED QUALITY WITHOUT INFORMED POLICY

Geva Blenkin and Vic Kelly

This book set out to attempt an evaluation of the impact of the National Curriculum on the early years of education and on children's experiences during this crucial stage in their development. The evaluation has been undertaken by way of a series of contributions from people with well established expertise and experience in the field of early education and with a deep familiarity with the research evidence, especially as it relates to their own special interests.

Three general themes have constantly recurred in the contributions of every one of these experts, and we must emphasize these in this concluding chapter as being the major conclusions to which we are all led by a consideration of such evidence as there is of the impact of the National Curriculum, and in the light of what more extensive research has told us about education in the early years.

The first of these themes is that from every angle from which we have sought to view the National Curriculum, whether from that of the major subjects it requires us to teach or from the point of view of particular groups of children, especially those who may be felt to be especially vulnerable, such as non-native speakers of English and those deemed to have special educational needs, from every one of these viewpoints the National Curriculum has revealed itself as inadequate as a recipe for education in the early years.

The second recurring theme is the failure of those responsible for the National Curriculum to take any account of what has been learnt about the school curriculum and, especially, an appropriate curriculum for the early years of schooling, from the inter-related research and practice of half a century or more. It is crass to be planning a curriculum for the twenty-first century on what is (proudly even!) described as a 'back to basics' policy, to be imposing on the school system a curriculum which is fundamentally Victorian in both style and content.

And the third, and consequent, theme is the constant attempts to cover up the realities of these policies. We noted in Chapter 1 that the strategy adopted for the implementation of the National Curriculum has been one of power-coercion through the use of rhetoric and the control of the discourse of the educational 'debate'. And we noted both there and in Chapter 2 that this has been done through official publications which make claims and assertions for which there is no supporting evidence, and by the suppression, always attempted and often successful, of contrary evidence. Such contrary evidence as is already in the public domain has been dealt with by a 'discourse of derision' (Ball, 1990), by an attempt to 'rubbish' it and to suggest that it is misguided, irrelevant, 'ideological'. Yet we also saw in Chapter 2 that it is this misguided, irrelevant, 'ideological' research which provides a very sound theoretical base for the approach to the curriculum adopted traditionally by most, if not all, early years specialists, the kind of firm theoretical base the National Curriculum itself manifestly lacks.

Finally, in drawing these three themes together, we must note again that it is the resulting conflict between the solid research-based approach of the early years specialists and the rhetoric of the political policy-makers that is at the root of that tension and stress which currently characterizes teaching in the early years. It is also this which explains the use of rhetoric to impose these policies; for there is no empirical/rational basis for them and thus no hope of teachers being influenced in their favour by normative/re-educative means.

These three themes, then, will form the core of this final chapter, as it seeks to summarize the main concerns which earlier chapters have identified.

THE INADEQUACIES OF THE NATIONAL CURRICULUM AS A PROGRAMME FOR EARLY LEARNING

No one who has read carefully through the earlier chapters of this book can fail to appreciate what a complex and subtle matter is the learning of pupils in their early, formative years. No one can thus be unaware of the complexities of providing adequate support for that learning. The learning, the thinking, the intellectual processes generally of young children are qualitatively different from those of older pupils, and especially of the mature adult. They thus require a form of support which is qualitatively different – not merely a watered-down version of the same.

This is what is meant by those who press the claims for a developmentally appropriate curriculum for the early years. And those claims are not ideological, in the sense of stemming from some political adherence to a particular doctrinal stance. They are an inevitable consequence of the recognition that young children are not mini-adults but are, in a fundamental sense, different. Nor does one need to be an expert or to study the research intensively to be able to recognize that; one only has to observe the behaviour and listen to the talk of young children for a very short time.

One of the reasons for the fundamental inadequacy of the National Curriculum in the early years, then, is its complete failure to recognize this. It was suggested in Chapter 2 that the architects of current policies seem not even to like children. Whether that is true or not, it is quite clear that they either do not possess the wit or common sense to learn anything from their observations of children, or they have such little contact with them that they have no such observations to learn from.

Hence, as a recipe for supporting the learning of children in the early years, the National Curriculum is far too simplistic in its conception to provide adequate guidance or advice. Taking, as it does, models of teaching and of learning which are derived from a view of what happens in secondary schools or in higher or further education, it imposes those models on a sector of education where massive research evidence shows them to be unsuitable.

It thus ignores the manifest educational advantages of play, which have emerged very clearly in several of the earlier chapters, and the merits of a holistic approach to the curriculum at this stage. It lacks the subtlety to recognize the significance of the fact that young children must be assisted to structure their own knowledge, to make their own sense of their own worlds, rather than be exposed at too early a stage to the formalized structures which adults have built into what they (but not the children) recognize as 'subjects'. And, in failing to see this, it does violence to those very subjects it misguidedly is seeking to impose. For we saw in Chapter 5 what a poor thing National Curriculum English is in comparison to what we know properly supported language development can be. We saw this reinforced by what was said in Chapter 8 about the language learning – and indeed the learning generally – of non-native speakers of English. Chapter 6 revealed similar inadequacies and shortcomings in the concept of mathematics teaching which underpins National Curriculum mathematics, when this is compared to what earlier studies have revealed of the potential of mathematical learning and development. And Chapter 7 said much the same of scientific and technological learning.

Even when evaluated on its own terms, therefore, as a curriculum designed to improve the quality of learning in those subjects it has selected for emphasis, it is revealed as inadequate because it takes a limited and simplistic view of what the teaching and learning of those subjects entails in the early years of schooling.

It is this fundamental simplicity and lack of subtlety which can be seen to be leading to a lowering of standards rather than to that raising of them which the documentation continues to promise. The National Curriculum is clearly not delivering what we are told it sets out to deliver. And the evidence for this is again to be found in our earlier chapters, in the tendency of children to 'play it safe', for example, in any task which they perceive to be part of formal summative assessment, in the reduction of ambition for the improvement of their own levels of performance which this suggests, or rather the change in their perception of what constitutes quality of performance – full stops and accuracy of spelling, for example, rather than imagination and creativity of thinking or expression. It is a poor substitute for the kind of provision that might really stimulate the intellectual growth of children and fully develop their capacities and their potential.

It is only if one takes a limited view of standards, as meaning little more than the short-term demonstration of a temporary knowledge and mastery of a limited array of facts, that one can claim that the evidence supports such a raising of standards. This is clearly the kind of criterion which is used by those who would have us believe that things are getting better. Certainly, this is now the central concern of the SATs, as several earlier chapters have made plain. And this must be the basis of those claims to improvement which are emerging from Ofsted. For, if these simplistic criteria are not those they are using, then their assertions lose all claim to honesty.

On any more subtle definition, standards are clearly falling. And this is the clear message of earlier chapters, which have not merely asserted this, but also explained in some detail both how and why this is occurring.

The same is true if we return to a consideration of that other major claim of the National Curriculum which we considered in Chapter 1, its claim to increase entitlement for all pupils. There can be no doubt, from what we have seen in Chapters 8 and 9, that its effects on those children for whom entitlement might be seen as most problematic and difficult to achieve, those who are not native speakers of English and those who are deemed to have other kinds of special educational need, far from being beneficial are the precise opposite of this. For such children, the National Curriculum has built-in disadvantages, to be added to the existing disadvantages that their special requirements create. The evidence of this offered in those two chapters seems overwhelming.

Of particular concern perhaps is the fact that being a non-native speaker of English, and thus enjoying that potential for enhanced language development that the necessity to communicate in more than one language offers, has, as we saw in Chapter 8, through the National Curriculum, and perhaps especially through its testing arrangements, been turned from an educational advantage into a serious disadvantage. In Orwellian terms, it is a matter of 'Two languages good. One language better', or even 'All children are equal but some are more equal than others'. Such pupils have special educational needs, but not in the sense that a child with an identifiable physical or mental disability has. It is a serious indictment of the National Curriculum that such pupils are now being regarded as disabled rather than as advantaged. For it is only in the context of a narrowly conceived curriculum that their needs become weaknesses rather than strengths.

Nor are the disadvantages which are now being experienced by all pupils who have special needs of whatever kind merely a matter of resources, although that is clearly a not inconsiderable factor. Again, as both Chapters 8 and 9 revealed, they are a further result of the way in which learning in the early years is conceived, or rather misconceived, in current policies. For, if all children need carefully planned and tailored support for their learning at this stage, as we have seen the research evidence clearly indicates, then those children whose learning needs are complex in differernt ways have need of this even more. There are particular advantages for them in opportunities for play, for example, as we have seen; for experimentation in non-threatening contexts; for being offered a holistic set of educational experiences rather than a fragmented programme of subjects; and for using well prepared teachers as a resource to support the individual forms of learning they require.

If we accept that their needs are different, then we must recognize, as the corollary of that, that they must be placed at a particular disadvantage if they are merely offered the same educational diet as every other child, especially when that diet is so narrowly conceived. This is again a simplistic, even simple-minded, notion of entitlement. And it leads, as we have seen, to the appearance of entitlement rather than its reality. For that reality is clearly the opposite of entitlement; it is disadvantage, inequality and ultimate alienation.

We also noted on several occasions the increased potential for the alienation of many children through the premature formalization of their learning experiences. We have seen again the massive evidence that points us away from too early a formalization of this kind. This is a further dimension of that general point we noted earlier concerning the qualitative differences in the young child's thinking. Yet the National Curriculum is founded on the notion that all learning, from the earliest stage, must be formalized – into levels, programmes of study, attainment targets, etc. – and that educational provision must be matched to the structures of the subjects to be taught and learnt rather than to those of the minds which are attempting to assimilate them. And there is already evidence (Barrett, 1989) that such early formalization is leading to forms of alienation and disaffection from schooling among young pupils of a kind which can be conducive neither to a raising of standards – however these are conceived – nor to the achievement of entitlement. There is much in our earlier chapters which confirms and illustrates this.

On many counts, then, we must conclude that the National Curriculum is a very poor vehicle for the provision of high-quality education in the early years, by whatever criteria one defines that quality.

A COMPLETE DISREGARD OF THE RESEARCH EVIDENCE

We have seen in every chapter of this book that a major reason for the inadequacy of the National Curriculum, along with its associated policies, as a basis for quality provision in the early years is its failure to take any account of research evidence, and especially that evidence which demonstrates that early education must be planned in quite a different way from that which comes later.

We have seen too that what is happening in England and Wales is in stark contrast to policy developments in almost every other country in the world, including many which, it might be claimed, are less well established economically than the UK. For almost everywhere else the research evidence is being taken very seriously and every effort is being made to develop high-quality provision for children from birth to 8 years of age.

Enough has probably been said about this in earlier chapters, and especially in Chapter 2, to make it unnecessary to repeat it here. It is well attested as a bizarre phenomenon of current policies, and earlier chapters have offered conclusive evidence of its existence and its influence.

It may be worthwhile, however, to spend a moment seeking for an explanation of it. It is difficult to explain it in rational terms. It can hardly be that the architects of the National Curriculum regard as cranks, crackpots or bimbos such people as Rousseau, Pestalozzi, Froebel, Montessori, Dewey, Piaget, Susan Isaacs, Bruner or Vygotsky. Yet these are among the major figures from whose work that substantial body of theory to which we have made constant reference is derived. And it is their work which is swept away unceremoniously as not worthy of attention by those who wish to replace it with a set of policies which, as we have seen over and over again, have little or no intellectual base.

Nor surely can it be that they believe that Gradgrind and Wackford Squeers, far from being the products of Charles Dickens's fertile literary imagination, were in reality educational theorists with a genuine alternative philosophy of early education to offer.

One might be generous and attempt to explain it in terms of that general ignorance of early education which most people in our society appear to evince, although one has to assert that such ignorance is not acceptable in those who are claiming the right to make policy for this sector. Such an explanation, however, does not explain the energy and even the dishonesty and shabby dealing which has characterized the attempt to oust current policies for early education and replace them with the National Curriculum.

The only explanation of this that carries conviction is that the hidden agenda of these policies is a reduction in expenditure on education; that the assertion of raising standards, providing entitlement and all the rest of it is indeed rhetoric, designed to conceal the inevitable loss in quality, entitlement and all else which earlier chapters have shown to be salient features which can be increasingly recognized in early education in England and Wales; and that the denigrating of the developmentally appropriate curriculum and the promotion of the National Curriculum constitute an attempt to do no more than to get some kind of educational provision for children in the early years in the maintained sector on the cheap.

What other reason could there be for rejecting the possibility of providing the sort of high-quality curriculum every other country is currently planning? And what other explanation could there be for the attempts to cover up the effects of these policies, which is the third, and final, major issue this chapter sets out to address.

Before we turn to that, however, we should note one final point. A major reason why most other countries, even some who can hardly afford it, are putting resources into the provision of high-quality early education is that they have recognized the long-term benefits of doing so. And they have even recognized what the research overwhelmingly suggests, that those long-term benefits are to be measured in financial as well as in social, humanitarian or educational terms, that, as we saw in Chapter 2, the provision of high-quality early education literally 'pays off' in that those children who have the benefit of it cost society far less in later life. In the USA study, for example, it was estimated that 'for every $1000 invested in the children who attended the pre-school programme, $4130 was returned to the taxpayer (after controlling for inflation) by the way of savings on educational or social provision required . . . later in life' (Sylva, 1992a, p. 685). In the light of that, it was suggested that society could not afford *not* to provide adequately for its young children (Beruetta-Clement *et al.*, 1984).

To fail to recognize the strength of this case, then, is to be guilty of the most damaging kind of short-termism. And it puts into perspective any claims that are being made to planning for the twenty-first century. And the damage is compounded by the necessity it creates for the kinds of devious practices we have seen associated with the attempts to suppress the evidence which would support a developmental approach to the early years curriculum and to replace it with the vastly inferior offerings of the National Curriculum.

THE COVER-UP

We turn finally to a consideration of the devices our political masters and mistresses, and their aides, have been forced to resort to in order to try to impose this ill-conceived curriculum on teachers in the early years.

Chapter 1 discussed in some detail the use of rhetoric and the attempt to gain control of our educational discourse which have been major features of their strategies. It drew attention to the devices of assertion without evidence, of the attempted suppression of contrary evidence and of the denigration of the views of those who take an alternative or critical stance. Subsequent chapters have given examples of all of these practices. One has to ask what confidence these people have in the goods they are trying to foist on us if they have to resort to barrow-boy strategems of this kind to persuade us to accept them. For we all know that for someone to assert, shout, spout, hit one over the head with his or her views is a sure sign of the weakness rather than of the strength of those views.

As the inadequacies of the National Curriculum as an early years curriculum become increasingly apparent, they are met by assertions to the contrary rather than by significant attempts at change or adjustment. It is the Magnus Magnusson principle of policy-making and implementation – 'I've started, so I'll go on'. How long can it go on, one is inclined to ask.

Nor is this only true of the educrats, the amateurs, the civil servants and lay persons of NCC, SEAC and now SCAA. One has learnt also to deal very guardedly with the comparable claims which come from what should be the professional source of Ofsted. For it is clear that the judgements made there are at best made in the light of official political policies.

One's response, for example to the claims of inspectors that *x* per cent of lessons in primary schools, or in secondary schools, are satisfactory or are unsatisfactory, or the recent claim (Ofsted, 1993c) that 4-year-olds are making significant gains from being placed in reception classes (quite the opposite of what we saw was being claimed in Chapter 3) has to be 'according to whose criteria?' or 'according to what criteria?' A major weakness of HMI inspections over the years has been the unwillingness to declare or reveal their criteria of judgement. Too often, however, it has been quite clear that those criteria have made no reference to, and even shown a mismatch with, the principles underpinning the work on which they have been making their judgement – clearly an intellectually illicit process, unless declared openly (in which case the clash of principles and criteria itself must be debated).

In the present cases, it is plain that such judgements concerning the satisfactory or unsatisfactory nature of lessons observed, or the quality of the 4-year-olds' experience in reception classes, have often been made less in relation to the educational value of what has been observed and more in respect of the effectiveness with which National Curriculum subjects have been 'delivered', or attainment targets addressed, since these are now the main concerns and preoccupations of schooling at every level, and thus they provide the (not always acknowledged) criteria by which inspectors make their judgements. The criticisms offered by inspectors, for example, of some of the lessons in primary schools they have observed relate in almost every case to the teacher's knowledge of the subject and thus to the quality of the subject 'delivery'. They thus have little significance or relevance for the quality of the experiences the pupils are being offered in wider educational terms.

It is in this light that we must view such pronouncements, and this is the perspective in which we must place them. Quality, like beauty, resides in the eye of the beholder or in the eye of those who make the policies he or she is obliged to implement. What is satisfactory, or unsatisfactory, then, to Ofsted may not appear in the same light when evaluated by those different criteria which must derive from a commitment to a developmentally appropriate curriculum. If in doubt, ask those poor 4-year-olds.

This is a further example, then, of that tension we have noted throughout between what is being imposed and what is already in place, another source of stress for teachers and another example of how their work is often derided and denigrated unfairly.

However, it is not only what HMSO publishes that gives this kind of cause for concern. One can see even more sinister implications in what it refuses to publish. For one hears almost daily of researchers whose findings HMSO will not publish, or who are being asked to write and rewrite their findings until they have put them into a form that is politically correct or acceptable (an experience with which we are not ourselves unfamiliar); and who are prevented by the small print of their contracts from having them published elsewhere. Indeed, at a recent conference of the British Educational Research Association (BERA), it was felt necessary to launch new ethical guidelines for research: 'For even the most senior researchers have had to face . . . sponsors (particularly government quangos) trying to increase their control over contracts, the publication of results and even the research methods' (O'Connor, 1993b, p. 16). It all adds up to a shiftiness that gives one no confidence in either the medium or the message.

In essence, what we are identifying here is a subtle (not always that subtle, merely unpublicized) form of censorship, another, slightly old-fashioned term for the 'legitimation of discourse'. And there are further dangerous dimensions of this when it becomes what Richard Hoggart (1992, p. 260) (albeit in a different context) has called 'the most difficult of all types of censorship: self-censorship'. This is the kind of censorship which begins to have its impact when we allow ourselves to accede to the controls placed on our thinking and our action, to accept the discourse which is officially legitimated, to abandon the beliefs and values we once adhered to because they are no longer fashionable, i.e. officially approved. As Hoggart goes on to say (*op. cit.*, pp. 260–1),

> You would not perhaps yield to explicit directives or bullying [although, heaven knows, in education we have seen enough of both in recent times], and they are rarely needed. You do begin instinctively to evade issues, opinions, positions not acceptable to those above or the body of those out there. All this is hugely practised in totalitarian states; but like persistent bad drains it also haunts open societies.

If we are tempted to feel that this is not the kind of situation that early educators are currently in, we have only to note the degree to which the jargon of the official documents and, in particular, the commercial metaphor we noted in Chapter 1, has entered, and perhaps now dominates, the language in which many of us now discuss our professional concerns – how readily we talk of 'delivering' a curriculum, for example. And we have only to note the reluctance and caution some of us display at the prospect of debating the kinds of educational values we have been concerned to reiterate in this book. Furthermore, there are few of us who have not experienced attempts to silence us when we seek to discuss educational issues in these terms, to discourage us, for example, from sharing with parents any doubts we may have about the experiences their children are having, or missing, as a result of current policies.

Finally, those of us who are involved in the examination of teachers, on both initial training and award-bearing in-service courses, are only too aware that, if every effort is not made to obviate this, many of them will debate and write essays and other assignments about deeply controversial educational issues with reference only to what they have read in the official documentation, and thus merely scratch the surface of the issues in the politically sanitized style and at the intellectually superficial level which characterizes that documentation.

And so, there is little doubt that, in addition to the attraction of reduced expenditure, it is the desire to maintain the professional 'debate' of teachers within these narrow confines that is a major motivating factor behind current proposals for further reductions in the intellectual and academic content of teacher training courses and, now, even higher degree study and research in education. The rhetoric here is that of 'practical relevance'; the derision is directed at 'all that theory'; the underlying message, therefore, is 'Do not think before you act – especially when supporting the learning of young children'.

The cover-up is extensive and well under way. We must resist it – in the interests of our own professional status, in the interests of the quality of our provision for the children for whom we have responsibility and, indeed, in the interests of the democratic health of our society. Teachers need to get beyond, and stay beyond, the rhetoric, the legitimated discourse, the limited and limiting language of the official documents, the National Curriculum speak. Education, especially in a society which purports to be democratic, is a highly complex matter. It has many dimensions which require, and deserve, a level of sophistication of debate of a kind which is currently being suppressed. In a democratic society, teachers, like all professionals, have a duty not, of course, to direct society's policies on the issues which fall within their own expertise, but to provide society with the understandings it needs to make sensible and informed decisions, to advise it on those complex issues and on the sophistications of the debate. Current policies are not only preventing early years teachers from making what they, as trained professionals, would see as adequate provision for their pupils; they are also preventing them from offering society a lead in the framing of its educational policies for that important sector of schooling.

Teachers, then, must not allow themselves to be seduced, cajoled or bullied into becoming themselves a part of the cover-up. On the contrary, they have a professional and public duty to get beyond the rhetoric, and to take the rest of society, and especially the parents, with them. For it is not only the teaching profession which is being sold short by current policies; it is society as a whole and, in particular, those young children who will form, and be responsible for, the society of the future.

SUMMARY AND CONCLUSIONS

This concluding chapter has attempted to draw some threads together by identifying the major themes which permeate the book's earlier chapters. It has suggested that there are three major themes, or threads, which are common to all, and that these are closely interwoven.

First, it was suggested that earlier chapters have offered comprehensive evidence that the National Curriculum has already proved to be an inadequate vehicle for the provision of high-quality education for children in the earlier years of schooling.

Second, it was claimed that there is little doubt about what high-quality education is at this stage; that there is massive research evidence to demonstrate its value; that most other countries, including some which are manifestly less healthy economically than the UK, are currently recognizing this and investing major resources in it; but that the research evidence is being ignored completely in the framing of policies for early education in England and Wales.

Third, we noted the evidence in earlier chapters of the elaborate cover-up that is currently being perpetrated. Not only is the research evidence being ignored; it is, wherever possible, being suppressed, and replaced by assertions without evidence or even without anything more than a highly tenuous basis in truth.

And we noted the danger that the teaching profession itself might become a part of this cover-up process – by too readily accepting the parameters placed on the discussion of educational issues by the educrats, by failing themselves to see beyond the superficialities of the official documents and by accepting the strictures laid on them in relation to sharing their doubts about the current policies with their pupils' parents.

Finally, it was suggested that teachers, like every other professional body in a democratic society, have a responsibility not only to their pupils but also to society itself, to ensure that it has the best advice and information available to it when it is planning its educational provision.

It has been said (probably many times) that education is too important to be left to teachers. The evidence of this book is that it is even more dangerous to leave it to the politicians. For the policies hatched out by the present holders of political power in England and Wales have not only put education, and especially early education at risk, they have also placed in jeopardy some fundamental principles of democracy.

REFERENCES

Adams, F. (1990) *Special Education in the 1990s*, Longman, London.

Alatis, J. E. (ed.) (1980) *Georgetown University Round Table on Languages and Linguistics*, Georgetown University Press, Washington, DC.

Alexander, R. (1992) *Policy and Practice in Primary Education,* Routledge, London.

Alexander, R., Rose, J. and Woodhead, C. (1992) *Curriculum Organisation and Classroom Practice in Primary Schools*, DES, London.

Andersson, B.-E. (1992) Effects of day-care on cognitive and socioemotional competence of thirteen-year-old Swedish schoolchildren, *Child Development*, Vol. 63, pp. 20–36.

Archer, M. (1993) Here is the good news: help is at hand, *The Sunday Times,* 15 August.

Armstrong, M. (1980) *Closely Observed Children*, Writers & Readers Co-operative, Chameleon Books, London.

Armstrong, M. (1993) Much too proper English, *The Times Educational Supplement*, 28 May.

Arnot, M. and Barton, L. (eds.) (1992) *Voicing Concerns,* Triangle, Wallingford.

Association for Science Education (1992a) *Primary Science: A Shared Experience*, ASE, Hatfield.

Association for Science Education (1992b) *Change in Our Future: A Challenge for Science Education*, ASE, Hatfield.

Athey, C. (1990) *Extending Thought in Young Children*, Paul Chapman, London.

Baker, K. (1987) Speech to annual Conservative Party conference, Blackpool, 7 October.

Ball, S. J. (1990) *Politics and Policy Making in Education: Exploration in Policy Sociology,* Routledge, London.

Barber, M. (1993a) Teachers and the National Curriculum: learning to love it?, in Barber and Graham (eds.) (1993) *op. cit.,* pp. 10–25.

Barber, M. (1993b) Think quality in science, not quantity, *The Times Educational Supplement,* 27 August.

Barber, M. and Graham, D. (eds.) (1993) *Sense, Nonsense and the National Curriculum*, Falmer, London.

Barrett, G. (1986) *Starting School: An Evaluation of the Experience*, AMMA and Centre for Applied Research in Education, Norwich.
Barrett, G. (1989) *Disaffection from School. The Early Years*, Falmer, London.
Barsamian, D. (ed.) (1992) *Chronicles of Dissent. Interviews with Noam Chomsky*, Common Courage Press, Maine/AK Press, Stirling.
Barton, L. (ed.) (1989) *Disability and Dependency*, Falmer, London.
Barton, L. and Tomlinson, S. (1981) *Special Education Policy and Special Issues*, Falmer, London.
Bassey, M. (1983) Pedagogic research: case studies, probes and curriculum innovations, *Oxford Review of Education*, no. 7, pp. 73–94.
Baxter, J. (1993) Children's astronomy, *Topic*, no. 9, NFER, Slough.
BBC TV (1991) *Children with Special Needs in Danger of Neglect*, May.
BBC TV (1993) *Children with Special Needs*, July.
Beard, R. (ed.) (1993) *Teaching Literacy, Balancing Perspectives*, Hodder & Stoughton, Sevenoaks.
Bell, G. and Colbeck, B. (1989) *Experiencing Integration*, Falmer, London.
Bennett, N. and Kell, J. (1989) *A Good Start?*, Blackwell, Oxford.
Bennis, W. G., Benne, K. D. and Chin, R. (eds.) (1969) *The Planning of Change*, Holt, Rinehart & Winston, New York.
Bentley, M., Campbell, J., Lewis, A. and Sullivan, M. (eds.) (1990) *Primary Design and Technology in Practice*, Longman, London.
Bernhardt, E. B. (ed.) (1992) *Life in Language Immersion Classrooms*, Multilingual Matters, Clevedon.
Bernstein, J. R. (1973) *Einstein*, Collins, London.
Beruetta-Clement, J., Schweinhart, L. J., Barnett, W. S., Epstein, A. S. and Weikart, D. P. (1984) Changed lives: the effects of the Perry pre-school programme on youths through age 19, *Monographs of the High/Scope Educational Research Foundation*, no. 8.
Beveridge, M. (ed.) (1982) *Children Thinking Through Language*, Edward Arnold, London.
Beynon, J. and Mackay, H. (eds.) (1992) *Technological Literacy and the Curriculum*, Falmer, London.
Blenkin, G., Edwards, G. and Kelly, A. V. (1992) *Change and the Curriculum*, Paul Chapman, London.
Blenkin, G. M. and Kelly, A. V. (eds.) (1988) *Early Childhood Education: A Developmental Curriculum*, Paul Chapman, London.
Blenkin, G. M. and Kelly, A. V. (eds.) (1992) *Assessment in Early Childhood Education*, Paul Chapman, London.
Blenkin, G. M. and Kelly, A. V. (1993) Never mind the quality: feel the breadth and balance, in Campbell (ed.) (1993) *op. cit.*, pp. 49–66.
Blenkin, G. M. and Whitehead, M. R. (1988) Creating a context for development, in Blenkin and Kelly (eds.) (1988) *op. cit.*, pp. 32–60.
Bloom, D. (1988) What is the return on the investment? Child Care – The Bottom Line, conference, New York Child Care Action Group.
Booth, T., Swann, W., Masterson, M. and Potts, P. (1992a) *Policies for Diversity in Education*, Open University Press in association with Routledge, London.
Booth, T., Swann, W., Masterson, M. and Potts, P. (1992b) *Curricula for Diversity in Education*, Open University Press in association with Routledge, London.

Bredekamp, S. (ed.) (1987) *Developmentally Appropriate Practice in Early Child-hood Programs Serving Children Through Age 8*, National Association for the Education of Young Children, Washington, DC.

Bretherton, I. (ed.) (1984) *Symbolic Play: The Development of Social Understand-ing*, Academic Press, New York.

Briggs, M. (1993) Bags and baggage revisited (or another suitcase for the rack), *Mathematics Education Review*, no. 2, pp. 6–20.

Britton, J. (1970) *Language and Learning*, Allen Lane, London.

Britton, J. (1992) *Language and Learning* (second edition), Penguin Books, Harmondsworth.

Broadbent, L. (1993) A spiritual concern, *Nursery World*, 15 July, pp. 14–15.

Broadhead, P. (ed.) *Researching the Early Years Continuum*, British Educational Research Association Dialogues, forthcoming.

Bruce, T. (1987) *Early Childhood Education*, Hodder & Stoughton, Sevenoaks.

Bruce, T. (1987) *Time to Play in Early Childhood Education*, Hodder & Stoughton, Sevenoaks.

Bruner, J. S. (1973) *Beyond the Information Given. Studies in the Psychology of Knowing*, Allen & Unwin, London.

Bruner, J. S. (1986) *Actual Minds, Possible Worlds*, Harvard University Press, Cambridge, Mass.

Bruner, J. S. (1990) *Acts of Meaning*, Harvard University Press, Cambridge, Mass.

Bryant, P. and Bradley, L. (1985) *Children's Reading Problems*, Blackwell, Oxford.

Butterworth, G. E., Harris, P. L., Leslie, A. M. and Wellman, H. M. (eds.) (1991) *Perspectives on the Child's theories of Mind*, Oxford University Press.

Buxton, L. G. (1981) *Do You Panic About Maths?*, Heinemann, London.

Byram, M. and Leman, J. (eds.) (1990) *Bicultural and Trilingual Education*, Multi-cultural Matters, Clevedon.

Campbell, R. J. (1989) In search of evidence, *Junior Education*, July, pp. 10–1.

Campbell, R. J. (ed.) (1993) *Breadth and Balance in the Primary Curriculum*, Falmer, London.

Carter, R. (ed.) (1990) *Knowledge about Language and the Curriculum*, Hodder & Stoughton, Sevenoaks.

Cassidy, D. J. (1989) Questioning the young child: process and function, *Childhood Education*, Vol. 65, no. 3, pp. 146–9.

Cato, V., Fernandes, C., Gorman, T., Kispal, A. and White, J. (1992) *The Teaching of Initial Literacy: How do Teachers do it?*, NFER, Slough.

Cherryholmes, C. H. (1987) A social project for curriculum: post-structural perspec-tives, *Journal of Curriculum Studies*, Vol. 19, no. 4, pp. 295–316.

Chukovsky, K. (1963) *From Two to Five*, University of California Press, Berkeley, Calif.

Clarke, M. A. and Handscome, J. (eds.) (1983) *On TESOL '82: Pacific Perspectives on Language Learning and Teaching*, TESOL, Washington, DC.

Coard, B. (1971) *How the West Indian Child is Made Educationally Subnormal in the British School System*, New Beacon Books, London.

Cockburn, A. (1992) Introduction, in Barsamian (ed.) (1992) *op. cit.*, pp. i–xi.

Cohen, A. and Cohen, L. (1986a) *Primary Education*, Harper & Row, London.

Cohen, A. and Cohen, L. (1986b) *Special Educational Needs in Ordinary Schools*, Harper & Row, London.

Cohen, A. and Cohen, L. (1988) *Early Education in the PreSchool Years*, Paul Chapman, London.

Cortazzi, M. (1991) *Primary Teaching How It Is. A Narrative Account*, David Fulton, London.

Cousins, J. (1990) Are your little Humpty Dumpties floating or sinking? What sense do children of four make of the reception class at school? Different conceptions at that time of transition, *Early Years*, Vol. 10, no. 2, pp. 28–38.

Cox, B. (1991) *Cox on Cox. An English Curriculum for the 1990s*, Hodder & Stoughton, Sevenoaks.

Cox, R. W. (1986) Social forces, states and world orders: beyond international relations theory, in Keohane (ed.) (1986) *op. cit.*, pp. 205–49.

Crowe, B. (1983) *Play is Feeling*, Unwin, London.

Cummins, J. (1979) Linguistic interdependence and the educational development of bilingual children, *Review of Educational Research*, Vol. 49, pp. 222–51.

Cummins, J. (1980) The construct of language proficiency in bilingual children, in Alatis (ed.) (1980) *op. cit.*

Cummins, J. (1981) *Bilingualism and Minority Language Children,* Ontario Institute for Studies in Education, Ontario.

Cummins, J. (1991) Language development and academic learning, in Malave and Duquette (eds.) (1991) *op. cit.*, pp. 161–75.

Cummins, J. (1992) Heritage language teaching in Canadian schools, *Journal of Curriculum Studies*, Vol. 24, no. 3, pp. 281–6.

Daniels, H. and Ware, J. (1990) *Special Education and the National Curriculum*, Kogan Page in association with the University of London Institute of Education, London.

David, T., Curtis, A. and Siraj-Blatchford, I. (1992) *Effective Teaching in the Early Years: Fostering Children's Learning in Nurseries and in Infant Classes*, Organisation Mondiale pour l'Education Prescolaire (OMEP), London.

Davis, R. (1983) *Learning Mathematics: The Cognitive Science Approach to Mathematics Education*, Croom Helm, Beckenham.

de Bóo, M. (1990) Supporting science, in Bentley *et al.* (eds.) (1990) *op. cit.*, pp. 80–4.

de Bóo, M. (1991) Vive la difference, *Primary Science Review*, Vol. 18, p. 24.

Deci, E. L. and Ryan, R. M. (1982) Curiosity and self-directed learning: the role of motivation in education, in Katz (ed.) (1982) *op. cit.*, pp. 71–85.

Desforges, C. and Cockburn, A. (1987) *Understanding the Mathematics Teacher*, Falmer, London.

Dessent, T. (1987) *Making the Ordinary School Special*, Falmer, London.

DeVries, R. with Kohlberg, L. (1987) *Programs of Early Learning: The Constructivist View*, Longman, New York.

Donaldson, M. (1978) *Children's Minds*, Fontana/Open Books, London.

Donaldson, M., Grieve, R. and Pratt, C. (eds.) (1983) *Early Childhood Development and Education*, Blackwell, Oxford.

Dore, A. (1993) Painted black by the Greens, *The Times Educational Supplement*, 27 August.

Dowling, M. (1992) *Education 3–5* (second edition), Paul Chapman, London.

Duckworth, E. (1987) *The Having of Wonderful Ideas*, Teachers College Press, Columbia University, New York.

Dunn, J. (1988) *The Beginnings of Social Understanding*, Blackwell, Oxford.

Duquette, G. (1992) The home culture of minority children in the assessment and development of their first language, *Language, Culture and Curriculum*, Vol. 5, no. 1, pp. 11–23.

Durant, J. R., Evans, G. A. and Thomas, G. P. (1989) The public understanding of science, *Nature*, Vol. 340, pp. 11–13.

Early Years Curriculum Group (1989) *Early Childhood Education: The Early Years Curriculum and the National Curriculum*, Trentham, Stoke-on-Trent.

Early Years Curriculum Group (1982) *First Things First, Educating Young Children. A Guide for Parents and Governors*, Madeleine Lindley, Oldham.

Early Years Curriculum Group (1993) *Early Years Education in Jeopardy* (available from V. Hurst, Goldsmiths' College, London).

Egan, K. and Nadaner, D. (eds.) (1988) *Imagination and Education*, Open University Press, Milton Keynes.

Eisner, E. W. (1982) *Cognition and the Curriculum*, Longman, New York.

Eisner, E. W. (1985) *The Art of Educational Evaluation: A Personal View*, Falmer, London.

Eisner, E. W. (1990) The role of art and play in children's cognitive development, in Klugman and Smilansky (eds.) (1990) *op. cit.*, pp. 43–56.

Elkin, S. (1993) Three Rs and a bit of common sense, *The Independent*, 1 September.

Elkind, D. (1989) Developmentally appropriate education for 4-year olds, *Theory into Practice*, Vol. 28, no. 1, pp. 47–52.

Elkind, D. (1990) Academic pressures – too much, too soon. The demise of play, in Klugman and Smilansky (eds.) (1990) *op. cit.*, pp. 3–17.

Elliot, J. (ed.) (1993) *Reconstructing Teacher Education*, Falmer, London.

Engel, D. M. and Whitehead, M. R. (1993) More first words: a comparative study of bilingual siblings, *Early Years*, Vol. 14, no. 1, pp. 27–35.

Ervin-Tripp, S. M. (1974) Is second language learning like the first? *TESOL Quarterly*, Vol. 8, pp. 111–24.

Fantini, A. E. (1991) Bilingualism: exploring language and culture, in Malave and Duquette (eds.) *op. cit.*, pp. 110–20.

Feasey, R. and Thompson, L. (1992) *Effective Questioning in Science*, School of Education, University of Durham.

Feynman, R. P. (1988) *What Do You Care What Other People Think?*, Unwin Hyman, London.

Filer, A. (1993) The assessment of classroom language: challenging the rhetoric of objectivity, *International Studies in the Sociology of Education*, in press.

Finch, J. (1988) Ethnography and public policy, in Pollard, Purvis and Walford (eds.) (1988) *op. cit.*, pp. 185–200.

Fisher, R. (ed.) (1987) *Problem Solving in Primary Schools*, Blackwell, Oxford.

Fishman, J. A. (1970) Bilingual education in sociological perspective, *TESOL Quarterly*, Vol. 4, pp. 215–22.

Fishman, J. A. (1972) *Advances in the Sociology of Language. Vol. II. Selected Studies and Applications*, Mouton & Co., The Hague.

Fishman, J. A. (1976) *Bilingual Education. An International Sociological Perspective*, Newbury House, Rowley, Mass.

Floyd, A. (ed.) (1981) *Developing Mathematical Thinking*, Addison-Wesley, London.

Foucault, M. (1980) *Language, Counter-Meaning, Practice*, Cornell University Press, New York.

Freire, P. and Macedo, D. (1987) *Literacy, Reading the Word and the World*, Routledge & Kegan Paul, London.

Friesen, J. W. (1987) *Reforming the Schools for Teachers*, University Press of America, Lanham, NY.

Froebel Blockplay Research Group (1992) Being scientific and solving problems, in Gura (ed.) (1992) *op. cit.*, pp. 107–31.

Fromberg, D. P. (1990) An agenda for research on play in early childhood education, in Klugman and Smilansky (eds.) (1990) *op. cit.*, pp. 235–49.

Fulcher, G. (1989) *Disabling Policies*, Falmer, London.

Gammage, P. (1992) *Quality: The Tension between Conflict and Process*, Occasional Paper 1, University of Nottingham.

Gammage, P. and Meighan, J. (eds.) (1993) *Early Childhood Education: Taking Stock*, Education Now Publishing Co-operative, Ticknall, Derbyshire.

Gardner, H. (1991) *The Unschooled Mind*, Basic Books, New York.

Geertz, C. (1973) *The Interpretation of Cultures*, Basic Books, New York.

Gelman, R. and Gallistel, C. R. (1978) *The Child's Understanding of Number*, Harvard University Press, Cambridge, Mass.

Gilbert, C. (1989) *A Guide to Primary Technology Policy*, Oliver & Boyd, London.

Giles, H. (1973) Accent mobility: a model and some data, *Anthropological Linguistics*, Vol. 15, pp. 87–105.

Goelman, H., Oberg, A. and Smith, F. (eds.) (1984) *Awakening to Literacy*, Heinemann Education, Portsmouth, NH.

Goldstream, J. M. (1972) *Education: Elementary Education 1780–1900*, David Charles, Newton Abbot.

Graff, H. J. (1987) *The Labyrinths of Literacy. Reflections on Literacy Past and Present*, Falmer, London.

Graham, D. with Tytler, D. (1993) *A Lesson for Us All: The Making of the National Curriculum*, Routledge, London and New York.

Gray, E. and Tall, D. (1993) Success and failure in mathematics: the flexible meaning of symbols as process and concept, *Mathematics Teaching*, no. 142, pp. 6–10.

Gregory, E. (1993) What counts as reading in the early years classroom, *British Journal of Educational Psychology*, Vol. 63, pp. 214–30.

Gregory, E. and Kelly, C. (1992) Bilingualism and assessment, in Blenkin and Kelly (eds.) (1992) *op. cit.*, pp. 144–62.

Gregson, D. (1990) Why do pirates have peg legs? A study of reading for information, in Webb (ed.) (1990) *op. cit.*, pp. 34–54.

Greven, P. J. (1973) *Child-Rearing Concepts, 1628–1861*, Peacock, Itasca, Ill.

Grosjean, F. (1982) *Life with Two Languages. An Introduction to Bilingualism*, Harvard University Press, Cambridge, Mass.

Guha, M. (1988) Play in school, in Blenkin and Kelly (eds.) (1988) *op. cit.*, pp. 61–79.

Gura, P. (ed.) with the Froebel Blockplay Research Group, directed by Tina Bruce (1992) *Exploring Learning: Young Children and Blockplay*, Paul Chapman, London.

H.M.I./D.E.S. (1989) *Provision for Primary Aged Pupils with Statements of Special Educational Needs in Mainstream Schools*. D.E.S. Jan–July 1989.

Hall, E. J. (1959) *The Silent Language*, Doubleday, New York.
Hall, N. and Abbott, L. (1991) *Play in the Primary Curriculum*, Hodder & Stoughton, Sevenoaks.
Hamers, J. F. and Blanc, M. H. (1989) *Bilinguality and Bilingualism*, Cambridge University Press.
Harlen, W. (1993) Changing the goal posts, *Primary Science Review*, no. 28, pp. 2–3.
Harris, D. (1988) Dilemma and difference, *The Times Educational Supplement*, 4 November.
Harris, P. (1989) *Children and Emotion*, Blackwell, Oxford.
Harris, P. L., Brown, E., Marriot, C., Whittal, S. and Harmer, S. (1991) Monsters, ghosts and witches: testing the limits of the fantasy-reality distinction in young children, in Butterworth *et al.* (eds.) (1991) *op. cit.*, pp. 105–25.
Hart, S. (1992) Differentiation: part of the problem or part of the solution?, *The Curriculum Journal*, Vol. 3, no. 2, pp. 131–42.
Hartley, D. (1993) *Understanding the Nursery School*, Cassell, London.
Hatch, E. M. (1983) *Psycholinguistics: A Second Language Perspective*, Newbury House, Rowley, Mass.
Heath, S. B. (1983) *Ways with Words. Language, Life and Work in Communities and Classrooms*, Cambridge University Press.
Heath, S. B. (1987) Foreword, in Graff (1987) *op. cit.*, pp. vii–ix.
Hennessy, S., McCormick, R. and Murphy, P. (1993) The myth of general problem-solving capability: design and technology as an example, *The Curriculum Journal*, Vol. 4, no. 1, pp. 73–89.
Hoggart, R. (1992) *An Imagined Life (Life and Times Volume III: 1959–91)*, Chatto & Windus, London.
Hohmann, M., Banet, B. and Weikart, D. P. (1979) *Young Children in Action: A Manual for Preschool Educators*, High/Scope Educational Research Foundation, Ypsilanti, Mich.
Holt, J. (1984) *How Children Fail* (revised edition), Penguin Books, Harmondsworth.
Howson, A. G. (1983) *A Review of Research in Mathematical Education Part C: Curriculum Development and Curriculum Research*, NFER, Windsor.
Hughes, M. (1983) What is difficult about learning arithmetic?, in Donaldson, Grieve and Pratt (eds.) (1983) *op. cit.*, pp. 204–21.
Hughes, M. (1986) *Children and Number Difficulties in Learning Mathematics*, Blackwell, Oxford.
Hughes, M. (1993) Teachers' perceptions of the role of parents in the education of young children, a report of current research at the University of Exeter, conference paper, Early Childhood Organization (ECHO), Worcester, 16 January.
Hurst, V. (1991) *Planning for Early Learning*, Paul Chapman, London.
Hurst, V. (1993) Observing play in early childhood, in Moyles (ed.) (1993) *op. cit.*, forthcoming.
Hurst, V. (forthcoming) Coming up or going down; how do we conceptualise the early years?, in Broadhead (ed.) *op. cit.*
Hurst, V. and Lally, M. (1992) Assessment and the nursery curriculum, in Blenkin and Kelly (eds.) (1992) *op. cit.*, pp. 46–68.
Hutt, J. S., Tyler, S., Hutt, C. and Christopherson, H. (1988) *Play, Exploration and Learning: A Natural History of the Preschool*, Routledge & Kegan Paul, London.

Jackson, B. (1979) *Starting School,* Croom Helm, London.

John-Steiner, V. (1985) The road to competence in an alien land: a Vygotskian perspective on bilingualism, in Wertsch (ed.) (1985) *op. cit.,* pp. 348–73.

Jowett, S. and Sylva, K. (1986) Does kind of pre-school matter?, *Educational Research,* Vol. 28, no. 1, p. 21.

Kagen, S. and Zigler, E. (eds.) (1987) *Early Schooling: The National Debate,* Yale University Press, New Haven, Conn.

Katz, L. G. (1977) *Talks with Teachers,* National Association for the Education of the Young Child, Washington, DC.

Katz, L. G. (ed.) (1982) *Current Topics in Early Childhood Education,* Vol. IV, Ablex Publishing Corporation, New York.

Katz, L. G. and Chard, S. C. (1989) *Engaging Children's Minds,* Ablex Publishing Corporation, New York.

Katz, L. G. and Chard, S. C. (1989) *Engaging Chidlren's Minds: The Project Approach,* Ablex Publishing Corporation, Norwood, NJ.

Kelly, A. V. (1986) *Knowledge and Curriculum Planning,* Harper & Row, London.

Kelly, A. V. (1989) *The Curriculum: Theory and Practice* (third edition), Paul Chapman, London.

Kelly, A. V. (1990) *The National Curriculum: A Critical Review,* Paul Chapman, London.

Kelly, A. V. (1992) Concepts of assessment: an overview, in Blenkin and Kelly (eds.) (1992) *op. cit.,* pp. 1–23.

Kelly, L. G. (ed.) (1969) *Description and Measurement of Bilingualism: An International Seminar,* University of Toronto Press, Toronto.

Keohane, R. (ed.) (1986) *Neo-Realism and Its Critics,* Columbia University Press, New York.

King, A. S. and Reiss, M. J. (eds.) (1993) *The Multicultural Dimension of the National Curriculum,* Falmer, London.

Kirkman, S. (1992) SATs 'improved teaching methods', *The Times Educational Supplement,* 6 March.

Klugman, E. and Smilansky, S. (eds.) (1990) *Children's Play and Learning: Policy Implications,* Teachers College Press, Columbia University, New York.

Krashen, S. (1982) *Second Language Acquisition and Second Language Learning,* Pergamon, Oxford.

Lally, M. (1991) *The Nursery Teacher in Action,* Paul Chapman, London.

Lally, M. and Hurst, V. (1992) Assessment in nursery education: a review of approaches, in Blenkin and Kelly (eds.) (1992) *op. cit.,* pp. 69–92.

Lally, M. and Hurst, V. (forthcoming) *Practitioners Learning from Observation,* National Primary Centre, Oxford.

Lawton, D. and Chitty, C. (eds.) (1988) *The National Curriculum,* Bedford Way Paper 33, Institute of Education, London.

Legaretta-Marcaida, D. (1981) Effective use of the primary language in the classroom, in Skutnabb-Kangas (ed.) (1981) *op. cit.,* pp. 83–116.

Lurie, A. (1990) *Don't Tell the Grown-Ups. Subversive Children's Literature,* Bloomsbury, London.

Macnamara, J. (1969) How can one measure the extent of a person's bilingual proficiency?, in Kelly (ed.) (1969) *op. cit.,* pp. 80–98.

Major, J. (1992) *Good Housekeeping,* June (quoted in editorial).

Malave, L. M. and Duquette, G. (eds.) (1991) *Language, Culture and Cognition*, Multilingual Matters, Clevedon.

Malkus, U. C., Feldman, F. H. and Gardner, H. (1988) Dimensions of minds in early childhood, in Pellegrini (ed.) (1988) *op. cit.*, pp. 25–38.

Mandelbaum, G. (ed.) (1970) *Language, Culture and Personality*, University of California Press, Berkeley, Calif.

Mant, J. and Summers, M. (1993) Some primary school teachers' understanding of the earth's place in the universe, *Research Papers in Education: Policy and Practice*, Vol. 8, no. 1, pp. 101–29.

McAuley, H. J. (1990) Classroom-based research: dialogical structures, *Early Child Development and Care*, Vol. 64, pp. 85–98.

McIntosh, A. (1977) When will they ever learn, in Floyd (ed.) (1981) *op. cit.*, pp. 6–11.

McLaughlin, B. (1988) *Theories of Second Language Learning*, Edward Arnold, London.

Mead, M. (1927) Group intelligence and linguistic disability among Italian children, *School and Society*, Vol. 25, pp. 465–8.

Medawar, P. B. (1979) *Advice to a Young Scientist*, Harper & Row, New York.

Medway, P. (1992) Constructions of technology: reflections on a new subject, in Beynon and Mackay (eds.) (1992) *op. cit.*, pp. 65–83.

Meek, M. (1991) *On Being Literate*, The Bodley Head, London.

Metz, M. (1988) The development of mathematical understanding, in Blenkin and Kelly (eds.) (1988) *op. cit.*, pp. 184–201.

Mills, R. W. and Mills, J. (1993) *Bilingualism in the Primary School*, Routledge, London.

Moore, J. (1993) Science co-ordination in primary schools: a survey of current practice in Humberside schools, *Curriculum*, Vol. 13, no. 1, pp. 52–7.

Morgan, C. (1992) Can you count on the number SAT?, *British Journal of Curriculum and Assessment*, Vol. 3, no. 1, pp. 8–9.

Moyles, J. (ed.) (forthcoming) *The Excellence of Play*, Open University Press, Milton Keynes.

Nash, I. (1992) Heaven knows where earth is, *The Times Educational Supplement*, 3 January.

Nash, I. (1993) Scientists buckle under the backlash, *The Times Educational Supplement*, 8 January.

National Association for the Teaching of English (NATE) (1992) *'Made Tongue-Tied by Authority'. New Orders for English?*, Longman, York.

National Union of Teachers and University of Leeds (1993) *Testing and Assessing 6 and 7 years olds*, NUT, London.

Nelson, K. (1989) *Narratives from the Crib*, Harvard University Press, Cambridge, Mass.

Nelson, K. and Seidman, S. (1984) Playing with scripts, in Bretherton (ed.) (1984) *op. cit.*, pp. 45–70.

Oberg, A. and McCutcheon, G. (1989) Teachers' experience doing action research, *Peabody Journal of Education*, Vol. 64, no. 2, pp. 116–27.

O'Connor, M. (1993a) Teachers forced to bow to tradition, *The Times Educational Supplement*, 17 September, p. 6.

O'Connor, M. (1993b) First steps out of the twilight zone, *The Times Educational Supplement*, 24 September, p. 16.

O'Hear, A. (1991) *Father of Child-Centredness: John Dewey and the Ideology of Modern Education*, Centre for Policy Studies, London.
Oliver, M. (1990a) Intellectual masturbation. A rejoinder to Soder and Booth, *European Journal of Special Needs Education*, Vol. 7, no. 1, pp. 20–30.
Oliver, M. (1990b) *The Politics of Disablement*, Macmillan, London.
Opie, I. (1993) *The People in the Playground*, Oxford University Press.
Ortony, A. (1979a) Metaphor: a multidimensional problem, in Ortony (ed.) (1979) *op. cit.*, pp. 1–16.
Ortony, A. (1979b) *Metaphor and Thought*, Cambridge University Press.
Osborn, A. and Milbank, J. (1987) *The Effects of Early Education*, Clarendon Press, Oxford.
Ovens, P. (1993) The development of primary school teachers' thinking about the teaching and learning of science, in Elliot (ed.) (1993) *op. cit.*, pp. 211–28.
Paley, V. G. (1981) *Wally's Stories. Conversations in the Kindergarten*, Harvard University Press, Cambridge, Mass.
Paley, V. G. (1986) *Molly is Three. Growing up in School*, University of Chicago Press, Chicago, Ill.
Paley, V. G. (1988) *Bad Guys Don't Have Birthdays: Fantasy Play at Four*, University of Chicago Press, Chicago, Ill.
Paley, V. G. (1990) *The Boy who Would be a Helicopter*, Harvard University Press, Cambridge, Mass.
Pascal, C. and Bertram, A. D. (1993) The education of young children and their teachers in Europe, *European Early Childhood Education Research Journal*, Vol. 1, no. 2, pp. 27–38.
Pellegrini, D. (ed.) (1988) *Psychological Bases for Early Education*, Wiley, Chichester.
Peters, D. L. and Klinzing, D. G. (1990) The content of early childhood teacher education programs, in Spodek and Saracho (eds.) (1990) *op. cit.*, pp. 67–81.
Piaget, J. (1926) *The Language and Thought of the Child*, Routledge & Kegan Paul, London.
Pollard, A. (1985) *The Social World of the Primary School*, Cassell, London.
Pollard, A., Purvis, J. and Walford, G. (eds.) (1988) *Education, Training and the New Vocationalism*, Open University Press, Milton Keynes.
Pound, L., Cook, L., Court, J., Stevenson, J. and Wadsworth, J. (1992) *The Early Years Mathematics*, Harcourt Brace Jovanovitch, London.
Powell, D. R. and Sigel, I. E. (1991) Searches for validity in evaluating young children and early childhood programs, in Spodek and Saracho (eds.) (1991) *op. cit.*, pp. 190–212.
PriME (1991) *Calculators, Children and Mathematics: The Calculator-Aware Number Curriculum*, Simon Schuster, Hemel Hempstead.
Revell, M. (1993) Test tube baby, *The Times Educational Supplement*, 21 May.
Richards, M. and Light, P. (eds.) (1986) *Children of Social Worlds*, Polity Press, Cambridge.
Rivers, W. (1969) Commentary on R. M. Jones' paper, in Kelly (ed.) *op. cit.*, pp. 35–40.
Roaf, C. and Bines, H. (1989) *Needs, Rights and Opportunities in Special Education*, Falmer, London.
Romaine, S. (1989) *Bilingualism*, Blackwell, Oxford.

Rosen, B. (1988) *And None of it was Nonsense. The Power of Storytelling in School*, Mary Glasgow, London.

Saer, D. J. (1924) An inquiry into the effect of bilingualism upon the intelligence of young children *Journal of Experimental Psychology*, Vol. 6, pp. 232–40 and 266–74.

Sapir, E. (1970) Linguistics as a science, in Mandelbaum (ed.) (1970) *op. cit.*, p. 8.

Sassoon, R. (1990a) *Handwriting: The Way to Teach it*, Stanley Thornes, Cheltenham.

Sassoon, R. (1990b) *Handwriting: A New Perspective*, Stanley Thornes, Cheltenham.

Sassoon, R. (1993) Handwriting, in Beard (ed.) (1993) *op. cit.*, pp. 187–201.

Schieffelin, B. B. and Cochran-Smith, M. (1984) Learning to read culturally: literacy before schooling, in Goelman, Oberg and Smith (eds.) (1984) *op. cit.*, pp. 3–23.

Schmidt-Rohr, G. (1931) Liebe zur Muttersprache, in Simon (ed.) (1931) *op. cit.*, pp. 203–204.

Schweinhart, L. J. and Weikart, D. P. (1993) *A Summary of Significant Benefits: the High/Scope Perry Preschool Study through age 27*, High/Scope Institute, London.

Selinker, L. (1992) *Rediscovering Interlanguage*, Longman, London.

Shakespeare, S. (1993) Let parents see exactly whose top of the class, *The Daily Telegraph*, 11 August, p. 14.

Shorrocks, D. (1992a) *Evaluation of National Curriculum Assessment at Key Stage 1*, SEAC, London.

Shorrocks, D. (1992b) Evaluating Key Stage 1 assessments; the testing time of May 1991, *Early Years*, Vol. 13, no. 1, pp. 16–20.

Shorrocks, D., Frobisher, L., Nelson, N., Turner, L. and Waterson, A. (1993) *Implementing National Curriculum Assessment in the Primary School*, Hodder & Stoughton, Sevenoaks.

Shuard, H. (1986) *Primary Mathematics Today and Tomorrow*, Longman, London.

Simon, G. (ed.) (1931) *Sprachwissenschaft und politisches Engagement*, Beltz Verlag, Basel.

Skemp, R. (1971) *The Psychology of Learning Mathematics*, Penguin Books, Harmondsworth.

Skemp, R. (1989) *Mathematics in the Primary School*, Routledge, London.

Skutnabb-Kangas, T. *Bilingualism or Not?*, Multilingual Matters 7, Clevedon.

Slaughter, R. A. (1989) Cultural reconstruction in the post-modern world, *Journal of Curriculum Studies* Vol. 21, no. 3, pp. 255–70.

Smith, F. (1988) *Joining the Literacy Club*, Heinemann, London.

Smithers, A. and Robinson, P. (1992) *Technology and the National Curriculum*, Engineering Council, London.

Spodek, B. and Saracho, O. N. (eds.) (1990) *Early Childhood Teacher Preparation, Yearbook in Early Childhood Education Vol. 1*, Teachers College Press, Columbia University, New York.

Spodek, B. and Saracho, O. N. (eds.) (1991) *Issues in Early Childhood Curriculum, Yearbook in Early Childhood Education Vol. 2*, Teachers College Press, Columbia University, New York.

Stables, K. (1992a) The role of fantasy in contextualizing and resourcing design and technological activity, conference paper, IDATER, Loughborough University.

Stables, K. (1992b) Issues surrounding the development of technological capability in children in the first years of schooling (ages 5–7), conference paper, International Conference on Technological Education (INCOTE), Weimar.

Stables, K. (1992c) Big pictures, small steps: an approach to the assessment of design and technological capability, conference paper, DATA Primary conference.

Stenhouse, L. (1975) An Introduction to Curriculum Research and Development, Heinemann, London.

Straker, A. (1987) The challenge to change, abridged version of the presidential address to the Mathematics Association Conference, Leicester.

Sutcliffe, J. (1991) SATs study points finger at teachers, The Times Educational Supplement, 20 September.

Swann, R. and Gammage, P. (1993) Early childhood education . . . where are we now?, in Gammage and Meighan (eds.) op. cit., pp. 31–45.

Swatton, P. (1993) What does it mean to be scientific and how should we assess it?, The Curriculum Journal, Vol. 4, no. 1, pp. 59–71.

Sylva, K. (1992a) Quality care for the under-fives: is it worth it?, RSA Journal, Vol. CXL, No. 5433, pp. 683–90.

Sylva, K. (1992b) Seminar paper, Goldsmiths' Association for Early Childhood (GAEC), London.

Sylva, K. (1993) The impact of early education on children's development, OMEP Current Research in Early Childhood Update, no. 60, OMEP, London.

Sylva, K., Roy, C. and Painter, M. (1980) Childwatching at Playgroup and Nursery School, Grant McIntyre, London.

Tajfel, H. (1974) Social identity and intergroup behaviour, Social Science Information, Vol. 13, pp. 65–93.

Thomas, A. (1989) Ability and achievement expectations: implications for classroom practice, Childhood Education, Vol. 66, no. 2, pp. 235–41.

Thompson, P. (1993) Getting back to first principles, The Times Educational Supplement, 21 May.

Threlfall, J. (1992) No sums, please, we're infants, Education 3–13, Vol. 20, no. 2, pp. 15–17.

Tizard, B., Blatchford, P., Burke, J., Farquar, C. and Plewis, I. (1988) Young Children in the Inner City, Inner London Education Authority, London.

Tizard, B. and Hughes, M. (1984) Young Children Learning: Talking and Thinking at Home and at School, Fontana, London.

Tomlinson, S. (1982) A Sociology of Special Education, Routledge & Kegan Paul, London.

Tomlinson, S. (1993) The multicultural task group: the group that never was, in King and Reiss (eds.) (1993) op. cit., pp. 21–31.

Trevarthen, C. (1992) Playing into Reality: Conversations with the Infant Communicator, pp. 67–84 in Winnicot Studies no. 7, Spring 1993, London, Karnac Books.

Vygotsky, L. S. (1962) Thought and Language, MIT Press, Cambridge, Mass.

Vygotsky, L. S. (1971) The Psychology of Art, MIT Press, Cambridge, Mass.

Vygotsky, L. S. (1978) Mind in Society. The Development of Higher Psychological Processes, Harvard University Press, Cambridge, Mass.

Vygotsky, L. S. (1986) Thought and Language (revised and edited by A. Kozulin), MIT Press, Cambridge, Mass.

Walkerdine, V. (1988) *The Mastery of Reason. Cognitive Development and the Production of Rationality*, Routledge, London.

Warnock, M. (1977) *Schools of Thought*, Faber & Faber, London.

Warnock, M. (1986) Children with special needs in ordinary schools: integration revisited, *Education Today*, Vol. 32, p. 56.

Wasserman, S. (1991) The art of the question, *Childhood Education*, Vol. 67, no. 4, pp. 257–9.

Wasserman, S. (1992) Serious play in the classroom, *Childhood Education*, Vol. 68, no. 3, pp. 133–9.

Watts, M. (1991) *The Science of Problem-Solving*, Cassell Education, London.

Webb, R. (ed.) (1990) *Practitioner Research in the Primary School*, Falmer, London.

Weikart, D. (1987) Curriculum quality in early education, in Kagen and Zigler (eds.) (1987) *op. cit.*

Weir, R. H. (1962) *Language in the Crib*, Mouton, The Hague.

Wells, G. (1985) *Language, Learning and Education*, NFER/Nelson, Slough.

Wells, G. (1987) *The Meaning Makers: Children Learning Language and Using Language to Learn*, Hodder & Stoughton, Sevenoaks.

Wertsch, J. V. (ed.) (1985) *Culture, Communication and Cognition, Vygotskian Perspectives*, Cambridge University Press, London.

Whitehead, M. (1990) *Language and Literacy in the Early Years*, Paul Chapman, London.

Whitehead, M. (1992a) Failures, cranks and fads: revisiting the reading debate, *English in Education*, Vol. 26, no. 1, pp. 3–14.

Whitehead, M. (1992b) Assessment at Key Stage 1; core subjects and the developmental curriculum, in Blenkin and Kelly (eds.) (1992) *op. cit.*, pp. 93–121.

Whitehead, M. (1993) Born again phonics and the nursery rhyme revival, *English in Education*, Vol. 27, no. 3, pp. 42–51.

Willes, M. J. (1983) *Children into Pupils: A Study of Language in Early Schooling*, Routledge & Kegan Paul, London.

Wilson, J. and Cowell, B. (1986) The development and implementation of special education policy; where did the 1981 Act fit in?, in Cohen and Cohen (eds.) (1986b) *op. cit.*, pp. 53–63.

Wolfendale, S. (1993) Baseline assessment – notes and discussion, *OMEP Current Research in Early Childhood*, update no. 58, OMEP, London.

Wong-Fillmore, L. (1983) The language learner as an individual: implications of research on individual differences for the ESL teacher, in Clarke and Handscombe (eds.) (1983) *op. cit.*, pp. 203–28.

Wood, D. (1986) Teaching and learning, in Richards and Light (eds.) (1986) *op. cit.*, pp. 191–212.

Wood, D. (1988) *How Children Think and Learn*, Blackwell, Oxford.

Wood, H. and Wood, D. (1983) Questioning the preschool child, *Educational Review*, Vol. 35, no. 2, pp. 149–62.

Wragg, T. (1992) Light shed on leading questions, *The Times Educational Supplement*, 21 February.

Yang, K. S. and Bond, M. H. (1980) Ethnic confirmation by Chinese bilinguals, *Journal of Cross-Cultural Psychology*, Vol. 1, pp. 411–25.

Yorke, M. (1986) *A Dormal Nay*, Edward Arnold, London.

OFFICIAL PUBLICATIONS REFERRED TO IN THE TEXT

Central Advisory Council for Education (1954) *Early Leaving,* HMSO, London.
Central Advisory Council for Education (1959) *15 to 18* (The Crowther Report), HMSO, London.
Central Advisory Council for Education (1967) *Children and Their Primary Schools* (The Plowden Report), HMSO, London.
Department of Education and Science (1975) *A Language for Life* (The Bullock Report), HMSO, London.
Department of Education and Science (1978a) *Primary Education in England: A Survey by HM Inspectors of Schools,* HMSO, London.
Department of Education and Science (1978b) *Special Educational Needs* (The Warnock Report), HMSO, London.
Department of Education and Science (1982) *Mathematics Counts* (The Cockcroft Report), HMSO, London.
Department of Education and Science (1985) *Mathematics from 5 to 16: Curriculum Matters 3: An HMI Series,* HMSO, London.
Department of Education and Science (1987) *The National Curriculum 5–16: A Consultation Document,* HMSO, London.
Department of Education and Science (1988a) *Report of the Committee of Enquiry into the Teaching of English Language* (The Kingman Report), HMSO, London.
Department of Education and Science (1988b) *English for Ages 5–11, Proposals of the Secretaries of State* (The Cox Report, November), NCC/HMSO, London.
Department of Education and Science (1989a) *National Curriculum: From Policy to Practice,* HMSO, London.
Department of Education and Science (1989b) *English for Ages 5–16, Proposals of the Secretaries of State* (The Cox Report, June), NCC/HMSO, London.
Department of Education and Science (1989c) *Aspects of Primary Education: The Teaching and Learning of Primary Science,* HMSO, London.
Department of Education and Science (1989d) *Provision for Primary Aged Pupils with Statements in Mainstream Schools,* HMSO, London.
Department of Education and Science (1990) *Starting with Quality* (The Rumbold Report), HMSO, London.
Department of Education and Science (1991a) *The Implementation of the Curricular Requirements of the Education Reform Act: English Key Stage 1 and Mathematics Key Stage 1,* Reports by HM Inspectorate on the First Year, 1989–90, HMSO, London.
Department of Education and Science (1991b) *Mathematics in the National Curriculum,* HMSO, London.
Department of Education and Science (1991c) *Aspects of Primary Education: The Teaching and Learning of Technology,* HMSO, London.
Department of Education and Science (1992) *Curriculum Organisation and Classroom Practice in Primary Schools: A Discussion Paper,* HMSO, London.
Department of Education and Science (1993) *Statistical Bulletin,* HMSO, London.
Department of Education and Science/Her Majesty's Inspectorate (1992) *Getting in on the Act: Provision for Pupils with Special Educational Needs,* HMSO, London.

Department of Education and Science and the Welsh Office (1988) *Mathematics for ages 5 to 16,* HMSO, London.

Department of Education and Science and the Welsh Office (1989) *Mathematics in the National Curriculum,* HMSO, London.

Department for Education (1993a) *English for Ages 5–16. Proposals of the Secretaries of State,* NCC/HMSO, London.

Department for Education (1993b) *The Initial Training of Primary School Teachers: New Criteria for Course Approval,* draft paper, HMSO, London.

Department for Education/School Examinations and Assessment Council (1993a) *English Anthology: KS3,* HMSO, London.

Department for Education/School Examinations and Assessment Council (1993b) *Assessment Handbook Mathematics: MA2 Number: MA3 Algebra,* HMSO, London.

Early Childhood Care and Education Working Group (1988) *Education to Be More,* Ministry of Education, Wellington, New Zealand.

Ministère de l'Education Nationale (1992a) Aide à l'évaluation des élèves: Cycle des Approfondissements (Thevenet, M. S., Roche, J. and Reces, M. C., Imprimerie Nationale, France).

Ministère de l'Education Nationale (1992b) Aide à l'évaluation des élèves: Cycle des Apprentissages Premiers (Thevenet, M. S., Roche, J. and Reces, M. C., Imprimeries Nationale, France).

Ministerio de Educacion y Ciencia (1992) Proyecto Curricular de Educacion Primarim: Que, Como, Cuando Ensenar y Evaluar.

Ministerium fur Kultus und Sport, Baden-Württemburg (1993) Bildsung plan fur die Grundschule.

Ministry of Education, Province of British Columbia (1990) *Year 2000: A Curriculum and Assessment Framework for the Future,* Victoria, BC.

National Board of Employment, Education and Training (1992) *A Snapshot of the Early Years of Schooling,* Compulsory Years of Schooling Project, Australian Government Publishing Service, Canberra.

National Curriculum Council (1988) *Introducing the National Curriculum Council,* NCC, London.

National Curriculum Council (1990) *Curriculum Guidance 3: The Whole Curriculum,* NCC, York.

National Curriculum Council (1991a) *Report on Monitoring the Implementation of the National Curriculum Core Subjects, 1989–90,* NCC, York.

National Curriculum Council (1991b) *Mathematics Non-Statutory Guidance,* NCC, York.

National Curriculum Council (1991c) *Circular No. 11: Linguistic Diversity and the National Curriculum,* NCC, York.

National Curriculum Council (1992a) *National Curriculum English: The Case for Revising the Order. Advice to the Secretary of State for Education, July 1992,* NCC, York.

National Curriculum Council (1992b) *Starting out with the National Curriculum,* NCC, York.

National Curriculum Council (1993) *Special Needs in the National Curriculum: Opportunity and Challenge,* NCC, York.

National Curriculum Council/National Oracy Project (1990) *Teaching, Talking and Learning in Key Stage One,* NCC, York.

National Curriculum Council/School Examinations and Assessment Council (1993) *The National Curriculum and its Assessment: An Interim Report*, NCC/SEAC, York/London.

National Union of Teachers (1991) *Miss, the Rabbit Ate the 'Floating' Apple! The Case against SATs*, a report on the 1991 Key Stage 1 SATs, NUT, London.

National Union of Teachers/University of Leeds (1993) *Testing and Assessing 6 and 7 Year Olds. The Evaluation of the 1992 Key Stage 1 National Curriculum Assessment. Final Report*, NUT, London.

Office for Standards in Education (1993a) *The Teaching and Learning of Number in Primary Schools. National Curriculum Mathematics Attainment Target 2*, HMSO, London.

Office for Standards in Education (1993b) *Curriculum Organisation and Classroom Practice in Primary Schools: A Follow-Up Report*, HMSO, London.

Office for Standards in Education (1993c) *First Class: Standards and Quality of Education in Reception Classes*, HMSO, London.

Schools Council (1965) *Curriculum Bulletin 1. Mathematics in Primary Schools* (fourth edition 1972), HMSO, London.

School Examinations and Assessment Council (1989) *An Introduction to SEAC*, HMSO, London.

School Examinations and Assessment Council (1992) *Technology 1–4: Suggested Guidelines for a more Standardised Approach to Design and Technology in Teacher Assessment, Key Stage 1*, SEAC, London.

LITERATURE REFERRED TO IN THE TEXT

Ahlberg, J. and Ahlberg, A. (1977) *Each Peach Pear Plum*, Kestrel/Penguin Books, Harmondsworth.

Ahlberg, J. and Ahlberg, A. (1989) *Bye Bye Baby*, Heinemann, London.

Eliot, T. S. (1942) *Little Gidding*, Faber & Faber, London and Boston, Mass.

Frost, R. (1955) *Selected Poems*, Penguin Books, Harmondsworth.

Hutchins, P. (1968) *Rosie's Walk*, The Bodley Head, London.

Sendak, M. (1967) *Where the Wild Things Are*, The Bodley Head, London.

Wagner, J. (1977) *John Brown, Rose and the Midnight Cat*, Kestrel/Penguin Books, Harmondsworth.

Woolf, V. (1931) *The Waves*, Penguin Books, Harmondsworth (1951).

Indexes

INDEX OF AUTHORS

INDEX OF SUBJECTS